BATTLE OF BRITAIN
PILOT

Dedicated, with respect, to the late Mrs Dorothy Barclay, and to all those mothers whose sons were brave and selfless when bravery and selflessness were the qualities most required.

BATTLE OF BRITAIN
PILOT

THE SELF-PORTRAIT OF AN RAF FIGHTER PILOT AND ESCAPER

GEORGE BARCLAY
EDITED BY HUMPHREY WYNN

Haynes

HAYNES
PUBLISHING

First published by William Kimber & Co., 1976
Revised edition published by Crécy Books Ltd, 1994
This fully revised and re-illustrated edition first published in 2012 by Haynes Publishing.

A catalogue record for this book is available from the British Library.

ISBN 978 0 85733 239 4

Library of Congress control no. 2012933485

Published by Haynes Publishing,
Sparkford, Yeovil,
Somerset BA22 7JJ, UK.
Tel: 01963 442030 Fax: 01963 440001
Int. tel: +44 1963 442030 Int. fax: +44 1963 440001
E-mail: sales@haynes.co.uk
Website: www.haynes.co.uk

Haynes North America Inc.
861 Lawrence Drive, Newbury Park,
California 91320, USA.

All images courtesy of the Barclay family except where stated.

Page design and layout by Dominic Stickland.
Edited by Sophie Blackman and Jonathan Falconer.

Printed in the USA by Odcombe Press LP,
1299 Bridgestone Parkway, La Vergne, TN 37086.

Contents

Foreword to the first edition   6

Foreword to the new edition   8

Acknowledgements to the first edition   10

Acknowledgements to the new edition   11

Introduction   12

1: The Making of a Fighter Pilot   14

2: The Battle of Britain   40

3: Recovery and Back to Operations   88

4: France and Spain   104

5: Down the Line and Back to the UK   118

6: Journey to El Alamein   134

7: My Brother George – Stories of the Resistance   156

Bibliography   174

Details of Aircraft Mentioned   175

Index   177

John Grandy, second from left, when
commanding No 249 Squadron.

Foreword to the first edition

Marshal of the Royal Air Force
Sir John Grandy, GCB, KBE, DSO

Sir John Grandy (1913–2004) was Chief of the Air Staff from 1967 to 1971. During his distinguished RAF career, which began in 1931, he commanded No 249 Squadron, in which George Barclay served, in the Battle of Britain. Prior to becoming CAS he was C-in-C, RAF Germany, and Commander, 2nd Allied Tactical Air Force, 1961–63; AOC-in-C RAF Bomber Command, 1963–65; and C-in-C, British Forces Far East and UK Military Adviser to SEATO (South-East Asia Treaty Organisation), 1965–67. Grandy served as Governor of Gibraltar from 1973 to 1978 and then Constable and Governor of Windsor Castle. He was also Chairman of the Trustees of the Imperial War Museum.

In the spring of 1940 I was fortunate enough to be appointed to form a new day fighter squadron at Royal Air Force Station Leconfield in Yorkshire. My orders were to get No 249 Squadron formed and trained up to a standard acceptable to day fighter operations in the shortest possible time. Our period of training is briefly referred to in the early pages of this book, which Mr Humphrey Wynn has put together with such care.

One of my first moves was to fly to Cranwell. At that time I had had some experience of our University Air Squadrons and had formed a high opinion of the calibre of undergraduate who chose to learn to fly in those splendid volunteer units. I knew that a number of these stalwarts were by then continuing their training at Cranwell, and it was quite clear to me that if my squadron was to be as good as I wanted it to be, some of them would be a great asset and, furthermore, make my operational training task that much easier and quicker of

achievement. Amongst those who joined 249 as a result of this visit was George Barclay.

I was lucky; Barclay rapidly became one of the most balanced and sensible, yet dashing, highly courageous and skilful fighter pilots. I doubt whether any of his service friends knew that he kept a diary; I certainly did not. The story his writings tell makes exciting reading, and is a remarkable and valuable contribution to Royal Air Force literature and to our knowledge of air fighting and its development in the early years of the Second World War. It is of the greatest interest and importance to have this personal account, written at the time, of a fighter pilot's view of the changing tactics and nuances of air combat. It is striking too to perceive how Barclay's own skill and cunning develop as the Battle unfolds.

There follows the description of his escape and subsequent posting to the Middle East, but there is far more to these writings than that. The other aspect of the story is the quite unconscious revelation of the man. As one reads this book, one meets again George Barclay; modest in the extreme, invariably courteous, brimming over with humour. A man who loved flying and whose one determination in those days was to fight and destroy the enemy in the air. His infectious personality and flair for leadership would undoubtedly have moulded him into becoming one of our most distinguished fighting commanders. It was a great privilege to have known and flown with him.

His family are rightly very proud of him. We are indebted to them for allowing these diaries and letters to be published.

John Grandy
MRAF

Foreword to
the new edition

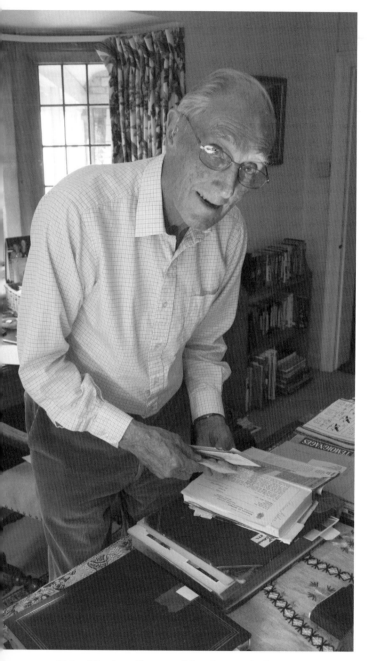

Richard Barclay with some of the photograph albums and
ephemera that belonged to his brother George.

Richard Barclay

During the Battle of Britain my brother George
came home for a 48-hour leave straight from the
Battle. As the house was full of family who had
rallied to greet him, George and I shared a bedroom. Our
day started early as George was used to a 5am 'stand-to'
before daylight. To my huge delight (I was seven years
younger than him) he enthralled me with tales of aerial
and other adventures. I was sorry when the time came to
join our family round my parents' bed for cups of tea and
morning prayers.

It was only when the war was over, three years after
George's death, we learnt that he had kept a diary during
the Battle of Britain – apparently it is the only one written
day-to-day on either side. It also recorded his crash in France
the following year, and escape, or 'evasion', through the
Zones – the Forbidden Sector, Occupied and Unoccupied
France – each with patrolled frontiers, and then on
through Franco Spain. We knew nothing of the existence
of George's diary and never anticipated it as, of course, it
was strictly against orders for Servicemen to keep diaries
during the war. Despite this, several senior officers seem to
have disregarded this rule – they probably felt the enemy
would have no chance of seeing their diaries kept safe in a
remote headquarters, and like George, needed the relief of
expressing their version of events and their inner feelings.

In 1946 my parents felt they could no longer bear the pressure of the large parish of Cromer, nor the constant reminders of the two sons and an especially close nephew they had lost in the war. A few days before they were due to move to the small parish of Langley near Maidstone, the bank manager in Cromer rang my father to say, 'Mr Barclay what do you want done with your son George's parcel?' Father asked, 'What parcel?' and was told that there was one in the strong room. Father replied, 'I can't understand this. When we were clearing up George's affairs in 1942 you were meant to advise us of anything of his you held.' The manager replied that he could not say whether or not the bank had reported the parcel earlier, but could my Father come and claim it.

Father did so and found in it not only the diary but also George's Battle of Britain Distinguished Flying Cross (DFC). This was a slightly embarrassing though pleasing find. When George was killed, Father asked his Battle of Britain Commander, John Grandy, if he could discover what had happened to George's DFC. After a considerable investigation John reported it had not been found but that he enclosed a replacement. Of course it had not got George's name engraved on it. I suspect that John had used his own seniority to obtain another one. So now I have the two DFCs – one is on display with George's campaign medals at Tangmere Military Aviation Museum and the other in my 'strong box'.

Also, I should report how the diary came to be published. When it was discovered I had it typed up by my secretary in her private time. My aim was to show it to any publishers I came across, as the family felt it was an important historical document as the only diary written actually day-to-day during the Battle of Britain. The response in each case was that there was insufficient material to justify publishing it as a book.

Then in about 1970 a most interesting article by H. Montgomery Hyde appeared in *The Times* about what Lord Trenchard had anticipated before the coming air conflict in 1940. I wrote to Dr Montgomery Hyde saying that some of his conjectures would be confirmed by reference to George's diary. He responded by inviting me to lunch at the Garrick Club where I met Group

Captain Haslam, the head of the Royal Air Force Air Historical Branch. He confirmed that the RAF would like to see the diary in print and suggested that one of his staff would be willing to edit it and offer the resulting book to publishers. Thus we met and were delighted by Humphrey Wynn, an ex-RAF fighter pilot himself, and were pleased with what was eventually published in 1976. George's diary was republished a couple of times, but it then went out of print. Last year I discovered that the publishing rights had reverted to me and thanks to Haynes Publishing this new edition is the result.

After the Liberation of France my parents received messages addressed to George from the few survivors of the Escape Line that had helped him. Through them over the following years we learnt bit-by-bit of the tragic and terrible betrayal of the Line that cost so many French lives. Some of George's helpers came to visit us in England and joined us for the launch of the diary, and later on my three sons and I visited them in France.

Gradually, the full story fell into place, but it was not until 1989 that it was completed, when a stroke of luck enabled Mauricette Ghoris to contact us. Her parents had hidden George for his first two nights in France, and as a 14-year-old she had partnered her father in his Underground work, including escorting George on an adventurous transfer from one safe house to another. In the intervening years she had attempted to contact George, first by learning English, and then by taking her holidays in England searching for his home, which she remembered was called Cromer. Unfortunately she thought Cromer was in London so spent money and precious holiday time there to no avail.

When I was laid up during the winter of 2010–11 I thought I would jot down my memories of these events of some 70 years ago for my family. Extracts from these have been added to this new edition of my brother George's diary.

We feel honoured to pay a proud tribute to those gallant helpers, and to George himself.

Richard Barclay
December 2011

Acknowledgements to the first edition

During 1974 a remarkable diary, written during the Battle of Britain by a No 249 Squadron pilot Flying Officer R.G.A. Barclay, was lent to the Ministry of Defence Air Historical Branch (AHB) by the diary-keeper's brother Richard. The latter had been prompted to send this document to the AHB for perusal after correspondence with Dr H. Montgomery Hyde, following his article on 'Lord Trenchard – Architect of Victory in 1940' in *The Times* for 15 September 1973, to commemorate the Battle of Britain. Richard Barclay felt that it would be of interest to the public 'to read an account written at the time which expresses the atmosphere so clearly'.

Such diaries are rare – largely because, in the interests of wartime security, RAF officers were discouraged from keeping them. Such rarity itself gives a high value to George Barclay's account of 1940 fighter operations, while the fact that it is a first-hand narrative by a participant in one of the world's major battles gives it even greater worth. It is like having a diary kept by a soldier at Waterloo, or a sailor at Trafalgar.

One of the AHB historians, Humphrey Wynn, was so impressed by George's diary that he wrote an article on its author for the September 1974 issue of the *Royal Air Forces Quarterly*, and expressed the view that the complete text should be published. It contains the whole of George Barclay's Battle of Britain diary as its centrepiece, followed by his more fragmentary account of his escape through France and Spain after being shot down in September 1941. Before and after these diaries occur a Prologue and Epilogue, detailing George's background and RAF career up to his emergence as a

fighter pilot, and his final tour of operations in the Middle East up to the time when he was shot down over El Alamein in July 1942.

As far as possible, the story is told in George's own words and in those of his friends, through his diaries, combat reports, squadron Operations Record Books (ORBs), flying log book and letters, the existence of which was not known to George's family until after his death, as he had deposited them in his bank, thus ensuring their safety and security.

The editor acknowledges assistance from many quarters in drawing together the material for this self-portrait by George Barclay – in particular, unstinted kindness and helpfulness from Mrs Dorothy Barclay, her daughters Mrs Ann Asher and Mrs Mary Bosanquet, and her son Mr Richard Barclay; courtesy and warm hospitality from Mme Henriette and M André Fardel and M and Mme Fernand and Elisa Salingue; advice and comment from Marshal of the Royal Air Force Sir John Grandy, and for contributing the Foreword; support for the idea of the book from Dr Montgomery Hyde; aid in its preparation from many official bodies – the MoD Air Historical Branch (Group Captain E.B. Haslam, Mr H.H. Edmonds, Mrs L.R. Robinson and Mr J. Spottiswood), the MoD Air Library (Mr F.S. White), the Public Record Office (Mr N.E. Evans and Mrs Anna Knowles), the Imperial War Museum (Mr E. Hine) and the Royal Geographical Society map room. Photographs, except where otherwise acknowledged, have been provided by the Barclay family; the pictorial maps were specially drawn by Mike Badrocke, and Mrs Moreen Knight ably deciphered and typed the editor's manuscript.

H.W.

Acknowledgements to the new edition

The Barclay family were delighted when Jeremy Yates-Round and Jonathan Falconer saw the original edition of my brother George's diaries, together with the additional photographs in our albums, and told us that Haynes would be willing to republish them in this enlarged format.

We wish to thank them most warmly, and also to thank and congratulate the editor, Sophie Blackman, for an excellent production, which we heartily recommend to you the readers. My wife, Joan, has been heavily involved and of the greatest help and encouragement to me – thanks a million!!

Richard Barclay
July 2012

NOTE ON ABBREVIATIONS
A 'Glossary of Terms Used in the Diary', compiled by George Barclay himself, has been included. For the sake of consistency, ranks have been given in full where abbreviated in George's diaries and log book.

GLOSSARY OF TERMS USED IN THE DIARY
AA (Ack-ack) Anti-aircraft guns and/or the shell bursts.
A.1. First class.
Caterpillar A green caterpillar with a ruby eye was presented to any airman who escaped by parachute by the Irving Co. who made the 'chutes. The caterpillar represented the silk worms.
Clare A 'C' Class (Imperial Airways/BOAC) four-engined flying-boat, built by Short Brothers.
Controller An Air Force officer controlling fighters in the air from an Operations Room to which was fed all information about own and enemy forces from radar, Observer Corps, etc.
D/F Direction-finding.
'Dingbat' A fast-moving type of tramp!
Dispersal The huts and parking places for aircraft scattered round the airfield where the squadron awaited orders to take off.
e/a Enemy aircraft.

Flight Six aircraft.
Haywire Crazy, unpredictable, useless.
IF Flying by instruments.
Link Trainer A simulated aircraft cockpit used for practising instrument flying procedure, etc.
Mae West Inflatable life jacket.
Pancake To land an aircraft either normally, or (original meaning) with wheels retracted.
Pip, squeak, zero A form of radio position-finding, using radar.
Plug To pull the plug is to put the throttle beyond the normal permissible maximum boost position, only allowed in combat because of the wear on the engine.
Scramble Take off (originally in emergency).
Rhubarb Low-level freelance fighter operation against ground targets.
Section Three aircraft in formation.
Squadron 12 aircraft (in fighter squadrons).
State A board announcing who would fly on operations and the state of readiness.
Tannoy Loudspeaker system.
U/S Unserviceable – out of action.
Vector Turn into new course or the course itself.
VHF Very-high-frequency radio telephone.
Wing Two squadrons during Battle of Britain; normally three.

Introduction

George in flying kit beside No 249 Squadron's dispersal hut turns to look at the photographer.

From 1 September 1939, when he was called up for service, until 17 July 1942, when he was shot down over El Alamein, George Barclay's life was contained in, and devoted to, the Royal Air Force. Even though he wholeheartedly enjoyed the resumption of family life and sporting activities when on leave, he was only really happy when he got back to his squadron. When off operations he chafed to be back on them. He was par excellence a young Englishman destined for one of the professions – banking, the law, perhaps the Foreign Office or the Church – who by force of circumstance became a professional warrior.

His sister Ann recalls that in about 1937, talking with a friend of hers who had fought in the Spanish Civil War, George said he would eventually like to become a mercenary – following the tradition of some of his fighting forebears, like Colonel David Barclay who served King Gustavus Adolphus of Sweden and General Barclay de Tolly, who commanded the Russian army in the retreat on Moscow before Napoleon, emerging from the campaign with honour and promotion.

Once in the RAF, he had no doubts about wanting to be a fighter pilot; he took naturally to the individual combats of the Battle of Britain, making his contribution to that crucial defeat of the Luftwaffe and surviving being twice shot down. He came back into Fighter Command when it was on the offensive, carrying the war into German-held skies. He was shot down a third time when on a sweep over northern France, and immediately became a cool, quick-witted and courageous escaper – going 'down the line' through France, into Spain and back home via Gibraltar. As if these experiences were not enough, he started a third tour of fighter operations – this time as commanding officer of a squadron being sent out to the Western Desert. He commanded it briefly in the period of confusion during the last withdrawal, to El Alamein; it had Spitfires, but he was asked to take over a squadron of Hurricanes, in which he had fought in the Battle of Britain.

He had commanded it only a fortnight when, leading his pilots over the battlefield one early evening in July 1942, they were 'jumped' by Me109Fs and he was shot down – but this time there was no return, no brave escape.

Such a story might be paralleled a hundred times, but for one thing. George Barclay kept an incomparable diary of his Battle of Britain experiences. As a document it is as important as a personal account of a great battle as the diary of an Elizabethan seaman in the Armada engagement, or of one of Nelson's officers at Trafalgar; it is sensitive and perceptive, and realistic in its comments upon air fighting tactics. He also wrote a diary about his escape through France, though this was not completed for the whole journey to Gibraltar; nevertheless it conveys vividly the thoughts and actions of a young RAF pilot who finds himself in the middle of a French field, in uniform, only an hour after having lunch in the officers' mess at his home airfield – suddenly on the run, with only his wits between him and the enemy.

It is these two diaries which form the core of this book, and through which George Barclay tells his own story as a fighter pilot, with the beginning and the end of his operational career told also in his own words – through letters and through combat reports – and in those of his friends, particularly those who wrote the epilogue to his short-lived but devoted and impressive spells of command in the Western Desert. 'His leadership was of the highest quality', wrote one of the pilots on his last squadron, 'both on the ground and in the air. ... One of my friends said that although he didn't believe in hero worship he would follow him anywhere, because he felt he was giving everything he'd got.'

How this quality of fighting leadership developed in a young Englishman, whose life until September 1939 had been notably peaceful and happy, emerges in the letters and diaries that form George Barclay's self-portrait.

Humphrey Wynn

El Alamein War Cemetery: George's grave.

CHAPTER ONE

The Making
of a Fighter Pilot

The notice from the Royal Air Force requiring 754320 Sergeant Barclay, R.G.A., Cromer Vicarage, Norfolk, to join the Volunteer Reserve Town Centre at Cambridge on 1 September 1939 – similar to hundreds of others plopping through letter-boxes all over the country notifying Royal Air Force Volunteer Reservists to join for service in the Royal Air Force – meant for George Barclay, as for his fellow reservists, the end of civilian employment or university life; the end of boyhood and youth in the 1930s, and swift translation from amateur airmen into professionals.

For George Barclay at his father's vicarage, it meant the end of an extremely happy boyhood in which enduring

George with his favourite pigeons at Great Holland, Essex, in 1935. 'George was always mad on flying,' says a handwritten note on the back of this photograph. 'He trained his fantails!'

family links had been formed, but the beginning of a brief wartime career as a fighter pilot, in which the qualities he had inherited from his parents and their progenitors stood him in excellent stead during operations and when evading capture on enemy territory.

Cromer had only recently become his father's living; the Reverend G.A. Barclay had been inducted there on 29 March 1939. The Barclay sons and daughters – George had an elder brother, Charles, and a younger one, Richard, and two sisters, Ann and Mary – had spent a happy childhood in the charming rectory at Great Holland (which George could see, and refers to in his diary, when he was flying from North Weald in the Battle of Britain) on the Essex coast near Frinton-on-Sea. 'An idyllic existence', as Richard Barclay recalls, 'with horses and a huge fruit garden, ducks, pigs, etc, and marvellous bathing and summer activities.'

The Barclay family had inherited a strong vein of military, sporting and missionary zeal, which characterised them with both fighting and gentle qualities. On the Barclay side there had been Colonel David Barclay, in the army of the Swedish king Gustavus Adolphus in the 17th-century Thirty Years War, later becoming a Quaker; there had been bankers and churchmen, an alliance between shrewd business and strong religious interests. On the maternal side there were the Studds, the famous cricketing and missionary family – three brothers who all played for Eton and one of whom (C.T., George Barclay's grandfather) played for England. After C.T.'s father, a passionate racehorse owner, had been converted by the American missioners

This portrait photograph of George was probably taken on his passing out from RAF Cranwell in April 1940.

Cromer Vicarage and Church, where George's father, Gilbert, was Vicar from 1939 to 1946.

Charlie, Richard and George in 1929. This picture was taken from an album George gave to his mother for Christmas in 1941, after his escape from Occupied France. His mother, Dorothy Barclay, collected material but never completed it, so her son Richard (84 in 2010) and daughter Mary (92 in 2010) completed the album in 2010.

Moody and Sankey, C.T. gave up cricket and all he held dear to become a missionary – first in China, where his four daughters were born, then in India and finally in the Belgian Congo, where he died. It was such antecedents – adventurous but of Christian scrupulousness, of steel-like courage and determination but also gentle, sporting but practical – that George Barclay inherited.

Before the period at Great Holland rectory – that 'idyllic existence' his brother Richard recalls, 'a marvellous lull before the storm. ... a time of perpetual sunshine and family fun' – George had first been educated at home by a governess, Miss Marjorie Wright, and then at a prep school, Hawtreys, Westgate-on-Sea, where he won a wooden spoon prize for catching cricket balls hit high into the air by the headmaster at the nets on summer Sunday evenings, and also proved to be a good rugby three-quarter; then at Stowe School, where he had the companionship of two cousins, Lionel Buxton and Ian Munro.

He mentions Lionel in a letter from school to his mother, postmarked 23 September 1935 – a letter that reveals much of his character, both in his love for his parents and in his conscientiousness:

*What a superb holiday you and Father gave us all.
We can never thank you enough. You both spent
your time slaving for us and got no return. Thank
you so, so much.*

Reverend G.A. Barclay with his family, their dogs and a cat at Great Holland Rectory, Frinton-on-Sea, Essex. From left, standing: Mary, Charles, Ann and George; seated with him: Richard and Mrs Barclay.

A parson in wartime – Richard Barclay remembers

My father, Gilbert Barclay, was 57 when he moved to the parish of Cromer in 1939. He had two major concerns. He was to lose his parish curate to the Forces, and having himself served in the trenches in the First World War, where his regiment was all but wiped out twice in one year, he had to anticipate a similar experience for his young family. He had three sons and two daughters, and a special relationship with two nephews and a niece who spent their school holidays with us, as their parents were missionaries serving abroad.

I was 12 when war was declared, and my first duty was to listen to the Prime Minister's broadcast at 11am on Sunday 3 September and then bicycle – for the first time ever on a Sunday! – down to the church so that my father could tell the outcome to the congregation. As he did so, the first air-raid warning of the war sounded, yet the service continued with an even greater intensity. It was finally relieved by the 'all clear' – it had been a false alarm.

Father's work increased rapidly as his flock was affected by worries and losses. In addition, he was

appointed as a chaplain to the Forces and ministered to many isolated defence units scattered around the countryside. One Easter Day, probably 1940, he took eight communion services.

Cromer itself was bombed 'lightly', by the measurement of the times, on about six occasions. The house at the bottom of our garden was hit and we lost windows and tiles. During a daylight raid, after the bombs had exploded, my father and my sister Ann rushed to the front door as Ann's son, Gillie, was in a pram on the far side of the wide front lawn. When they heard the aircraft returning at rooftop level, Father ran out to pick up Gillie. The aircraft was machine-gunning any movement on the ground and Ann was horrified to see tracer bullets hit the lawn, the drive, and ricochet into the flowerbeds. (Afterwards I searched diligently for them but found none.) As a result of Ann's experience we obtained a Morrison shelter – a very solid steel table-like structure placed in the nursery, and whenever the warning was sounded, as it frequently was on the East Coast, Gillie and his sister, Rosalind, were popped into their cage.

The church itself was made uninhabitable for a time, but was actually spared complete destruction as a bomb bounced against the tower, only to explode further on. The fire-watchers on the tower emerged considerably shaken! The local Baptists had two chapels and lent us one.

Father was determined to be available when any of his flock suffered, so took no leave. Eventually, he was persuaded to take a few days off in a bungalow on a hilltop a few miles out of Cromer. One night we heard explosions out at sea, and saw red streaks of tracer bullets rising in the air against aircraft and along the sea against torpedo boats – another convoy was being attacked, and our lifeboats would soon be out on rescue missions. As we watched, a huge explosion lit the sky in the direction of Cromer. Father wanted to go there at once but we were not allowed to use the roads at night. Next day we found that a German naval mine dropped by parachute had drifted inland and blown the roof off a friend's house in Beeston. It left a great crater, which exists to this day as a rather charming garden pond.

Father's anxieties for his family were to be justified. Of his sons, Charles was killed in the Royal Norfolks at Kohima, Burma (a brother officer was awarded a posthumous Victoria Cross). George, after fighting in the Battle of Britain and over France, had been shot down over El Alamein. Of my Father's nephews, Lionel was killed in the Guards at Salerno, but Ian survived, though wounded. Of the girls, Ann, whose husband served on the ground in the RAF in the Middle East for most of the war, was left with two babies and no home. Charlie's widow was left with two babies, one of whom he never saw. My sister Mary served first in MI5, but when her eyesight was affected by long days underground, she left for the Land Army and became an enthusiastic carter and plough woman behind massive shire horses. My cousin Susan became a nurse.

I could tell many stories of receiving telegrams or telephone calls at home; 'we regret to inform you…' such devastating news, yet my parents soldiered on with their ministry. I joined the Navy in 1944 and only learnt many years later that my parents feared they were saying a final goodbye to me too. They never gave me any inkling of their anxiety.

HERE KNELT
before giving their lives that we might live
GILBERT CHARLES BARCLAY
Lieut·The Royal Norfolk Regiment · Born
11ῆ June 1916 · Fell at Norfolk Ridge Kohima
5ῆ May 1944 in the decisive battle for India
Darling Husband of Rome Flora
AND
RICHARD GEORGE
ARTHUR BARCLAY D·F·C
Squadron Leader R·A·F·V·R
Born 7th· December 1919 · Fought in the
decisive battles of Britain and Egypt
Shot down and escaped from France
1941 · Fell at El Alamein 17ῆ July 1942
Beloved Sons of Gilbert and Dorothy Barclay
Cromer Vicarage

WHOSOEVER LIVETH AND BELIEVETH
IN ME SHALL NEVER DIE

Remember also GILBERT ARTHUR BARCLAY their father
much loved Vicar of this parish 1939 -1946
Born 21 February 1882 Ordained 24 February 1907 Died 10 May 1972

Commemorative plaque in Cromer Parish Church, where George and his elder brother Charles were together with their mother and father for the last time on 5 April 1942. Beneath the plaque is a memorial to their father, previous Vicar of the parish.

The model of Sir Francis Drake's ship the *Golden Hind* built by George in 1935 while he was home from school recovering from an operation. Mary, Charles, and George holding the dog Whiskey.

We all arrived safely here. Lionel is a 'settler', ie a very junior monitor with very little power. This means that he has completely superseded me. He will be a monitor next term probably.

Please send me some more money as I have 4/6 (or less) left over from the 30/-. Am sending accounts.

Please don't send study furniture until I write for some. Tons of love, George.

While at Stowe he suffered from mastoids, from which he nearly died. The operation he underwent left a scar along about one-third of the left-hand side of his neck, and he spent a whole month in bed at Great Holland. But this didn't prevent his subsequent acceptance as aircrew, nor hold back his studies seriously; he had, as his brother puts it, 'a good average academic and sporting existence' at Stowe. From school he went to Trinity College, Cambridge, to read geography; and it was there he got his first experience of flying when he joined the University Air Squadron (CUAS).

His godfather and first cousin, Sandy (Alexander) Barclay-Russell, recalls how he learnt of this decision one day in 1938 when they were shooting together – this was the sport in which George Barclay was at his happiest, and to which he refers time and again in his Battle of Britain diary.

I remember with appalling clarity', says Sandy Barclay-Russell, 'his telling me in 1938 that he had joined the University Air Squadron, as I had knowledge more than usual that war was inevitable and knew at once how inevitable the consequence must be.

He told me this when we were shooting at the "family shoot" belonging to my uncle Robin Barclay, possibly one of the finest partridge and mixed game shoots and estates in England. It had all the character of East Anglia, and of George's and my joint background. Those vast fen skies that towered over one, giving a sort of monumental scale to life. The fields, too (a hundred acres at times, and the superb Scotch fir belts – not hedges – that surrounded them), were a never-tiring source of strength to the spirit. Higham, this place between Newmarket and Bury St Edmunds, was very much part of our family tradition.

It was when we were both shooting there that George told me of his decision to fly and asked me what I thought. That, of course, I could not tell him. I had a vivid certainty of the result that at the time was devastating.

Gilbert Barclay off shooting with his sons at Triminhgam during the war. The two elder boys, Charles and George, were home on leave before postings abroad.

'Three ancient mariners' on board the houseboat *Whale*, Blakeney Point, 27–29 June 1939.

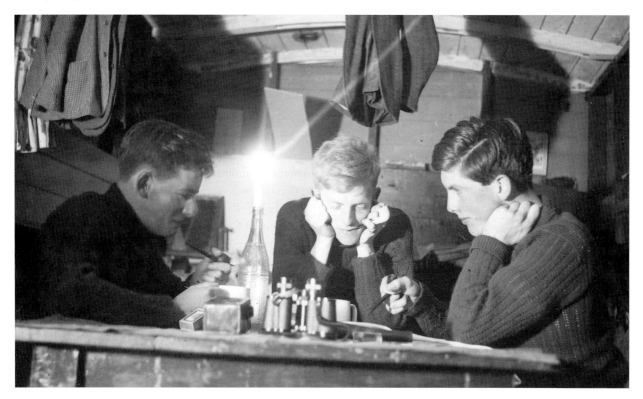

Before the war

In the 1930s we lived in a large rectory at Great Holland in Essex. In addition to my two brothers and two sisters, three first cousins of similar age joined us for their holidays from boarding school. All of them were much older than me and I felt detached from their vigorous activities, like the tail of an active dog that occasionally got a wag! If some of them did include me in simple games, such as French cricket, or on walks, my performance was so outclassed that I generally retired frustrated.

When George was in his early teens and I was still under Nannie's care in the schoolroom, I was vaguely aware that he was gravely ill. Following an operation on his mastoid he was left with a scar round his neck from his Adam's apple to near his spine. It must have happened in midsummer, as when he came home from hospital he was in bed in our revolving summerhouse on the lawn, tended by two nurses with whom he exchanged jokes and teases beyond my comprehension. There was one thrilling day after he recovered when he decided to practise his skills of leadership and field craft for Officers' Training Corps purposes, and I was given the task of representing his platoon. We crawled through woods and cornfields, using ditches and 'dead land' to ensure the enemy would not spot us, and we both thought we had done very well, though our knees and clothes suffered. Already George was mad on aeroplanes – models galore were suspended from his bedroom ceiling.

George and I shared another experience. It was decided that we both should have our tonsils out and share a room in the hospital. The night before, we were taken to a play of *The Wind in the Willows*, and all I remember of it was the naughty weasels being put over Ratty's knee and spanked, as I had been terrified by the only time my father spanked me for stealing my favourite medicine, Milk of Magnesia; this memory spoiled my evening. The following day was not too good either, as I woke up vomiting quantities of blood and had to go back into the operating theatre to be re-sewn up.

When we left Great Holland for Cromer, George was in his second year at Cambridge, and spending all his spare time learning to fly with the University Air Squadron.

In 1942, Sandy Barclay-Russell was serving with the Army in the Middle East when George Barclay was killed at El Alamein. Later he brought back to England the simple wooden cross that had marked his first grave.

The Barclay family were extremely close-knit, and George anxiously consulted his father before making up his mind to join Cambridge UAS. In a letter dated 16 October 1938 (the month in which he joined), written from 67 Jesus Lane, Cambridge, he said diffidently:

I enclose a pamphlet about the Cambridge University Air Squadron. Now, if you (or Mummie) should prefer that I didn't join please return the pamphlet and let me know as soon as possible. I have not said anything about it to Mummie. If you don't mind my joining, please fill up the pamphlet and also send it to me as quick as possible. You see the longer the delay the less chance I have of getting in. I shall have to take the very stiff medical anyway, and of course there is the possibility that my heart will get me thrown out. Anyway, if you prefer that I don't join, please tell me quickly, so that I can join the engineers.

Apparently there was no parental veto; he didn't go into the Army (unlike his elder brother Charles, killed in action at Kohima on 5 May 1944) but joined Cambridge UAS, which flew Avro Tutors at Duxford aerodrome.

George's determination to fly seemed to have stemmed, curiously, from an aircraft crash that occurred at Great Glen in Leicestershire, where his father had a parish before going to Great Holland. He made models and read books about the air, as most boys do; but those were days of great aviation activity, most of it far more visible from the ground than flying is nowadays – little biplanes and monoplanes scudding round Britain in the King's Cup Air Race; the Schneider Trophy world speed record-breaking seaplanes; Sir Alan Cobham's 'Circus' performing from local fields; the Air League's Empire Air Days; the annual RAF Pageant at Hendon; the great silver airships; formation of Auxiliary Air Force squadrons and UASs, and recruitment for the RAFVR; record-breaking

Cambridge University
Air Squadron

Cambridge University Air Squadron (CUAS),
1938–39. Third attachment, Duxford, July 1939.
George Barclay is back row second from right.

George beside his Hawker Hind training plane while
he was in the CUAS.

Formation flying at CUAS on Empire Air Day, 1939.
Avro Tutors in line abreast.

CUAS Tutors are over-flown by Spitfires of No 19
Squadron from Duxford.

solo flights, like those of Jim Mollison, Bert Hinkler, Amy Johnson and Jean Batten; and, behind all these enterprises, ever-increasing war clouds on the horizon and rearmament at home.

At Duxford, that famous old Cambridgeshire airfield where George Barclay had his first experience of flying, the UAS formed a small part of a station whose prime function was the training and deployment of fighter squadrons.

At Duxford, too, George would have seen the Spitfire for the first time: No 19 Squadron at the station became the first RAF squadron (in 1938) to be equipped with this fighter. Later, in his Battle of Britain diary, he was to compare its merits professionally with those of the Hurricanes he flew. Perhaps the sight of the beautiful new monoplane fighters (up to 1937, the RAF had operated biplane fighters) and the presence of two fighter squadrons, for No 66 had been formed there in 1936 under the RAF expansion scheme,

Spitfire Mk Is of No 19 Squadron refuel at Duxford. Note the pre-war 'WZ' squadron codes, two-blade propellers, pre-war black and white underside colour scheme, and the 'trolley acc' starters placed next to each aircraft ready for engine start-up.

helped to form George's ambition to become a fighter pilot. Two other reasons probably contributed: the fact that, as his subsequent flying training showed, he had a natural aptitude for single-engined aircraft; and, more subconsciously, that he had a chivalric desire to defend his own country and people against their enemies.

There wasn't much time for him to enjoy the pre-war atmosphere of a pleasant station like Duxford, where shooting and hunting were available as leisure pursuits. By the time George joined the UAS the Munich Agreement had been signed, and most people realised that the threat of war had only been postponed. In June 1939 all members of the University Squadron subject to the Military Training Act were attested into the RAFVR, and from 18 June to 28 July the annual UAS attachment – when all members did a concentrated period of full-time training – took place at Duxford, with 80 members attending and the aircraft available being increased by four Tutors and two Hinds. This was the last CUAS attachment before the war, and on 5 September 1939 the squadron closed down. In his time on the squadron, George did over 93 hours of flying – 44hr 10min dual instruction and 49hr 30min solo.

```
                    Cambridge University Air Squadron,
                      Fen Causeway,
                      Cambridge.

                      25.10.38.


Dear Sir,

            I have been instructed by the Selection Committee
to inform you that you have been selected for membership
of this Squadron, subject to your medical fitness.

            Will you, therefore, please call and make an
appointment with -
                  Dr. E.M.Billington, Bevan,
                        3,Trinity Street,
                              Cambridge.
for your medical examination.  I would add that there is
no charge for this examination.

            When this examination has taken place will
you please call at this office.

                      Yours very truly,



                      Flight Lieutenant,
                      Instructor, C.U.AIR SQUADRON.



    R.G.A.Barclay, Esq.,
            67,Jesus Lane.
```

The letter informing George that he had been selected for the Cambridge University Air Squadron.

When George Barclay received his instruction on 1 September to report to the VR Town Centre in Cambridge, he expected to start training at once; but the organisation for training hundreds of aircrew inevitably took time to get into gear.

In recalling that last brief peacetime summer and subsequent frustration at the delay in getting into the RAF, his brother Richard recalls that:

George adored flying and, with the clouds of war on the horizon, threw himself into the squadron's activities [both at Duxford and at the town headquarters in Fen Causeway]. It was therefore

George Barclay, newly commissioned into the RAFVR in 1939.

very frustrating for him on the outbreak of war to have to mark time for what I remember as months, but perhaps it was only weeks [actually just over two months], before he could resume his air training. During this period he furiously "double dug" up the lawn at Cromer Vicarage for a vegetable garden, feeding the succulent wire worms to our ducks and chickens and no doubt getting some shooting on the family estates in the vicinity. My father was an extremely keen and able shot and George was probably the keenest sportsman of the three brothers, being a good shot and an excellent dry fly fisherman.

In another way, this interim period was productive, for on 28 September 1939 he was informed that his application for a commission in the RAFVR had been approved and that he would be appointed a Pilot Officer from 3 October 1939; so from that date 754320 Sergeant R.G.A. Barclay became 74661 Pilot Officer R.G.A. Barclay – the first rung on the ladder he was to climb to Acting Squadron Leader by March 1942. Then, on 2 November, came the notice he had

been waiting for – ordering him to report before noon on Wednesday 8 November 1939, to No 3 Initial Training Wing (ITW) at Marine Court, Hastings, Sussex.

No 3 ITW was one of several initial training wings set up in coastal resorts to give potential pilots and observers their first training in navigation, armament, Air Force law, aircraft recognition, signals and other practical subjects; they were also given drill, PT and organised games, and many a young man became fitter at ITW than he had ever been before or ever was subsequently. No 3 ITW, notably, numbered among its PTIs the famous heavyweight boxers Sergeant Len Harvey and Corporal Eddie Phillips, while its instructors included the Walker Cup team golfer Pilot Officer L.G. Crawley and Test cricketer Pilot Officer W.R. Hammond.

Located in the requisitioned Marine Court Flats at St Leonards-on-Sea from 9 September 1939, the ITW was prepared for an intake of 1,000 trainees. Its operations record book notes that the Palace Pier had also been requisitioned 'to be used for educational and instructional purposes. The promenade immediately facing Marine Court provides a suitable Parade Ground for Drill and Physical Training and in inclement weather the underground car park adjacent to Marine Court is to be used for this purpose.' The syllabus provided for eight weeks' instruction, and the trainees must have been kept busy, with so much to be crammed in. George Barclay was there from the second week in November to about mid-December; then he had leave, probably spending Christmas at Cromer Vicarage, before being posted to the RAF College at Cranwell, Lincolnshire. His real flying training was about to begin.

It started precisely on 1 January 1940, flying Hinds, those famous Hawker biplanes on which he had had some experience at Cambridge, and all went well for the first fortnight. Then, on 18 January, returning from a cross-country flight to South Cerney, Gloucestershire, he crashed on landing in poor visibility at Barkston Heath, Lincolnshire, the satellite landing ground. But this was only a temporary setback; the same day, he was given further practice in take-off and landing, both dual and solo. Then all went well until the snows of early 1940 intervened. At Cranwell, exposed on the flat Lincolnshire plains, there were frequent heavy

Marching to classes at No 3 Initial Training Wing, Hastings, in 1939. George is second from the right in the rank nearest the camera.

snowstorms, plus fog and drizzle, from the beginning of February 1940, lasting for nearly three weeks. Owing to the state of the aerodrome, and the impossibility of flying, instructors and pupils were given leave from the beginning of February to the 25th; and it wasn't until 10 April 1940 that the 35 pupil officers on No 5 Course – the first 'war' course at Cranwell – completed their initial flying training and were posted to other units. The unit's ORB records:

This course is the first "war" course. It is composed of RAFVR officers formerly in University Air Squadrons. They came to Cranwell from No 3 ITW Hastings and had not been to an Elementary Flying Training School.

The record book added, as a general assessment: 'An above average course'; and George's flying log book, now with nearly 150 hours' flying recorded in it, reflected this assessment with an 'above average' end-of-course rating.

Richard Barclay says that according to family tradition the instructor said, 'What was wrong with you? I'd hoped to mark you "exceptional"' after the final flying test, but George had the flu and knowingly took his test with a high temperature rather than postpone it.

Opposite: George, fully kitted out in Sidcot suit, B Type flying helmet with 'doughnut' ear phone covers, goggles and leather gauntlets – de rigueur for an RAF fighter pilot in 1939–40.

January 1940, Squad II. George is in the middle row, third from the left.

The Hawker Hind trainer that George crashed while landing in poor visibility at Barkston Heath.

He was posted, not away from Cranwell, but to the Advanced Training Squadron (ATS) there, to fly Hinds, the Hawker two-seat fighter-bomber used widely in the 1920s and '30s, and formerly a front-line RAF aircraft. From 10 April 1940, the very day after finishing his initial flying training at Cranwell, George flew in the ATS, learning gun-firing, bombing, aerobatics, pilot navigation, formation and night flying. Late in May he had four days at No 5 Service Flying Training School (SFTS) at Sealand, near Chester, to convert to the Miles Master, his first experience of a retractable-undercarriage monoplane; but by 27 May he was back at Cranwell for the last five days of his flying training, and at the end of May received his final assessments – above the average as a pilot, above average as pilot-navigator/navigator, and average in air gunnery. He had done 124hr 25min solo flying time and 77hr 40min dual and had flown five different types of Service aircraft – Tutor, Hart, Hind, Audax and Master. A good start, but the real tests were still to come.

Changes and challenges now began to occur quickly for the newly fledged RAFVR pilot. First, to his horror, as he had set his mind on fighters, George was posted to No 1 School of Army Co-operation at Old Sarum, Wiltshire, as were several of his Cranwell friends – Pilot Officers Pat Doorly, David Scott-Maiden (later Air Vice-Marshal F.D.S. Scott-Maiden, DSO, DFC), and Tom Lund; and with him at Old Sarum were Pilot

Officers Robert Fleming and Pat Wells, also ex-Cranwell, who were to join a Hurricane fighter squadron with him. All these names are carefully listed in the clear, precise records George kept throughout his RAF flying career.

It was a brief assignment – eight days overall – to No 1 School of Army Co-operation. George was one of 20 officers on No 8 (Army Co-operation) War Course, which lasted from 2 to 10 June 1940. During it he converted to two new types – the Westland Lysander, that high-wing STOL (short take-off and landing) monoplane much used later in the war for flying Special Operations Executive personnel into and out of Occupied territory, and the Hawker Hector biplane, from the same stable as the Harts and Hinds he had flown at Cranwell. In seven days he did 7hr 20min flying, including several exercises in pinpointing objects on the ground, and two of photographing them from a Hector. But after this brief incursion into Army Co-operation the 20 members of No 8 Course were sent northwards for sterner stuff – to begin their fighter pilot education at No 5 Operational Training Unit (OTU), Aston Down, Gloucestershire.

Richard Hillary, ex-Oxford UAS, followed the same path and in his classic *The Last Enemy* tells how while at Aston Down he flew his Spitfire under one of the bridges over the River Severn. Richard Barclay says that George told him he did this too.

The unit's ORB recorded on 10 June 1940 that 26 pilot officers and 12 sergeant pilots 'reported for instruction', the pilot officers including George Barclay and his close friends

In the crew room waiting for a flight. Tan-coloured Sidcot suits and white flying overalls are much in evidence.

from Cranwell days, Robert Fleming and Pat Wells. The course was to be a significant experience for them: they were to fly Spitfires for the first time, their initial taste of a current operational aircraft (No 5 OTU also had Battles, Defiants and Harvards), and in just under a fortnight they would be joining their first squadron.

George seems to have revelled in the Spitfire, which he experienced on his second day's flying at Aston Down. First he flew a little Magister, the latest RAF *ab initio* trainer, to get accustomed to the local geography; then he was given dual on a Fairey Battle, the obsolescent single-engined bomber which had so recently been the cause of such heavy RAF losses in the air war over France, and flew one solo for 40 minutes; then on 12 June came his first flight in a Spitfire, followed by three hour-long sessions of aerobatics. Flying the Mk I version of this beautiful elliptical-winged fighter, he must have revelled in its highly sensitive fore-and-aft control, its speed and its lissom manoeuvrability. But it was to be more than a year before he first flew Spitfires operationally, and much was to happen to him in the intervening 14 months.

The OTU course, moreover, was not just a matter of throwing Spitfires around the sky – although that increased the young pilots' confidence in handling their machines. They were given practice in formation flying (essential for a fighter squadron) and in making formation attacks (a tactic less likely to be used operationally), in dog-fighting and in firing the Spitfire's eight guns. On his last day's flying at Aston Down – 21 June – he took a Spitfire up to 28,000ft, much higher than he had ever flown before.

His end-of-course assessment as a fighter pilot was 'above average as a pupil' – and the same page in his log book that saw him 'signed off' at the end of his training was also marked: 'Seen on posting to 249 Squadron, John Grandy, S/L [Squadron Leader]'.[1] For on 23 June 1940 George Barclay and his friends Bob Fleming and Pat Wells completed their OTU course and were posted to No 249 Squadron at Leconfield, Yorkshire.

No 249 was then a new squadron, only five weeks old, and it had a chequered start because Fighter Command HQ couldn't decide at first whether to equip it with Hurricanes or Spitfires. It started off at Church Fenton, Yorkshire, on 16 May 1940 with an establishment for 16 Hurricanes. Its CO, Squadron Leader Grandy, had come from No 219 Squadron and the first of his two flight commanders, Flight Lieutenant

High jinks at Church Fenton. George was twice stationed at Church Fenton in Yorkshire with No 249 Squadron in 1940, first when the squadron was re-formed there on 16 May, and then from 8 July to 14 August.

R.G. Kellett, later to achieve legendary fame in the Battle of Britain in command of the famous No 303 (Polish) Squadron, from No 616 Squadron. Flight Lieutenant Kellett was made 'A' Flight commander and Flying Officer R.A. Barton (a week later made an acting flight lieutenant) 'B' Flight commander. At first the new fighter squadron

[1] *John Grandy formed and trained No 249 Squadron from 16 May 1940 onwards, as he explains in his Foreword to this book. He later became Marshal of the Royal Air Force.*

Leconfield, May–June 1940. George and fellow No 249 Squadron pilots imitate the stance of their CO, Squadron Leader John Grandy. George Barclay and Tom Neil are second and third from left.

72098 Pilot Officers Patrick Hardy Vesey Wells, 74661 Richard George Arthur Barclay, 74672 Robert David Spittal Fleming, posted from Cranwell and attached to No 5 OTU Aston Down for training.

was allotted eight Hurricane Is; then on 17 May a signal was received from its controlling formation, No 13 Group,[2] cancelling the equipment with Hurricanes and substituting Spitfires. On the same date the squadron was ordered to move to Leconfield, which it did on 18 May, when eight Spitfires were allotted to it; and the next day it began operational flying training.

The Spitfire period, however, lasted only three weeks. On 10 June the squadron received a signal from Fighter Command HQ saying that it was to be re-equipped with Hurricanes. The next day, eight were allotted to it from No 10 Maintenance Unit (MU), Brize Norton; and it was with this type that No 249 fought in the Battle of Britain.

The squadron knew that it was getting three young ex-Cranwell recruits, even while they were still at Aston Down, for on 15 June its ORB noted:

This training was pretty brief, it could be argued, to fit them for fighter operations against the Luftwaffe; at Cranwell they had flown obsolete biplanes, and in Aston Down's 10 days George had only got 15hrs flying on Spitfires.

But they were fortunate in that No 249 was a new squadron, and they would gain experience with it as it worked up to operational status. Their arrival at Leconfield on 23 June was meticulously recorded:

The following pilots were returned from No 5 OTU on completion of training, and internally posted as follows:

'A' Flight 72098 P/O Patrick Hardy Vesey Wells
74661 P/O Richard George Arthur Barclay
74672 P/O Robert David Spittal Fleming

[2] *Fighter Command was divided into Groups, their numbers and their areas covering England, Wales and Scotland in an anti-clockwise rotation, thus: Nos 9, North-west England and most of Wales; 10, South Wales and West of England; 11, South-east England; 12, Eastern England up to Yorkshire; 13, North-east England and Eastern Scotland; 14, North-east Scotland.*

No 249 Squadron equipped with the Hawker Hurricane fighter at Leconfield in June 1940.

In other words, they came under the experienced eye of Squadron Leader R.G. Kellett, who had been promoted from flight lieutenant on 12 June. (On 19 July he was posted to Northolt to command No 303 [Polish] Squadron.)

George, who had done 229hr 50min flying up to that date, spent his first few days at Leconfield learning how to fly a Hurricane, and on 25 June climbed one to 30,000ft – the highest he'd ever been. He fired the Hurricane's eight guns for the first time, flew in formation, made camera-gun attacks, practised R/T (radio telephony) and instrument flying. On 1 July he got his first squadron assessments – 'average' as a fighter pilot and as a pilot-navigator.

Meanwhile, No 249 Squadron was heading for its own first assessment – as to its fitness for day fighter operations. On 29 June a 13-strong formation of its Hurricanes flew up to Church Fenton for a test by the Air Officer Commanding (AOC) No 13 Group to qualify as an operational squadron. George, and probably his fellow newcomers, were not included.

The tests, supervised by the Senior Air Staff Officer (SASO) Air Commodore C.H. Nicholas, and his officers, were based on practice interceptions of three Blenheims – these 'targets' being provided by No 219 Squadron from Catterick. No 249 was ordered off the ground by flights, interceptions and attacks being made over the aerodrome. Each flight was then recovered separately and tested for quick refuelling and

rearming, which took 12 minutes. SASO expressed himself satisfied at the standard the squadron had reached, and this opinion was formally confirmed on 3 July when No 249 received a signal stating that it was now operationally trained by day.

As if to confirm this, George had his first experience of operational flying on the following day, 4 July, in an early morning offensive patrol with Squadron Leader Kellett and Pilot Officer Pat Wells – also receiving his 'baptism of fire'. They took off from Leconfield at 05:00hrs and were airborne for 45 minutes, but didn't encounter any enemy aircraft.

On 7 July the squadron was ordered to move to Church Fenton and next day scored its first operational success, when Green Section of 'B' Flight attacked a Ju88 some 15 miles north-east of Flamborough Head and shot it down at 11:30hrs.

George wasn't involved; he went to Church Fenton that day, when the squadron's move there was completed, and continued his practice attacks, scramble and formation flying. On 18 July he visited his 'old school', Cranwell, and must have felt proud to show himself there in a squadron Hurricane.

Meanwhile, No 249 had become qualified (on 9 July) for night operations; and on 22 July the squadron received an official pat on the back for the work done in becoming operational – a letter from the AOC (Air Officer Commanding) No 13 Group, Air Vice-Marshal R.E. Saul, to Squadron Leader John Grandy congratulating the squadron on doing 1,010hr 20min flying training in June. 'I do not remember a case', said the AOC, 'where a squadron has ever passed the 1,000hr mark in a month, and this intensive effort to become operational at the earliest possible moment reflects the greatest credit on all concerned.'

Clearly George Barclay and his ex-Cranwell friends had joined a good unit, and their loyalty to it grew as the weeks went by. Like the squadron as a whole, he worked hard to increase proficiency, and by the time July 1940 was out had qualified himself to do night patrols.

No 249's first big test was soon to come. With a kind of premonition, the squadron ORB noted on 6 August:

There seems to be very little activity in the north now, but things are boiling up in the south of England and attacks are being carried out by large numbers of enemy aircraft on convoys and south coast ports. We are all hoping to get a move south.

In expressing this brave hope, the writer could hardly have realised what was in store for 249 and the other Fighter Command squadrons; for these enemy attacks were the first rumbles of the biggest and longest air battle the world had ever seen up to that time – the Battle of Britain.

RAF Church Fenton came under the control of No 12 Group, whose AOC was Air Vice-Marshal Trafford Leigh-Mallory, from 10 August, and he had visited the station two days earlier. Then on 13 August the station commander (Group Captain C.F. Horsley, MC) telephoned Squadron Leader Grandy to say that he had heard from the AOC that the squadron would probably be moving to Boscombe Down, Wiltshire, the following day.

Group Captain Horsley's early warning was no doubt acted upon, for on the 14th, after lunch, No 249 flew off to Boscombe Down – a station in the Middle Wallop sector of No 10 Group with the defence of Portsmouth and Southampton as its prime concern – and the next day were in action, George taking part in an offensive patrol which lasted for 1hr 20min in the late afternoon.

The squadron spent 18 days at Boscombe Down and on only the third day there one of its pilots, Flight Lieutenant E.J.B. Nicolson, took part in an action that subsequently won for him the only Victoria Cross awarded to a Royal Air Force fighter pilot during the war – engaging and destroying an

Bare-headed but wearing his Mae West – George in a posed cockpit photograph at Church Fenton.

Opposite: Not long after their arrival at Boscombe Down, 249's pilots sit and wait amongst their kit.

Me110 near Southampton while his Hurricane was on fire. But, operationally, this was not a very successful period. The ORB entry for 24 August gives the reason why:

The controllers at Middle Wallop appear to be working under very difficult circumstances, with untrained personnel and lack of equipment. On many of the patrols so far carried out [George had done six from Boscombe Down up to that date], no information other than the original telephoned order and the order to land had been received.

Then on 31 August the ORB noted: 'Many patrols have been flown but the enemy nearly always appear to approach the coast then turn south.'

A royal visit to No 249 Squadron at Boscombe Down in August, from where the squadron operated from the 14th to the end of the month. From left to right: Group Captain (later Air Marshal Sir Ralph) Sorley, Squadron Leader John Grandy, HRH The Duke of Kent, No 249 pilots Flying Officer Percy Burton (in the doorway), Flying Officer Pat Wells and Pilot Officer George Barclay.

But No 249 Squadron was about to meet the biggest test in its short operational existence. It was to move to an area where the controllers were the best in Fighter Command, where Luftwaffe aircraft didn't 'approach the coast then turn south' but kept on coming, in their hundreds. It was to replace No 56 Squadron in the front line at North Weald, in No 11 Group; and Pilot Officer George Barclay, who on 24 August started pencilling vivid descriptive notes of operations in his log book –

Yellow Section, Flying Officer Parnall, Flying Officer Wells, and self, at 20,000ft over Isle of Wight. Flew into formation of 70 109s at 18,000–25,000ft! No shot fired by either side, as Dennis did not fall for the Hun decoys, and so averted certain destruction; I was livid, until I realised about the decoys!

– would be its superb chronicler for the Battle of Britain.

His diary starts when the squadron moved to North Weald, Essex, at the beginning of September 1940. At the end of that month he carefully listed No 249's personnel in his log book:

Above: Hurricane Mk I, P3870, GN-C, was a favourite squadron aircraft for George to fly. On 16 August 1940 it was being flown from Boscombe Down by Squadron Leader Bruce King when it was involved in the action that saw Flight Lieutenant James Nicolson (in P3576) shoot down a Messerschmitt Bf110 fighter and earn Fighter Command's only Victoria Cross of the war. Note George's parachute pack balanced on the tailplane and his helmet draped over the gun sight inside the cockpit.

Left: James 'Nick' Nicolson while recovering from his injuries in hospital at Torquay, before he was told he had won the Victoria Cross.

Below: Nick recuperates from his burns.

249 Squadron

Sept 1940

North Weald

CO, S/L John Grandy

Adj, F/O E.N. Lohmeyer, DFC; Engineering Officer,

P/O Tucker (Tom); Intelligence, F/O Woolmer (Woolly)

'A'	'B'
F/L Lofts, DFC (Keith)	*F/L Barton, DFC*
P/O Neil, DFC & Bar	*F/O Wells*
P/O Solak (Jersey)	*F/O Barclay*
P/O Thompson (The Rake)	*F/O Cassidy (Casserole)*
P/O McConnell (Mac)	*P/O Crossey*
	Worrall
W/O Bouquillard	*W/O Perrin*
Sgt Beard, DFM	*Sgt Smithson*
Sgt Palliser	*Sgt Killingback*
Sgt Stroud	*Sgt Davies*
Sgt Maciejowski	*Sgt Evans*
Sgt Mills (Dusty)	

Lasting from 10 July to 31 October 1940, the Battle of Britain was the first decisive military campaign ever to be fought exclusively by air forces. Had the German Luftwaffe – which at the start had about 1,200 fighters and 3,000 bombers, opposed by some 600 RAF Hurricanes and Spitfires – won the battle and gained air superiority over south-east England, the German Army would probably have attempted an invasion. RAF Fighter Command aircraft, directed by radar, were Britain's defensive weapon, and with the support of anti-aircraft artillery and barrage balloons, ensured her survival. In the Battle, whose crucial stage was reached during September 1940 when No 249 Squadron became involved, over 480 RAF and Allied Air Forces' pilots lost their lives and more than 420 were injured.

Steel-helmeted groundcrew rearm a Hurricane with belts of 0.303in ammunition. (*TopFoto*)

South-east England
in 1940, showing
towns, villages and
RAF airfields.

Dornier Do17
bombers were regularly
encountered by George.
Here, Do17s of
9./KG76 cross the
English coast near
Beachy Head on
18 August, heading at
low level to bomb the
RAF airfield at Kenley
in Surrey.

George being debriefed by E.L. Lohmeyer, squadron adjutant.

CHAPTER TWO

The Battle of Britain

Sunday, September 1st, 1940

Yesterday evening we were told we were to move to North Weald today to relieve the war-weary and much shot-up 56 Squadron. The morning was pretty hectic – packing, etc. Denis Parnall[1] took my luggage from dispersal up to the Mess. We gather we are really going to get some 'war' at last. Butch[2] in his usual pessimistic way said, 'I suppose some of us here will never return to Boscombe.' We are meant to be going for a week and I think everyone is quite sure *he* will survive for at least seven days! We are taking over the 56 aeroplanes with VHF radio and keeping the 56 crews, so only the pilots of 249 will be at North Weald.

We said goodbye to the Adjutant (Pilot Officer Lohmeyer) and CO and flew off after lunch. I flew No 3 on the CO[3] and Pat Wells. On landing one heard many derogatory remarks about the wireless masts near the aerodrome 350ft high.

After landing we had tea at the Mess and then returned to dispersal, where Squadron Leader John Cherry, the CO's brother-in-law and head Controller here, talked to us on VHF, etc. We took over our aeroplanes and 56 took off for Boscombe in ours. We did a short squadron flight to experiment with VHF. Mine didn't work and I was very disappointed with this so-called 'foolproof' R/T.

We grabbed beds in the hut and slept soundly, wondering what the morrow held in store.

Monday, September 2nd

I was off the state[4] in the morning and was very angry with Denis Parnall because of it! The squadron

---

[1] *Pilot Officer Denis Parnall was on 'B' Flight.*

[2] *Flight Lieutenant Barton, OC 'B' Flight.*

[3] *Squadron Leader John Grandy.*

[4] *Aircrew state – list of pilots who were to fly operationally.*

Percy Burton reads between sorties. Note the aircraft identification posters on the wall behind him. His parents played a major part in creating the great memorial at Capel le Ferne visible from high in the sky.

John Beazley relaxes with a book and a cigarette at North Weald.

scrambled and intercepted some Do215s and Me110s. Percy Burton crash-landed successfully. John Beazley baled out successfully. Nelg Wynn crash-landed successfully but was wounded in the neck. Several 215s were brought down, and 110s. Apparently the 215s put up some very good crossfire.

I came on the state after this scrap and we had three scrambles – the first over Rochford and the Estuary at 15,000ft, the second over North Weald at 15,000ft. We saw nothing. On the third scramble we ran into some 110s in defensive circles. They were above us, and we adopted the defensive snake formation. I did an upward full deflection attack from the front – went up into a loop and did an inverted spin out of it! I climbed up again but the 110s went off home hell for leather – one got left behind and I got in a long burst at long range, one of his engines pouring glycol as he drew away. I couldn't keep up, let alone catch him, so I left him to a Spitfire and

rejoined what was left of the snake. I saw one Spitfire shot down in the fight and I thought I saw 'J', the CO's machine, go down, but fortunately I was wrong.

Very shortly after his arrival at North Weald – possibly on 2 September – George wrote to his elder sister Ann:

Dearest Ann,
Thank you most awfully for such a grand holiday. It was most refreshing and the ideal 24 hours' leave. It did me an immense amount of good to get right into the country and well away from the RAF for a day. I think your little house is delightful and it was very nice to find you all so flourishing. I got back to the aerodrome at Colerne[1] with the assistance of a lorry driver who gave me a very useful lift up hill. We arrived back at Boscombe Down quite safely, to hear that the next morning (Sunday) we were to move to

[1] RAF station near Chippenham, Wiltshire.

my present address to defend London. We are having a bit of real 'war' now. We have been up four times today and twice had terrific battles with hundreds of Messerschmitts. It is all perfectly amazing, quite unlike anything else, I imagine. One forgets entirely what attitude one's aeroplane is in, in an effort to keep the sights on the enemy. And all this milling around of hundreds of aeroplanes, mostly with black crosses on, goes on at say 20,000ft with the Thames Estuary and surrounding country as far as Clacton displayed like a map below. We have shot down at least four for certain today and about half a dozen others probably destroyed or damaged. Our casualties – three shot down but all three pilots safe, one being wounded. We are here for a short time, replacing a squadron which needed a rest.

I must stop and go to bed, as I am pretty dead beat tonight.

North Weald – Flight Lieutenant R.A. 'Butch' Barton, who later became CO of No 249 Squadron – twice. December 1940–July 1941, then August–December 1941.

I'll come and visit you again when we return to Boscombe Down, if I may. I can't express how much I enjoyed my first stay.
With love to you all
from George.

Tuesday, September 3rd

What lovely partridge shooting weather! I was off the state today and missed some scrambles.

I had my first experience of large-scale bombing today. The squadron scrambled at about 9:45 and were pancaked at about 10:45 and told to refuel immediately. This was done and they were kept at readiness on the ground for ten minutes before going off again. Very soon after their take-off the Tannoy broadcast the 'take cover' and added, 'hostile aircraft approaching from south-east'. We took cover. I stood at the mouth of the shelter and watched. I saw AA fire and then almost directly overhead about 25 German bombers at 17,000ft. I hopped into the shelter and almost immediately hell was let loose. About 250 bombs were dropped – the noise quite unbelievable, and it seemed as if we were bound to get hit by at least one! The noise was utterly terrifying while it lasted. We came out of the shelter to see the aerodrome enveloped in a vast cloud of smoke and dust, the hangars on fire, and the sound of ammunition exploding. The whole place is covered in bits of anti-personnel bombs, yet the total casualties were only three killed! So much for the value of taking cover.

The WAAFs took the bombing as staunchly as did the men. The squadron was off the ground, which was the main thing, but they were scrambled too late to intercept.

When the fires were put out, etc, one saw that the real damage was comparatively small. The Mess is untouched. Half the aerodrome is u/s and there are some delayed action bombs scattered about. If bombs are going to be dropped, give me an aeroplane every time!

In the morning Butch Barton had to bale out when the squadron attacked some Do215s and Do17s. He landed quite OK and was brought back in an Army car. The Army couldn't make out why everyone just stood and laughed when Butch arrived, taunting him with the jibe, 'shot down by a bomber'!

'Ginger' Neil points a shotgun at the photographer.

Wednesday, September 4th

We had two scrambles today, nothing being seen. The first at 15,000ft over North Weald and the second over Gravesend at 20,000ft. I am very dissatisfied with only being on the state every other day. It can't be helped – at the moment we seem to have too many pilots – no doubt one day we shall be sick of the sight of an aeroplane. This sector is very easy to find one's way in – the Estuary is a great landmark.

Thursday, September 5th

I was off the state again today worse luck. The squadron ran into some bombers – He111s and

The squadron moved to North Weald on 1 September. Outside the dispersal hut Bill Millington holds Pipsqueak the puppy. Also in the picture are Squadron Leader John Grandy, the squadron CO (wearing side cap), Pilot Officer Crossey (behind Millington) and Pilot Officer Tom Neil standing (foreground).

Some downtime with a pipe and the puppy. From left: 'Butch' Barton, unknown, Terry 'Ossie' Crossey and Bill Millington.

Do215s. The CO was missing for an hour or two and everyone was very anxious. Pilot Officer Crossey (Ossie!)[1] was shot down and crash-landed OK. The CO, we heard later, was in hospital with some torn muscles in his leg and minor cannon-shell wounds. Apparently the squadron was told to re-form at 15,000ft over Eastchurch. The CO, on getting to the rendezvous, was told to pancake and as he dived down he got shot up by 109s. As is usually the case, he didn't see what got him.

We were all very relieved to hear the CO was OK and not badly wounded. Another 'caterpillar' for the squadron![2]

Friday, September 6th

We are having simply magnificent weather – I've never known anything like it – clear skies and brilliant sun. It must be the finest English summer for years, just when we would sometimes give our boots for a day of low cloud and rain! There's one advantage though and that's that we get to know the sector slightly. The Thames Estuary makes things easy, though the balloon barrage works in the other direction in bad weather.

We had two trips today – the first at 10,000ft over Rochford – quite uneventful, and the second in the evening at 20,000ft over the Isle of Sheppey. Though the weather was magnificent there was a bit of a haze at 10,000ft. The height of the raiders coming in was, for some unknown reason, not known, so all the squadrons were sent up high. Eight Junkers 87 dive bombers came in in the haze at 10,000ft and bombed Shellhaven. They were quite invisible from above – a very clever German manoeuvre. Wing Commander Beamish[3] was just climbing up to join us at 20,000ft when he ran into the 87s – the fighter pilot's dream came true! He shot a couple down, but they plugged Shellhaven good and proper, the immense clouds of black smoke rising to over 8,000ft.

Saturday, September 7th

Little did we realise what was in store for us today when we scrambled after lunch. Twelve aircraft took off to patrol Maidstone at 15,000ft, seven came back. We climbed up slowly in brilliant sun. Visibility was very good and I combined a sector recco with watching my tail. I saw Rochester, and thought of Aunt Chris and Tuppence![4] I looked over to the left and saw Burnham-on-Crouch where Norman Eddy the American[5] and I became photographer's assistants for

---

[1] 'B' Flight.

[2] Awarded to pilots who baled out; see glossary of terms used, page 11.

[3] Station Commander, North Weald.

[4] Miss C.O. Barclay, George's Godmother, who had helped to pay for his education at Stowe. Tuppence was her cat.

[5] An American contemporary of George's in Bruce House at Stowe, whose 'life was greatly changed by George's influence with the consequence that on his return to America he was ordained and went to work amongst the down-and-outs in Harlem, New York', as recorded by Richard Barclay.

a day! And I could just see Clacton pier and wondered whether the bumper cars were still running!

We got on patrol and drifted up and down the sky, while the No 3s in each section tended to weave less and less. Then suddenly 'Hullo, Ganer[1] leader; Hullo, Ganer leader, bandits on your right – over.' And there sure enough was a tiny slanting black line which we knew were bombers. We turned towards them. I turned the gun button to 'Fire' and looked to see that the reflector sight was working OK. I opened the hood, and immediately I could see 50 per cent better, though it is 50 per cent colder. I saw that the rapidly closing bombers were surrounded by black dots, which I knew to be Me109s. So we were in for it this time!

Before we knew where we were we were doing a beam attack on the Dornier 215s. All I remember is trying to avoid hitting anyone else as we attacked, and being conscious of Me109s coming down to attack us. I had a long burst at one section of Dorniers and as I broke away noticed at least two lagging behind and streaming glycol or white smoke. These weren't necessarily the ones I had fired at. I never saw another Hurricane anywhere near until I got back to the aerodrome.

As I broke off I turned and two yellow Me109s shot past underneath me. I turned back and fired at the nearest – no result. Had a burst at the farthest and immediately there was a puff of black smoke, a brilliant flame and down he went, slowly turning over on to his back. The whole hood and Perspex flew off and the fuselage began to disintegrate. But no time to stop. I turned sharply and found another yellow 109 on my tail, sitting pretty. I did an aileron turn in a dive to get away and then flattened out and had a good look round. I was about 7,000ft below the bombers, so I climbed up about a mile away on their starboard watching my tail carefully for Me109s.

Just when I was on the bombers' level and thinking about an attack, the whole formation turned towards me – so a head-on attack happened. All I saw as I broke away was the leader's port engine smoking, but I didn't wait to see as my windscreen was pitch black with oil and my engine dead as a gate post. I lost a lot of height to get away from the 109s and then set about making a forced-landing. Actually my immediate reaction with all this oil about the place and fumes and smoke was to bale out, but I decided to stay in, and everything went well until at 1,000ft I realised it was now too late to bale out! I landed safely, wheels up, in a field near Potterstreet village about four miles from North Weald. It was good to be on firm land again. The usual crowd collected and I put some soldiers on guard and got some others to take me back. I arrived shortly after the last Hurricane had landed. Seven of the twelve had come back – two of 'A' Flight's six. We heard later on that Robert Fleming[2] had baled out, had been very seriously burnt and had died as a result. Sergeants Killingback and Smithson[3] had both been wounded, presumably by cannon-shell fragments. Pat Wells is missing.[4]

When I got back, the pilots who could were preparing to take off again. One machine had gone u/s, so six took off. Meanwhile, three waves of Hun bombers flew over the aerodrome at about 16,000ft. We all thought they had come to finish off the job they had started on the 3rd. But no bombs were dropped – thank heavens. It was most depressing to watch them going over and being quite powerless to do anything. Five of the six aircraft that took off on the second sortie returned. Sergeant Beard[5] baled out – but we heard later that he was OK and will return tomorrow.

The odds today have been unbelievable (and we are all really very shaken!). There are bombs and things falling around tonight and a terrific gun barrage. Has a blitz begun? The Wing Commander's coolness is amazing and he does a lot to keep up our morale – very necessary tonight. We all wish the CO was here.

[1] *'Ganer' was the squadron's R/T call-sign.*

[2] *Pilot Officer R.D.S. Fleming, one of George's Cranwell contemporaries.*

[3] *Both 'B' Flight pilots.*

[4] *Pilot Officer P.H.V. Wells, another Cranwellian.*

[5] *'A' Flight.*

Sunday, September 8th

The weather was bad today, thank goodness, so we have had a valuable rest. I think we are all still a bit shaken after yesterday.

Monday, September 9th

The worst part of this job is the few minutes before we actually get scrambled – when we know we are going off shortly. Once we are in the air, everything is OK.

The weather was wonderful again today – a real blitzkrieg day, but it didn't materialise. We patrolled Sheppey at 15,000ft. Some He113s [single-seat fighters] passed over us in close formation, but we are out for bombers – anyway we couldn't get up to them and they went on their way.

Tuesday, September 10th

The weather was poor today and nothing much happened. Still no news of Pat Wells. We are afraid he must have been shot down into the Estuary. I am on the state practically all the time now owing to the shortage of pilots – a great improvement on the beginning of the month.

On this day George Barclay wrote to his parents about the fighting on 7 September. In this long letter he vividly relives that day's combats in an expanded version of his diary entry:

Tuesday North Weald

My darling Mummie and Far,

I'm afraid my sundry notes are often extremely reserved as to what we have been doing, but it is very difficult to know how much one can legitimately say in a letter. We have several times had some extremely exciting scraps with these vast Hun formations attacking London. Our fiercest hour was on Saturday, the 7th, or was the 7th a Friday? We lose all count of day and date! Anyway it was the day the Boche first attacked London Docks and the East End on a large scale.

We were sent up as a squadron (ie four sections of three aeroplanes) to patrol over Maidstone – it was a grand day and from 15,000ft the view was so delightful that one was tempted to sit there and admire it instead of searching for the Hun. I saw Westgate and couldn't help ruminating on Hawtreys.[1] I remembered flying model aeroplanes on the cliff while 'on leave' with particular clarity! Then there was Burnham-on-Crouch where Norman Eddy[2] and I became 'photographer's assistants' for a day with Douglas Went.[3] And there was Rochester and I thought of Aunt Chris's former home (and Tuppence!) and the Archdeaconry.

Then right on the horizon I could just see Clacton and in the haze I could just make out where Gt Holland[4] ought to be, though couldn't see it. And below us the balloon barrage and London – and that pulled me back to reality and I spent several minutes searching the sky for Huns and checking over the cockpit instruments.

Then over the wireless came a shout, 'Hullo, leader, Messerschmitt 109s behind us in the sun', and I'm sure twelve hearts suddenly beat double time! I looked extremely hard into the sun and cocked one wing up to cover it, so that I could look around without a glare, but I couldn't see anything. We started to climb hard, turning to get a good look around – and there several miles away was a black line in the sky – 35 Hun bombers in close formation – and I gradually began to distinguish about 70–100 other little dots – Hun fighters.

The squadron turned to attack and I switched on the electric sight and turned the gun button from 'Safe' to 'Fire'. And then things began to happen – we went in at the bombers and as I broke away I saw two dropping back from the formation, streaming white smoke from one engine. These weren't necessarily shot by me but by the squadron. But before one could take stock of the situation the Messerschmitts were on me – I say 'me' rather than

---

[1] *George's prep school at Westgate-on-Sea.*

[2] *The American referred to in a note under the 7 September diary entry.*

[3] *A professional photographer.*

[4] *The vicarage where he had spent his boyhood, between Frinton and Clacton.*

No 249 Squadron's Hurricanes get airborne from North Weald
in September 1940. The aircraft nearest the camera is George's
Hurricane, GN-C.

A Hurricane bursts into flames after being hit by enemy fire. (*TopFoto*)

'us' because from this time on I never noticed another Hurricane in the sky until the end of the fight – and probably it was the same with most of the other Hurricanes.

I turned quickly to see if there was anything on my tail and at the same moment two Messerschmitt 109s went past beneath my nose. I turned quickly, diving on one and gave him a burst – nothing happened – presumably missed him, but the noise of my eight guns gave me great confidence. I gave the second Me109 a burst and whoopee! A sudden burst of brilliant flame, a cloud of smoke, and a vast piece flew off it, and down he went. But no time to watch, there's something behind me shooting a grey line past me on the left (tracer bullets). I turned to the right and saw a Me109 go past with a vicious yellow nose and the large black crosses on the fuselage. At the same time I saw a Hurricane going vertically down pouring smoke (and later the pilot's parachute with another Hurricane circling it to protect him from the Huns).

But no time to stop, I couldn't see much owing to a spurt of oil on the windscreen. I dived to get away from the Me109s and levelled out at 6,000ft. And here a note on our Hurricanes – they are very strong and we have complete confidence in them. The other day I dived at 570mph and the aeroplane took the speed easily.

Having got rid of the 109s I could still see the bombers 10,000ft above, so I climbed up keeping my distance until I was again on their level to one side. They then made up my mind for me by turning straight towards me and I did a head-on attack on the leader. As I broke away my ammunition gave out, but I saw one of the leader's engines smoking. Now I couldn't see anything as oil was pouring out of the engine on to the windscreen and my engine gave signs of packing up altogether. I glided back over the Thames Estuary, noticing below a blazing oil tank with a thick cloud of black smoke up to 8,000ft, and a grey cloud of smoke over the Docks. I then realised I couldn't get back to the aerodrome and made a successful crash-landing in a field about five miles away from here – quite OK and the Hurricane not much damaged. I sat around and waited for some soldiers to guard the machine and then got a lift

back here. Meanwhile the whole local population had turned out to have a look.

I arrived back at the aerodrome to find the squadron just going off for a second crack at the Huns, but there was no machine for me so I sat in an air raid shelter and listened to two waves of Hun bombers go over after dropping bombs on London.

The section I was in was unfortunate that day as the other two pilots were both shot down and are now in hospital with slight wounds. We were on the outside of the first attack on the bombers and so bought it from the fighters.

This is all very badly written and heavens knows how many times I've used the word 'and'! But it may give some idea of a fight in the air. This is not for circulation; I'm afraid it's all about me, but of course the rest of the squadron did their stuff and went off again after rearming.
Best love,
from, George.

Wednesday, September 11th

We scrambled in the morning and climbed up to 17,000ft above haze over east London. We were vectored after various raids and it seemed as if we were going to miss them, when we saw ack-ack south of us. We opened up a bit and turned south. My windscreen became black with oil suddenly which meant I was useless.

Sunday, September 15th

We scrambled at about 11:30 and climbed up above 8/10–9/10 cloud over London to 16,000ft. (Percy Burton being up at Church Fenton in the Maggie,[1] his Irvin trousers[2] were not being used, so I bagged them and was able to fly with the hood open as a result. One can see much better like this.)

We cruised about above the clouds and chased some AA bursts without success and then suddenly sighted about 18 enemy bombers (Dornier 215s) on our right going in the opposite direction to ourselves. We turned and crossed beneath them but the squadron got split up. I followed three of our Hurricanes climbing up on the left of the bombers

[1] Miles Magister, a two-seat trainer.

[2] The Irvin suit (jacket and trousers) was made of leather-backed sheepskin, fleece-lined. The jacket zipped up and had a deep collar.

Flying Officer Pat Wells watches as his No 249 Squadron Hurricane is rearmed at North Weald.

for a head-on attack, lost patience and turned to do a beam attack on the leader. At the same time the leading Hurricane turned to do a head-on attack and we almost collided above the bomber. I broke over the bombers because I was too close to break away below. I remember diving earthwards in the middle of the bomber formation.

The attack was fairly successful. I opened fire with more than full deflection and let the Do[1] fly into the bullets like a partridge. I noticed his cannon firing from the top rear gun position. The Me109s escorting the bombers were far above and behind and did not trouble us – I believe due to Spitfires engaging them as I noticed a great dogfight going on – smoke trails, etc. Owing to lack of fighter opposition there was no need to break right away downwards, so I came back and did a short quarter attack. The Do215 then broke away from the formation and I saw that the engines were

just idling as it glided down. Then about eight of our fighters set on the lame duck about 3,000ft below me. On landing I claimed this as a 'probably destroyed'.

Meanwhile I was climbing to attack again, but a fighter came up behind and 'made a pass' at me. So I had to turn sharply to find out what he was – one of those confounded Spitfires again – Glamour Boys! By this time the bombers were too far away above me so I dived down through the clouds and found I was over the lower Thames. (I now noticed how painful my fingers were through cold. I find they get much worse if my fingertips are rammed right into the glove fingers. If gloves are on loosely it is much better.)

---

[1] Presumably Do215.

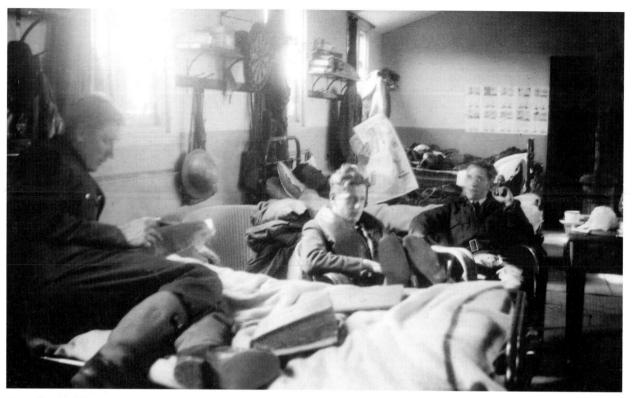

Time off in the billet.

A typical Dornier formation.

I returned to the aerodrome and gave the rearm sign over our dispersal area – a sideslip from side to side. I knew this would excite the crews enormously. They get almost more excited than the pilots about our fights. Pilot Officer Lofts, Pilot Officer Lewis, DFC, and Sergeant Palliser were all missing – three newcomers to the squadron, but they all turned up OK later on. We had a rotten lunch in our dispersal hut, sitting on our beds.

We were scrambled again at 2 o'clock and went to the same place as in the morning, joining 46 Squadron beneath the cloud layer. Butch Barton was leading the squadron owing to the CO (John Grandy's) absence at Boscombe Down. Very shortly after reaching our height (16,000ft) we sighted fighters above us, the usual heralds of approaching bombers, and then over the R/T came, 'Hullo Ganer leader – on your right, on your right – over.' No answer and again came 'Ganer leader – *on your right*' in a high-pitched excited shout. And sure enough there were about 20 Do215s, for once at the same height as ourselves. The squadron went into the attack on the beam. Denis Parnall, Red 1 (I was Red 2), we heard later did not attack with us but went into some Heinkel 111s that he saw coming up behind the Do215s. These Heinkels were the second wave – there was yet another behind them.

As we attacked I noted the cannon fire from the top rear gun positions of the Dorniers – little spurts of white smoke flicking back past the twin rudders in the slipstream, as if someone was giving intermittent squirts from a hose pipe. (Oh, the smell of cordite!)

After my attack the Do215 dropped behind the formation a bit and one parachute came out underneath. I couldn't wait to see what happened. In view of the above I claimed this Dornier as 'damaged', though I observed no effect of my fire. I then noticed all the Dorniers jettisoning their bombs.

The Dorniers had broken up on our first attack and some dived for the clouds, but for some inexplicable reason they stayed just skimming the clouds and did not go right into them and

Instrument Fly home. Inexperience? (I saw Sergeant Evans spin off a turn with two yellow 109s on his tail but was unable to warn him.) It seems improbable but I can't find any other reason.

I dived after one Do and gave it a longish burst (4 secs?) at about 200 yards. There was suddenly a flash of brilliant flame from the port engine (I nearly flew across the fire of another Hurricane) and, maimed, the Do went into the clouds. (Claimed as 'probably destroyed'.)

I transferred my attention to another Dornier skimming the top of the cloud, and closed in to a range of about 30yd, shooting all the time. The enemy aircraft took slight evasive action but I was able from my position above and to the left to keep the correct deflection on the glass-house of the pilot. As my ammo gave out the Do dived into the clouds. I followed him through and picked him up below, again over Shellhaven. He seemed quite OK so I did a feint attack on him. He did a gentle left-hand turn and began to dive more and more steeply towards the ground 7,000ft below. This beautifully streamlined aircraft seemed to gather speed steadily and I began to wonder when he was going to pull out of the dive. Then a gigantic flash several hundred feet high as the enemy aircraft went straight into the ground. A most memorable and rather awful sight. The bomber had just missed a bungalow and crashed on the track in front of it. This was about three miles west of Vange, north of Shellhaven. I noticed the smoke from at least two other crashed aircraft in the district.

All our aircraft returned safely, and we got about ten confirmed victories (Do215s and He111s) and the same number of probable victories, not to mention damaged enemy aircraft. Our best day so far since the squadron was formed in May. I had one bullet hole in the starboard wing of US-C,[1] but no damage done. (British fighters shot down 185 enemy aircraft today,[2] 131 bombers!) Boozy party this evening!

[1] *US were the code letters of No 56 Squadron. No 249's were GN.*

[2] *This figure appears in the ORB for 15 September 1940; it was widely publicised, but has subsequently been discounted. The now accepted figure is 56.*

Pilot Officer
Tom 'Ginger' Neil.

Monday, September 16th

Terrible weather today. We scrambled at about 7:00am and flew up to 21,000ft when we came out of cloud into brilliant sunlight and a circle of smoke trails made by enemy aircraft. We were over the Channel or France by this time. We stooged around a bit, saw enemy aircraft going home far above us with trails (probably Me110s). Pilot Officer Lofts, an auxiliary and newcomer to the squadron, led the section I was in. The whole squadron got split up. We descended through the cloud, flew around Maidstone a bit and then returned home in a mist. The kind of trip that leaves an annoyed feeling behind it.

The mist grew into a fog so that we couldn't see the wireless masts on the other side of the aerodrome and it poured with rain – no more flying. A few bombs were dropped around and on the 'drome during the night. Apparently a fifth columnist was signalling with a lamp in a wood nearby. A terrific AA barrage all night.

Tuesday, September 17th

'30 minutes available' all day today – but this means nothing except that we could get a long bath in the Mess. We scrambled at about 3:00pm and flew up over London, above clouds at 15,000ft. My thoughts wandered on to American air films as I turned on the oxygen, and I sang, 'Franklin D. Roosevelt Jones' lustily to myself. (Life now has some striking resemblances to that film *Dawn Patrol,* such as flying in our pyjamas!)

The sky was full of Hurricanes and we all got rather mixed up together. We saw some AA fire and some 109s above us. It was very bumpy. Once my engine stopped and my head hit the roof though my seat was as low as it would go. I am too big in flying kit really for Hurribags. I am about 6ft but my back is too long in proportion to my legs! I noticed a Hurricane with the letters RFB, which made me ruminate on Richard's[1] schooling problems – now to the fore at home.

---

[1] *Youngest of the three Barclay sons who significantly contributed to this edition of the book; his initials are R.F.B.*

Eventually the whole two squadrons split up all over the sky and Butch, Ginger Neil and self were all that was left! My (VHF) R/T was u/s today.

Wednesday, September 18th

We scrambled four times today. The first time at about 9:30 we saw nothing – there was some grand cumulus cloud about, as there has been on several days lately. The squadron looked grand against these cotton wool mountains. On the second sortie we came across about 20 He111s with 109 escort. We saw the 109s manoeuvring to attack us as we did a head-on attack at the He111s, whose position had been given away by ack-ack bursts.

There was only time for a quick burst as our speed of approach was of course colossal. We were with 46 Squadron and we heard on landing that the 109s had attacked their last two sections – two missing. After our first attack the He111s turned, having jettisoned their bombs, and made for home fast. I had another poop at the leader as they turned – no visible result. The bombers made off very fast and having broken right away because of 109s we were unable to catch them again. Pilot Officer Lewis, DFC, got a 109. The only observed result of the squadron's attack was two He111s damaged.

We saw nothing on the third scramble, only Shellhaven burning. It usually is nowadays! Just the odd tank burning, and they made a terrific cloud of black smoke, sometimes up to 8,000ft but the total damage done so far is very small. Denis (Flight Lieutenant Parnall, 'A' Flight Commander) has not turned up from the second trip. He has been missing ever since, but we recall the case of Pat (Flying Officer Wells) who was 'missing, believed killed' for five days and then was found slightly wounded in hospital.

On the fourth sortie we saw a lot of ack-ack fire high above us, and then about 12 He111s. They were below a high layer of cloud and we were above a lower layer. We tried to climb up but the bombers were climbing too and we couldn't catch them. We could distinctly see the Hurricanes attacking them far above and about four fell past us. One I noticed

North Weald 1941. Flight Lieutenant 'Lew' Lewis and Pilot Officer 'Ossie' Crossey.

in flames going down almost vertically – 20,000ft to ground level – what an explosion!! I then saw a lame Heinkel on the cloud layer below limping home.

Realising we wouldn't engage the main formation (very infuriating as they seemed to be almost unescorted) I dived down and closed to about 40yd range. The Heinkel turned left and I saw my bullets rake it from pilot's cabin to tail. A parachute appeared out of the top of the fuselage and flapped around; bits flew off, and a yellow rubber boat bobbed out of the rear top of the fuselage. Then he went down in a vertical dive into the clouds and straight on down, probably into the Estuary just off Shoeburyness.

Meanwhile, Sergeant Beard got an Me110 over Kent. We were the only two who fired any rounds. On the way home I joined the TP Squadron[1] –

---

[1] TP were the original wartime code letters of 73 Squadron.

The view from inside the cockpit of a Heinkel He111 of a Spitfire closing in for a stern attack on another He111. (*TopFoto*)

73 Squadron who were up at Church Fenton with us. I noticed a forced-landed Do215 in a field near Shoeburyness.

We got congratulatory telegrams yesterday from Archibald Sinclair, Secretary of State for Air, and from Sir Cyril Newall, Chief of Air Staff, for our bag on Sunday last. No 303 Squadron, led by Boozy Kellett (Squadron Leader Kellett, late of 249) and composed of Poles, beat us, getting 16 enemy aircraft destroyed to our 10. Boozy got DFC for this.

Thursday, September 19th

It is splendid to have the CO back again. He has been having treatment for the torn muscles in his leg, received when he baled out on September 6th.

Beazel (Pilot Officer Beazley) and I were scrambled this morning at about 9:45. The weather was very cloudy with high SW wind – just the day for single recco jobs to come over. We climbed up to 20,000ft between two layers of cloud, and for once my wireless was absolutely A1. We were vectored all over the place in the Southend area. Beazel's transmitter was u/s – I presumed he was not receiving Lumba (North Weald ground station) and passed on all Lumba's vectors to him quite unnecessarily.

We were suddenly told there was a bandit below us at 'Angels 10', *ie* 10,000ft. We dived and there was a Junkers 88, its engines sticking right out in front of the leading edge of the wing – very distinctive. We broke up and Beazel attacked from astern and got in about a 10-second burst. I did a sort of vertical full deflection attack from above, pulled out of the dive and did an astern attack of about seven seconds burst. The 88 turned slightly to the left and went into the cloud with the port engine pouring smoke and bits flying off. I dived after it into cloud and two black bits floated past – I noticed as usual the reek of cordite from my ammo. I never saw the 88 again, though I looked for it below cloud over the Estuary, where I saw several convoys and Thames barges. Beazel says both engines were smoking and bits flying off. Later we heard that the 88 had crashed off Deal.

Having lost Beazel in the clouds, I was vectored about a bit and then returned home to base – a thoroughly enjoyable trip. Practically the whole squadron went up in pairs throughout the morning, but we were the only ones to find anything. Nothing doing during the afternoon.

Friday, September 20th

We went off at about 11am, scrambled from '30 minutes available' – not even brought to readiness. There was a flap, and the Tannoy (loud speaker system) bawled, 'Take cover'. We eventually got into the air and Butch's R/T was dead! (He still leads as the CO is not fit yet). Added to this, Lumba wireless operator was a complete dimwit, and it took a very long time to give us a pip-squeak zero. We got no orders and just milled around over the 'drome at 14,000ft. It was a grand morning but everything went wrong that could go wrong, and I got furious!

A terrible night followed – bombs burst all around us, shrapnel whizzed and whistled, the ack-ack kept us awake, a cat meowed, the engines were run up right outside the door, and to cap the lot – the stooge (Pilot Officer Loweth) fell out of bed!

Saturday, September 21st

Beazel and I were scrambled in the middle of lunch to investigate what turned out to be an imaginary bandit and to get a report on the weather. It was a lovely day and we went out East and had a look at Clacton, Harwich and Ipswich. I just saw Gt Holland church and the white vicarage behind it in the field. On landing on the runway my port wheel sank in 18 inches in an ex-bomb crater and I went up on my nose. Was I livid!

It turns out that the Ju88 that Beazel and I destroyed on Thursday last was a Dornier 215. This just shows how one never recognises details on the aircraft one is attacking. A Do215 has two rudders, a Ju88 has one.[1]

The squadron took off again at about 6:15 (18:15) and joined up with 46. We chased about all over the

Thames Estuary and Kent, one time going out over the Channel by Folkestone and back over Dover, expecting the Dover ack-ack barrage to start up at any minute. We have already had two people shot down by ack-ack – Sergeant Rowell (Flash Alec) who did a crash landing at base and his aircraft burnt out, and Sergeant Beard who baled out successfully. When 46 Squadron lead they always go far too fast – a dangerous as well as infuriating procedure, as the last sections of the second squadron are bound to straggle and make easy meat for Me109s. This trip, however, was made very worthwhile by the glorious sunset. The clouds over France and the North Sea were quite pink while the other Hurricanes were brilliantly golden when they banked and caught the sun. The sun sank down to the sharp line where the black haze ended and continued down below it like a vast red ball, while the land below was already getting dark.[2]

We returned to find fog over London and we dived down through it, saying *auf wiedersehen* to that wonderful duck's egg green of the evening sky.

Sunday, September 22nd

A foul day – no activity except for a few 'two aircraft' patrols. Two Huns appeared in cloud gaps over the aerodrome. Beazel sighted one but it got away in cloud. I had the day off, so spent it in a long luxurious bath, and writing some letters.

The state of 'Alert I' is now in operation. This means that an invasion is expected within 12 hours. I personally don't think Hitler will invade at any rate until next spring.

Monday, September 23rd

I was off until 12 noon. We had to take cover at about 10:30, so I went down to dispersal just after the squadron scrambled. They saw 18 109s very high but made no contact. It is getting very cold at height. What is encouraging nowadays is the large number of friendly Spitfires and Hurricanes one finds floating around the sky, though one has to be extremely careful as the German fighters use every device to try to disguise the Me109 and He113 as Hurricanes and Spitfires respectively.

---

[1] *But see the entry for 23 September.*

[2] *George made a sketch of this sunset in his diary, as he did of the clouds mentioned in his 25 September entry.*

No 249 Squadron pilots at North Weald – a Press photograph taken on 21 September 1940 and made famous by its use in the Air Ministry's official published account of the Battle of Britain. Squadron Leader John Grandy, commanding officer, is third from the right and George Barclay (with checked scarf and pipe) is on his left. The other pilots are, from left: Pilot Officer Percy Burton (killed 27 September 1940), Flight Lieutenant Robert 'Butch' Barton, Flight Lieutenant Albert 'Lew' Lewis, Pilot Officer Terry 'Ossie' Crossey, Pilot Officer Tom 'Ginger' Neil, Pilot Officer John Beazley and Flight Lieutenant Keith Lofts – all of whom are mentioned in Barclay's diary. The photograph is also mentioned in *'Heaven Next Stop'* – *Impressions of a German Fighter Pilot* by Gunther Bloemertz, where one young Luftwaffe pilot says to another: 'Have a good look at those faces! They might just as well belong to us.'

No 1 Squadron Hurricanes lead a formation of Spitfires from an unidentified squadron. (*TopFoto*)

I slept in Ops last night; since the bombing on Sept 2nd the proper Operations Room has been moved out of the camp, and we use the old room to get a quiet and safe night.

It seems that I was quite right about the aircraft Beazel and I shot down on Thursday, 19th. It *was* an 88, as I swore it was at the time!

No other activity today.

Tuesday, September 24th

We scrambled at about 9:00 and patrolled above the Estuary. The ground from about 4,000ft looked exactly like a Japanese painting. There was mist hanging round, particularly over low ground, with woods appearing out of it and one couldn't see that they weren't fir trees. I have noticed this effect before – it is very lovely.

We saw 33 Hurricanes on patrol above us. They were all in close vics of three line astern, and making no provision for watching their tail. They circled above us, and then went into the cloud, leaving one below the layer. As we were still far away from them this looked like a cunning bit of Hun strategy but we felt very safe when we eventually discovered their identity. We went off again at about 11:15. London had a bank of fog over it with the balloon barrage poking through above it, so I informed Operations on landing. We patrolled over London at 20,000ft in a sort of haze cloud. We couldn't see anything above us or to one side but could see the ground – nor could we be seen from below. Fourteen He113s passed a long way ahead of us, going like dingbats.

We have a new occupation at dispersal – Totopoly, a very good racing game on the lines of Monopoly. We have had some very exciting races, though as far as I can see whether one makes or loses depends almost entirely on the bets one places.

Wednesday, September 25th

Everyone was rather expecting an invasion to break out at dawn this morning, because it was said that the Boche was sweeping the Channel of mines yesterday. Everyone was, therefore, very much at readiness at 5:50am though it was a bit of an effort as some pilots were rather the worse for wear after a hilarious evening at The Thatch, Epping, yesterday when the CO was in terrific form.

We went off at about 9:00 – a very cold trip indeed at 16,000ft in brilliant morning sun. I really must find some way of keeping my hands warm in extreme temperatures. We saw no enemy aircraft. There was a very large convoy in the Estuary and three destroyers steaming into Sheerness. I noticed what looked like three cruisers also near there.

I saw a broken-away balloon too. It looked like a half-opened parachute, very high up, and I thought there must be a dog-fight going on above us at first. I have several times seen Huns jump out and their 'chutes have not opened. One sees them out of the corner of one's eye in a fight and then, like so many other details that flash through one's mind, forgets all about them. Like ack-ack fire – we often get well into the ack-ack meant for the bombers we are attacking. It is interesting to observe this fire and note where the barrage is with respect to the bombers – usually a bit too low. One suddenly sees a puff of black smoke appear from nowhere, and the next moment one flies through it – it all seems very harmless if one is just out of range. Ack-ack is usually very useful in giving us the position of an enemy raid. We usually note the ack-ack fire, fly towards it and then find the bombers.

The second scramble of the day was at about 2:00pm. The squadron went off and split up into sections to try and find single Huns. I saw a Dornier 215 but it got away in cloud. The clouds were very fine (about 5,000ft to 7,000ft). Ginger (Pilot Officer Neil) led our section (yellow), his first trip as section leader.

I have a strangely opulent feeling today as my luggage has at last arrived from Boscombe Down and I have plenty of clothes for the first time this month!

The squadron got its first two DFCs today – Pilot Officer Ginger Neil and Pilot Officer Brian Meaker. The former has shot down six and the latter eight Jerries. The former thought he had four but a Pilot Officer from Hornchurch confirmed that two more he shot at crashed. Splendid! Four in one sortie. Actually we have two other DFCs in the squadron but they are replacements – Pilot Officer Millington and Pilot Officer Lewis – the former Australian, the latter South African.

We now have our own crews here. Until Tuesday last we had 56 Squadron crews, but they've now gone to Boscombe. We find our guns are in a terrible state – very bad maintenance by 56.

A land mine was dropped on the 'drome at about 11:00pm. It failed to explode.

Thursday, September 26th

Owing to the mine being on the 'drome we could not start up an engine even, let alone take off. We went to the Mess for breakfast, therefore, and bathed in peace. The Navy arrived and made the mine harmless, whereupon we came to readiness.

Red section damaged a Do215 but they thought it got back to France with a bit of luck.

I got a lift from the CO from Ops down to dispersal when we came to readiness at about 5:45am. It was a typical September morning – cold and fine, and I thought how many times we had started out at almost exactly the same hour from Gt Holland in previous Septembers to shoot partridges at Higham. How things have changed with the war. When shall I be able to cast a fly on Caladale[1] again?

I was going to fly home[2] this afternoon for 24 hours, but unfortunately the Maggie [Miles Magister, two-seat light aeroplane] was u/s. Very disappointing.

Friday, September 27th

A most momentous day. I was off the state in the morning and wandered down to dispersal when the squadron took off, cursing my luck to miss a scramble on my day off. The squadron came back in ones and twos, indicating they had been in action. And

[1] *Caladail (the gazetteer spelling) is a shallow loch south of Durness in Sutherland.*

[2] *To Cromer.*

how! They had met two defensive circles of 110s and had shot down about eight in 20 minutes!! Half the squadron didn't come back but arrived in driblets later. Pilot Officer Beazley (John) was wounded in the foot but got home, a good show. No news of Pilot Officer (Percy) Burton. Apparently the 110s were in a tight circle, ie a steep turn, and though the Hurribags came down from above they had a sitting shot at the bellies of the 110s.

We eventually reorganised the squadron and I led Red section on the next scramble. We went up to 15,000ft over Kent and stooged around in front of 46 Squadron. We saw a dog-fight going on on our left and then one lot of 109s came across in front of us and another lot came down on our tails. I went after a 109 that made a bolt for home. He dived steeply and I lost him in the haze but continued to dive, and the 109 suddenly shot up vertically in front of me – he saw me and dived again. Again I lost him, and pulled the plug in an effort to catch up. Again the 109 gave himself away by climbing vertically against the sky. I caught him this time and the superiority of manoeuvrability of the Hurricane over the 109 stood me in good stead. Every manoeuvre he did I could do but more tightly. I had a burst vertically up at him and another vertically down and a couple of deflection shots on the beam – and then the roof flew off and the pilot baled out successfully – the beautiful light green and yellow 109 crashing with a large explosion. I had chased him to the SW of Ashford. Sergeant Palliser, I found, had been an onlooker and had looked after my tail all the time. Nice work! We returned home to find that three 109s had been accounted for plus several probables.

While we had been up the remnants of the squadron from the first raid had returned – all except Percy Burton. If he's been shot up the tail it's bad luck as he's more careful and weaves more consistently than anyone else in the squadron.

We had pretty well a full squadron for the third scrap of the day. We met some Ju88s at about 18,000ft over London. They were very hard to catch (plug pulled, etc) and the roughest proposition in the bomber line we've come across – good crossfire, etc.

I did a beam attack on the leading four 88s and two left slight trails of smoke – two damaged. I then singled out one of the four and did another quarter attack. I could see the rounds hitting the fuselage, but these

88s are wonderfully armoured. I then did an astern attack – immediately both engines smoked and the 88 dropped out of formation. But immediately I ceased fire the smoke ceased also, and back into formation he shot! This whole process was repeated again. I got fed up then and gave the 88 a deliberately aimed burst at each engine. Clouds of black smoke poured out and he went down in a dive. Oil from his engines settled on my windscreen. Watchers on the ground confirm that it crashed. I saw no enemy fighters in the near vicinity during the engagement – presumably the 88s relied entirely on speed, armour plate and crossfire.

I then had to land at West Malling (trust the British to have an aerodrome that stands out for miles!) because my aileron control was very ham indeed. I discovered the starboard cable was completely severed by an explosive bullet – sundry other bullet holes too. I borrowed a Spitfire that had force landed earlier in the day and flew back home via the west of London.

It was nice to fly a Spitfire again but it gives one all the more confidence in the Hurricane for fighting purposes. (I don't think one can fight in a Spitfire with the hood open.)

On getting home I found that not one 88 got home to the Fatherland! Poor old Pilot Officer Brian Meaker, DFC, got shot down and was killed near Battle. A great loss – he was one of the best. He had shot down about 10 Huns. Pilot Officer Lewis, DFC, shot down six Huns today!! Some shooting. He's certain to get at least a bar to his DFC.

The ack-ack in the last engagement was not very good – almost nearer us than the Boche!

Our total today was 20 confirmed destroyed with about eight probables. More than twice as good as our previous best day!

By coming back in a Spitfire I graduated to the Glamour Boys! The Spitfires often hang around to get pickings while we are cracking into the bombers, and as a result we don't think much of them. Actually we are extremely grateful to them when they go at the escort fighters at the same time as we go for the bombers.

P/O Barclay's Combat Report for 27 September reproduced on page 63 read as follows:

I was flying as Red 1 when I saw a dogfight going on near by. Some 109s passed about 400ft on my

'A note on our Hurricanes – they are very strong and we have complete confidence in them.'

No 249 Squadron pilots Pilot Officer Bryan Meaker, DFC, and Flying Officer Percy Burton, were killed in action within hours of one another on 27 September. Meaker bailed out of his Hurricane after it was hit by return fire from a Ju88 over Dallington, East Sussex, but he struck the tailplane and was killed. Burton's Hurricane collided with a Bf110 during combat over Redhill, Surrey, and died when his aircraft crashed at Hailsham. George, too, was shot down on this day, but survived unhurt.

port side – there was no definite attack in squadron formation. I chased a 109 which dived very steeply. I had to use automatic boost cutout to catch up the 109. I lost the 109 in haze and owing to its camouflage against the ground, but it suddenly climbed almost vertically out of the haze. I closed to about 150 yards and fired about four bursts –

1 almost vertically up at the 109, 1 almost vertically down at the E/A – 2 bursts from the beam. The E/A poured glycol. The cockpit roof flew off. The pilot baled out successfully. The E/A crashed (confirmed by Sergeant Palliser) on a farm SW of Ashford.

Attacked E/A with squadron. First attack was on leading vic on the quarter – 5 second burst closing to 100 yards. Two of these four Ju88s left slight trails of smoke and I claim they were damaged. I then did quarter attack on one of the 4 E/A – saw the De Wilde ammunition hitting fuselage. Broke away and did a stern attack on same aircraft – it promptly dropped from formation and smoke came from both engines. I stopped firing and immediately the smoke ceased and the E/A rejoined the formation. I opened fire again from astern and again E/A smoked and lagged behind. When I stopped firing the E/A again ceased smoking and rejoined formation. I then closed up to about 100 yards and gave a deliberately aimed burst at each engine. A cloud of black smoke poured out of both and oil from E/A came on my windscreen. The E/A then went into a steep dive from which it had not pulled out when I last saw it. I had great difficulty in catching up the E/A until the end of the engagement – I had to use boost cutout. I force-landed at West Malling owing to a severed starboard aileron cable. The men at West Malling had seen the combat and confirm that a Ju88 with smoke pouring from each engine crashed in the vicinity. I claim E/A was destroyed. *Note.* The two damaged Ju88s I believe were subsequently shot down by other Hurricanes of 249 Squadron.

Saturday, September 28th
We had eggs with 'Holland' on them this morning! As Holland was over-run in May, these eggs certainly were veterans!!

We scrambled at about 10:30, joining up with 46 Squadron. We were sent up to 25,000ft (10,000ft too high for the Hurricane) and patrolled south of the Thames Estuary and London. It was bitterly cold though I had my Irvin suit on. I was very glad to get the order to pancake. We saw several batches of 109s on their way home. Sergeant Beard broke formation and shot one down.

J27/125

R E T.   FORM "F."

COMBAT REPORT.

Sector Serial No. .... (A) ——————

Serial No. of Order detailing Flight or Squadron to
Patrol .... (B) ——————

Date .... (C) 27 -9- 40 .

Flight, Squadron .... (D) Flight : A Sqdn. 249

Number of Enemy Aircraft .... (E) About 20 .

Type of Enemy Aircraft .... (F) ME · 109

Time Attack was delivered .... (G) About 12·50

Place Attack was delivered .... (H) Nr. Ashford.

Height of Enemy .... (J) 15000 ft.

Enemy Casualties .... (K) 1 ME 109 destroyed .

Our Casualties............... Aircraft .... (L) ⎫
                                                              ⎬ nil
                            Personnel .... (M) ⎭

GENERAL REPORT   P/O RGA BARCLAY . (R)

I was flying as Red 1 when I saw a dogfight going on near by. Some 109's passed about 400x on my port side – there was no definite attack in squadron formation. I chased a 109 which dived very steeply. I had to use automatic boost cut out to catch up the 109. I lost the 109 in haze and owing to its camouflage against the ground, but it suddenly climbed almost vertically out of the haze. I closed to about 150 yards and fired about five bursts. 1 almost vertically up at the 109. 1 almost vertically down at the E/A – 2 bursts from the beam. The E/A poured glycol.   Signature R.G.A. Barclay P/O .
The cockpit roof   O.C. ⎰ Section Red .
flew off. The pilot bailed out   ⎱ Flight
successfully. The E/A crashed   Squadron No. 249.
on a farm s.w. of Ashford .   (confirmed by Sgt. Palisser Red 3)

R.A.F. Form 1151.

(1611) Wt. 33246—2323 400 pads 12/38 T.S. 700
(3013—1611) Wt. 18604—1213 230 pads 7/39 T.S. 700

George's Combat Report for 27 September 1940, describing combat
with a Bf109; the cockpit roof flew off the enemy's plane, the pilot
bailed out and the plane crashed on a farm near Ashford in Kent.

I'm afraid it must now be presumed that Denis Parnall was shot down into the sea on the 18th.[1]

Air Vice-Marshal Sholto Douglas [Deputy Chief of the Air Staff] came to see us at lunchtime. We understood the visit was to congratulate us on yesterday's score, but he just stood and asked the usual questions and never mentioned yesterday.

We scrambled just after his visit and did another patrol at about 23,000ft. We saw 109s above us. Again, it seemed as if someone had left their R/T switch on 'transmit' and the result is that reception is bad with a great deal of interference. I'm inclined to think it's a technical fault rather than someone's stupidity. On the way back from this patrol two Messerschmitt 109s shot up our tails – I suppose we went to sleep because Lumba told us there were no enemy aircraft in the vicinity. The 109s had a squirt and broke straight down 10,000ft into the clouds. We chased them but it was quite hopeless, as they dived about 5,000ft before they attacked us. Angel squadron (46) took no avoiding action whatsoever – if there had been 20 Me109s most of them would have been shot down. As it was I saw one parachute and followed it down to the ground. It turned out to be Lewis who has about 16–18 Huns to his credit, so the 109s were no respecters of persons. Unfortunately we heard that Lewis had been badly burnt – a cannon shell in the reserve tank, I suppose. It will put him u/s for a few months.

Sunday, September 29th

Unfortunately we heard today that Percy Burton was killed on Friday – another great loss to the squadron. He was an amusing fellow and always had something to say! I am now the only one left of the five Cranwellians of the squadron:

Robert Fleming – killed Sept 7th
Pat Wells – wounded Sept 7th
John Beazley – wounded Sept 27th
Percy Burton – killed Sept 27th
Self – OK

We had two more congratulatory telegrams from Sir Archibald Sinclair, Secretary of State for Air, and Air Chief Marshal Sir Cyril Newall, Chief of the Air Staff, today, congratulating us on Friday's bag. It seems that 249 is making a very good reputation for itself – although a very new squadron (formed for the first time in history on about 15 May 1940). (Became operational on 28 June 1940.)

We got a Polish officer today – he seems a very good sort and speaks good English. He was in a Polish fighter squadron at the start of the war, but never fought as they were so short of aircraft. His name is George Solak – the George part in Polish sounds like 'Jersey' so he has been christened that already! We had all sorts of discussions on the war, the Air Force, etc, yesterday with the Wing Commander, Jersey, the CO and the pilots. The general conclusions reached and agreed upon were these:

(1) Someone in high places is wasting precious time in expanding the RAF
(2) It's no use having Cabinet reshuffles in times of emergency as it takes the new members at least one month to get a grip on the job
(3) The British people are still fast asleep. They haven't begun to realise the power of our enemies and that they have to give their 'all' as well as the forces to win
(4) That the threat of invasion is very real – and not a sort of flap or bluff, as the public seem to think
(5) That we need dictatorial methods to fight dictators
(6) That one German is nice, two Germans are swine[2]
(7) That we shall eventually win the war, but it will be the hell of a job and more so unless we pull ourselves together

The Station Commander is Wing Commander Beamish (Victor Beamish, DSO, AFC) and a wonderful man – he flies almost every time we take

[1] *Flt Lt Denis Parnall's Hurricane, V6685, was shot down during a patrol over Gravesend at 1.25pm on 18 September and crashed and burnt out at Margaretting, Essex. Parnall was killed. He was originally buried as an unknown airman at North Weald, but was exhumed and taken back to his native Cornwall for reburial at St Gennys, between Bude and Tintagel.*

[2] *George Barclay had visited Germany twice on pre-war holidays, and worked hard on German at school.*

off as a freelance and has a very large bag to his credit. He keeps up the morale of the pilots by his own complete disregard of nerves or fear.[1]

We had a quiet day today with one scramble at 4:00pm. We patrolled at 23,000ft over the Estuary and South London above 10/10ths cloud with 46 Squadron. The Wing formation went all haywire and we were really inviting the Me109s to take their pickings all the time, so we had 46 Squadron over to the Mess from Stapleford[2] after dinner to discuss things. We'll have to see how the things agreed upon work out in practice. On this afternoon's scramble we saw lots of fighters very high above us, leaving condensation trails, and we all fought as to whether they were Spitfires or He113s!

Monday, September 30th

What a day! Four sorties and nothing shot down though plenty seen. But it has been useful practice to get this formation with 46 Squadron going. The formation has been quite a success today. We now fly like this:

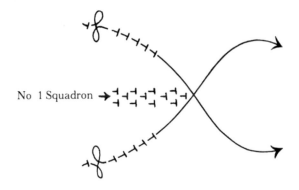

One squadron in section vics line astern – the other squadron in two sections of six weaving with the last of each six also weaving. On sighting enemy fighters above No 1 Squadron go into a defensive snake in close line astern and weaving.

The first trip was over 10/10ths cloud south of London and the Estuary. We saw some 109s above us – the yellow-nosed fellows. If we had had another three or four thousand feet we would have been on top of them.

Ginger Neil and I went off on the second trip looking for a bandit at 25,000ft. We went all over Kent and the Estuary. We could see a great deal of the French coast.

On the third trip we had hundreds of 109s above us. We were too high for the Hurricane anyway. We were shadowed by 109s all the time. No 46 were attacked by 109s but probably our snake saved us – an awful trip as we were quite helpless, just waiting to be attacked. I saw a Hurricane going down in flames and a parachute above us, possibly a Jerry. Apparently some Do215s with a large escort passed near us, but we missed them as we were watching the 109s.

On the fourth scramble we just floated around for about an hour and a quarter at 17,000ft. We saw Jerries making smoke trails above us in the sun but that is all. I quite enjoyed myself as I wasn't as cold as usual, and I amused myself by singing.

Tuesday, October 1st

An uneventful day. Two patrols at 20,000ft and 25,000ft above 10/10ths cloud over Kent. We saw the usual high Me109s – it was just as well there wasn't a fight as I had oil over the windscreen and couldn't see a thing.

Wednesday, October 2nd

We are very short of aeroplanes now – they nearly all have oil leaks, which means that after half-an-hour's flying one can't see anything through the windscreen. We had three trips in the morning – two patrols above the clouds south of London and one short scramble, which was cancelled as soon as we had joined up with 46 Squadron.

---

[1] *Then 37, an Irishman, an ex-Cranwell cadet and a pre-war Rugby international, Beamish went on to become station commander at RAF Kenley. A personification of RAF fighting spirit, he was awarded the DSO on 23 September 1940, the DFC on 22 October and a Bar to his DSO on 2 September 1941. He was one of the two fighter pilots who on 12 February 1942 spotted the German warships* Prinz Eugen, Scharnhorst *and* Gneisenau *during their 'Channel Dash'. He lost his life when, still fighting as Kenley's CO, he was shot down on 28 March 1942.*

[2] *Airfield where No 46 Squadron was based – about five miles south of North Weald.*

'Fighter pilots who are defending Britain. A typical pilot of a fighter squadron', reads the caption to this 1940 official press photograph of George in sheepskin flying jacket and scarf, against the backdrop of a No 249 Squadron Hurricane.

I led Yellow Section of two aircraft, the last section of the leading squadron. On the first scramble above the usual cloud layer at 20,000ft we saw some high 109s. On the second scramble 'A' Flight went off to investigate an unknown aircraft, leaving 'B' Flight and 46 Squadron on patrol. We climbed to 28,000ft!! and saw nothing. It was lucky we came down when we did, as my radiator was freezing up rapidly.

We had a visit from 'Stuffy' this afternoon [Air Chief Marshal Sir Hugh Dowding, AOC-in-C, Fighter Command]. He talked about the Hurricane II with Merlin XX engine, and 20mm cannons. Here's to the day we get both!!

My new Hurricane (GN-C as usual) has arrived today, the old GN-C having been shot up on 27 September – a good riddance too as it was badly rigged!

Some of us went to see Beazel [Pilot Officer Beazley] in Epping Hospital last night. His foot has been paining him, but he'll be all right again in time.

Pat Wells (wounded Sept 7th) arrived in the evening on his way on sick leave – good to see him again – he seems well. He says the Army types, mostly New Zealanders, who picked him up unconscious when he landed by parachute on Sept 7th, stole everything he'd got – cigarettes, etc, as well as Mae West and parachute.

Thursday, October 3rd

Some bombs were dropped near the Officers' Mess this morning at 5am. No damage! The weather was simply appalling today – low cloud and rain. Keith Lofts went off after a Hun that appeared over the aerodrome at 500ft but it was a hopeless chase. His pipsqueak didn't work and so he had a hectic half-hour being D/F-ed[1] home so that he would miss the wireless masts.

There was a test of German and British ammunition in the afternoon, but it was so badly carried out that it was valueless as a comparison. The Under-Secretary of State for Air, Captain Harold Balfour, came to tea in the Mess. He was very charming, and everyone was very impressed with his technical knowledge and interesting conversation.

[1] Direction-finding, a means of identifying aircraft and fixing their position.

He spoke of the grand time he had in his recent Canadian tour, and his flight in the *Clare*[1] across the Atlantic. We all got so browned-off in the evening that we went to Chelmsford – found it absolutely dead-beat and publess, so went to Brentwood where we ate at the White Hart.

Friday, October 4th

A lovely morning that clouded over after breakfast, and became a terrible day – low cloud, rain and fog. We did nothing all day except for Ginger and I who made a 15-minute trip into the fog in an attempt to intercept four bandits – needless to say fruitlessly. It was my first trip in my new GN-C – it seems very much nicer than the last, which had very tail-heavy elevator control.

It was announced that Butch and Keith (Pilot Officer Lofts) had got the DFC and that Lewis (now in hospital) had got a bar to his DFC. Sergeant Beard has the DFM. Great jubilations and a most monumental party was the result. The Thatch, Epping, and the Mess. Butch has led the squadron well for a long time in the CO's absence. Keith (or Koala, because he looks like one) had shot down five Huns before he came to the squadron and has since shot down about three more. Lewis has now about 17–18 Huns to his name. Sergeant Beard has been with the squadron since its inception and has about five Huns to his credit.

We all agreed that this squadron and probably every other one as well would be grounded for lack of machines after the first hour of an invasion. One has only to see what difficulty we have in putting up about nine machines after one good scrap. And sometimes we have difficulty just through the machines going unserviceable with oil leaks, etc. We wonder whether Hitler has thought of all this – because it seems to us that our fighter strength could be temporarily smashed so easily.

Saturday, October 5th

Mulligatawny (Pilot Officer Middleton, DFC) has secured a very nice terrier puppy for the squadron. We have named him 'Pipsqueak' but it tends to get shortened to 'Zero'! (Pipsqueak Zero is what the Controller gives to a pilot after take-off to tell him the exact second on which to set his Pipsqueak or contactor going. This mechanism emits a wireless signal for 15 seconds in every minute, thus giving the receiver of the signal a bearing and thus the position of the aircraft. Only four aircraft on the same frequency can of course be operated with pipsqueak at once.)

Boozy and Paizen, our kittens, were eventually captured in the dispersal wood at Boscombe Down and brought up here, but Butch refuses to have them in the hut so they have unfortunately been relegated to the men's hut.

We went off today for the first time at about 10:30 – half the squadron still carrying a hangover from last night with them! The oxygen was turned on fully the whole time in the aircraft of the unfortunates!

We patrolled over Kent at about 20,000ft, 46 Squadron leading the Wing. We always operate as a Wing formation nowadays. Two Me109s tried to jump on one of our sections but didn't succeed– no casualties to either side. I hoped we were going to have a scrap.

On the second flip, after lunch, we climbed up to 20,000ft over Kent and were then pancaked! On the way back we saw fighters on our own level for once, but unfortunately they turned out to be Spitfires. There was a high layer of cloud at about 23,000ft today. The 109s came out of it on the first trip.

In the afternoon some rather fine cumulus at about 4–5,000ft formed. Due to the high cloud the cumulus was not sunlit and it looked very white and ghostly. Two squadrons look very fine in such scenery.

This undated piece, possibly written on 5 October, describes the scene at dispersal in the early morning:

I woke as the airman orderly tapped my shoulder and repeated, 'Come along, Sir, come along Sir – four thirty', in my ear. It was very cold in the hut and dark so I wrestled with myself for a few minutes and then jumped out of bed and put on my flying kit quickly, Irvin trousers over my pyjamas, sweater, flying boots, scarf, Irvin jacket. I had won

---

[1] One of the BOAC 'C' Class Empire flying-boats.

North Weald – Flying Officer Bill Millington and Pipsqueak.

Pipsqueak puts up with a flea check. George applied the flea powder (see diary entry 5 October) with the assistance of Pilot Officer 'Ginger' Neil and Flying Officer Lohmeyer, the squadron adjutant and a veteran flier of the First World War.

the race with the cold by then and I added my Mae West more leisurely. With my gloves shoved into my pockets I was at last ready for whatever the day held in store. In the dark in the far end of the hut Pat and the CO were dressing too. I took down the blackout on one window and looked out – a lovely autumn morning with a duck egg blue sky half covered with high cloud. I thought of what I would have been doing with such a morning before the war. Obviously motoring the 60 miles to Higham from Cambridge to shoot partridge, to meet a large number of my relatives and consume an enormous shooting lunch!

John came and looked over my shoulder. 'Another bloody fine day,' he said with disgust. The weather had been terrific for the last few months. Oh boy, how we would have loved it normally but now a fine sunny day meant flying, flying, flying and terrific tension all day, gazing endlessly into a burning sun to see what wily Hun was lurking there. A fight or two, perhaps, and someone not there to join the drinking in the bar that evening. I am quite certain that whatever happens it won't be me who catches a packet. I feel invincible in the air; probably experienced and older people would call it gross over-confidence, but I'm sure the average pilot is invincible in his own mind until he gets beaten up.

A posed group of pilots at North Weald taking time out to read the newspaper. 'Lew' Lewis is on the left, Tom Neil is standing centre with newspaper.

The airscrew of the Hurricane outside was being turned slowly by the starter battery. Suddenly the silence of dawn was broken by a shattering noise as the engine woke and tried to make up time in apology for having been asleep.

I reawakened Ginger who was fast asleep again by this time, and then left the hut to look at my aeroplane. I walked almost in a sleep in the semi-darkness, enjoying the warmth of my Irvin suit, but the blast of cold air from the airscrew brought me

back to earth as I climbed into the cockpit out of which the fitter had just stepped. 'Morning, Parish,[1] morning Barnes, put my 'chute on the tail please.'

I checked the instruments one by one: petrol tanks full; tail trimming wheel neutral; airscrew fine pitch, directional gyro set; two pairs of gloves in their own crannies; helmet on reflector sight with oxygen and R/T leads connected – in fact everything set as I liked it for a quick getaway when we were scrambled.

Returning to the hut I found Kapan, the orderly, lighting the fire by the light of a hurricane lamp, while Ginger sat fast asleep in a deckchair, his head lolling on his yellow Mae West. I lay down and immediately became unconscious as if doped – the effect of sleeping in an Irvin suit. What seemed

[1] One of the squadron personnel who later in the war visited George's parents to express condolences on the loss of their son.

Sitting around waiting for the call to action that will inevitably come, North Weald, late 1940.

the next moment I woke with a terrific start to see everyone pouring out of the hut, putting on Mae Wests, silk gloves and other articles of flying kit. I could hear the telephone orderly repeating, 'Dover 26,000; 50-plus bandits approaching from south-east.' Percy shouted, 'Scramble George, lazy bastard', and automatically I ran out. Parachute on, pulled into cockpit by crew who had already started the engine. Straps, helmet, gloves, check the knobs, taxi out, get into right position in my section and take off. I put the R/T on, and only then do I wake up and realise I am in the air flying No 2 in Yellow Section. I tried to take an intelligent interest but my mouth was like the bottom of a birdcage as the result of last night's party! I'm not in the mood and it's too early in the morning anyway. We patrolled the Thames Estuary.

Sunday, October 6th

An awful day as regards weather. I did three-quarters of an hour's 'link' (Link Trainer) in the morning to fill up time – at the end of my ZZ landing[1] the squadron was scrambled so I took off late but caught up successfully and tacked on to a section with a spare place. We were sent up through the cloud as a squadron, which was quite ridiculous, and though we stuck together as a section we never saw the others again! We had a lot of adventures including nearly spinning in cloud because the section leader was instrument flying badly. In the end I took over the section and brought them home.

Monday, October 7th

We scrambled once before lunch, patrolling as usual and seeing the usual high Jerry fighters. The weather has changed completely since yesterday and today is lovely. Incidentally on account of the weather London had its first quiet night since Sept 6th or 7th.

We went off again twice in the afternoon – the first time we did an uneventful patrol, except for seeing something, I don't know what, shot down in the distance. On the second there was a slight mix-up with 109s – no casualties and Pilot Officer Millington, DFC, got a 'probable'.

Tuesday, October 8th

We scrambled three times in the morning and not at all in the afternoon. The first time Bill Millington took off first instead of the leader, Butch. The result was that everyone formed up on Bill, who tried to buzz off as soon as he realised this.

Everyone then thought, 'Oh, Butch's radio is u/s and he's indicating to someone else to lead.' I was leading Yellow Section and took over – my R/T u/s! So detailed Sergeant Beard, Yellow 2 (just got DFM), to take over. It took us the dickens of a time to straighten out the shambles, meanwhile we were grand pickings for Me109s! Mercifully we were pancaked soon. The second scramble was better, but not good enough as regards formation. Pilot Officer Worrall – his nickname is Screwball – was a bit dim on this occasion.

On the third scramble we had a pleasant jaunt up through cloud and down again. The weather was bad low down and it took some time to form up – and then we had to reform above the clouds. They were too thick to send squadron formations through, let alone Wing formations. On the first scramble we saw very high Jerry fighters, which made terrific smoke circles over south-east London. We were at 13,000ft but they were still a very long way above us. We heard later that London was bombed through cloud by Me109s carrying bombs.

On the second trip I had one of the two newly arrived French Sergeant Pilots in my Yellow Section. They are very good types and seem good at the job, like Jersey, the Pole. I now have a splendid white winged lion on my new GN-C. The work of a fitter-ex-draughtsman.

Wednesday, October 9th

257 Squadron [Hurricane squadron] have arrived to take the place of 25 (Blenheim night-fighter) Squadron. 257 was formed at the same time as 249 (May 1940). Most of the fellows in it have done quite a bit of fighting, but not with 257 Squadron, which has not seen much action. 257 strike me as being very proud of themselves, and quite determined they are the only squadron in the RAF. This is what I thought of them at first sight – let's hope I'm wrong.

---

[1] 'ZZ' was the codeword for a successful 'landing' in the trainer, which provided practice in instrument-flying procedures.

We went off just before tea by ourselves and climbed up to 23,000ft over Maidstone. We saw some ack-ack fire and a broken-away balloon (there's a very strong wind blowing). I was leading Yellow Section and looking after the squadron's tail. The Medway and Thames Estuary are perfectly wonderful in the sun – great designs in silver leaf. The clouds too were very fine. What the landlubber misses in the cloud line!

We have now worked out a Wing formation for when 249, 46 and 257 work together. Like this:

Pages from George's diary on 5 October showing a wing formation 'for when 249, 46 and 257 work together'.

We shall only find out if it's successful by trial in flight. I don't like the three tail-end (A, B and C) Sections being in open vics – I think weaving line astern would be better.

Thursday, October 10th

Some wonderful clouds today – great anvils reaching up to about 26,000ft. We had one scramble at about 3:00pm. We climbed up to 24,000ft with 46 Squadron and were not above the topmost clouds then. We saw some He113s above us – everyone except Millington and I thought they were Spitfires – but they had yellow noses and no roundels.

The scenery was magnificent and at one time the whole squadron was making white trails. Sergeant Bayley, my No 2 in Red Section, vanished, and apparently running short of oxygen, he lost consciousness and dived straight into the ground, knocking down two cottages, and unfortunately three people were killed. That is what we think happened – a most unfortunate accident. In peacetime it would have been a major tragedy – in war it is nothing. *C'est la guerre.* Shooting an aircraft down is not all fun and games – you've only got to see the havoc it causes when it hits the ground; and the bottom must be knocked out of the world of the individuals concerned.

On our trip today we came out of clouds right underneath some He113s. Though in a perfect position to attack they took no notice, and we couldn't gain on them. When we had landed there was a very loud and sudden clap of thunder – everyone thought it was a heavy bomb! Bombs are more common than thunder nowadays!

Friday, October 11th

I am 'A' Flight Commander for two days as Keith Lofts is on leave. I went off with some misgivings as to whether I was capable of leading a flight but as soon as we were in the air my fears subsided and I felt fit to lead a Wing! 'A' Flight was scrambled alone before breakfast. We sighted a bandit plus white trail at about 25,000ft almost as soon as we took off, but it was a hopeless chase. We therefore turned our attention to another photographic expedition, which we were told was at 20,000ft.

It passed over our heads about 5,000ft above, but we couldn't catch it, so we came home.

It was a perfect morning. The Estuary and Kent had about 50ft of ground mist. It looked like thick snow, but north of the Thames was clear. It was a wonderful spring morning.

Having a Section or Flight adds greatly to the interest of this flying, especially if there is no interception, when the flaps may be cold and dull.

Bill Millington and I went out to dinner at Epping Place in the evening with Captain Jones. The Colonel and Adjutant of the 13th/18th Hussars were there as well. Their revelations about the incompetence in the French Army in France were incredible. The Joneses know the Jack Pellys and Theresa and Blanch Buxton. Their son, Christopher, was apparently up at Trinity[1] at the same time as me. We spent a very pleasant evening.

Three other scrambles.

Saturday, October 12th

We went up before breakfast, climbing up to 23,000ft and patrolling all over Kent and south London. We were looking for some 109s, which for once were said to be below us. But no luck in the first hour – we were floating about over Dover with 257 Squadron, who were meant to be guarding our tails below us, when I happened to look back to the left and there was a glistening yellow nose pointed very much in my direction about 50 yards away. I immediately took action to avoid his quarter attack, in the shape of a violent turn to the left and lots of bottom rudder. The inevitable result at that height was a flick roll and spin. I got out, had a good look round and saw three 109s 2,000ft above.

I kept a good eye open for the 109s and rejoined the squadron. Unfortunately my No 2 (Red 2) has not been heard of since this short mêlée – he was Sergeant Perrin, a very nice Frenchman. No 257 have two blokes missing.

Sunday, October 13th

The two blokes from 257 Squadron who were missing yesterday are now safe. And I am glad to say, so is Perrin, the Frenchman [Capitaine G.C.M. Perrin]. He baled out and has slight leg wounds.

We went up three times today. The first time I took Sergeant Beard and we chased a bandit up the Estuary at 6,000ft but never saw it – very disappointing as we were close to it. I thought he was going to bomb a convoy that was steaming out of the Estuary. We then went off up to 25,000ft on a vector of 045, which took us up Debden way. We then went all over the upper atmosphere and apparently were very close to the Hun but again we didn't see him. It is amazing how when one has the whole of space to search the object searched for can pass quite near by without being seen, if the eyes of the searcher happen to be focussed on the distance – and the searcher cannot tell where his eyes are focussed unless there are clouds, etc. That was a lovely trip in brilliant sun but very disappointing. We finished up over Biggin Hill. London was very close and I noticed St Paul's for the first time.

On the second scramble, someone's wireless went haywire and stuck on 'transmit', so that we couldn't hear Lumba, and we had to pancake. It wrecked the whole scramble. Added to that the new sergeant pilots, of whom we have all too many, didn't take off in their right sections, the resulting chaos taking some time to sort out. We've almost got to train them in formation flying.

The third flap was a farce. As we took off we saw the trails of the Me109 bombers over London. In fact we were scrambled 20 minutes late. As usual this was due to Group's slowness. We climbed up to 20,000ft and then pancaked – it was ridiculous taking off at all.

Pipsqueak has selected Butch's bed as his private lavatory – much to Butch's fury!

[1] *Trinity College, University of Cambridge.*

Boozy Kellett has got the DSO. His Polish squadron, No 303, have destroyed 108 Huns! (in September). No 249 were second amongst the squadrons with 48 destroyed and 26 probably destroyed. First of the British squadrons. [No 249 Squadron was in No 11 Group.]

Ginger is on seven days' leave. I hope to follow him when he comes back. I shall probably be posted to 'B' Flight when I return, as they need another Section leader. Sergeant Smithson has arrived back (wounded Sept 7th) fit for flying. It's nice to have him back again – one of 249's original sergeant pilots.

I have been put in charge of the Link Trainer programmes on Mondays and Thursdays. I must get a scheme out for tomorrow.

Monday, October 14th

The weather was very bad today. Ossie (Pilot Officer Crossey) and I went up but an interception would have been lucky. We sailed around at about 4,000ft between two layers of cloud for about half-an-hour, and then came home at 900ft with very bad visibility, but a good vector from the Controller and my excellent wireless reception brought us home. A good wireless makes a flight in bad weather quite pleasant I/F practice and frees one's mind from all anxiety. Anyway we were glad to be safely down today.

We played Totopoly in the afternoon and went to a flick in the evening. While going to bed we heard the drone of engines and then the whistle of bombs. Although we heard them coming down I think they were some way away.

Tuesday, October 15th

I have now gone over to 'B' Flight, as they only have Butch and Bill [Flight Lieutenants Barton and Millington] as Section leaders and they need a third. Ops made the usual muddle about our state this morning. We came to readiness at 6:30am only to be told we were 15 minutes available. We needn't have been woken.

We scrambled with 257 Squadron and climbed to 22,000ft over Folkestone, where we were attacked by lots of 109s. The majority of the two squadrons dived down away with the result that the enemy aircraft immediately scored a decisive moral victory and it was left to a few Hurricanes to see what they could do at the original height. There was a good scrap over the Channel about eight miles off Folkestone. I'm glad to say both squadrons came out whole. I got a 'probable' 109. He flew straight across my bows – I gave him a long burst and he went over on his back and went down seemingly out of control. I continued to fire at various deflections and he streamed glycol. He was still upside down at about 2,000ft when I had to break off my attack owing to an attack by seven other 109s. They were quite easy to evade so low down (5,000ft). It was fun skimming back over Kent at 800ft below cloud. Had a wonderful view of Canterbury Cathedral on way back.

In the evening we had a conference with 257 and 46 and decided to work in sections of four and break away in pairs if attacked by 109s.

Wednesday, October 16th

We had an awful night, brilliant moonlight, which we think must have shown up the aerodrome to the Huns. Bombs whistled down on and off all night – the nearest 100–150 yards from our dispersal hut. An oil bomb burnt in the middle of the aerodrome. The Huns came over almost continually. Sometimes there were about five overhead at once.

We scrambled at 11:50 to do a standing patrol south of London as the AOC [Air Vice-Marshal K.R. (later Air Chief Marshal Sir Keith) Park] had a hunch that the Huns would try to bomb in the lunch hour. But nothing materialised. We tried out the new idea of sections of four, breaking into pairs when attacked, but as we weren't attacked it wasn't a real test. Keith Lofts and Bouquillard, the Frenchman, were despatched from the formation to shoot down a Do215. It is believed they succeeded, but Keith was shot down in the process. We hear he's quite OK though.

I felt very full of beans as we sailed over London, knowing Father and Mother were there.

Pilot Officers McConnell and Thompson have joined the squadron. They seem good types.

I was horrified to hear that Uncle Alfred[1] had

---

[1] *Alfred Buxton, who had been a missionary in the Congo and, until driven out by the Italian invasion, in Abyssinia. His story has been brilliantly told in his wife Edith's autobiographical* Reluctant Missionary *(Hodder & Stoughton, 1968).*

been killed by a bomb in London the night before last – what a very fine man he was, and what a tremendous loss to Aunt Edith, Susan and Lionel.

Thursday, October 17th

Nothing doing today except one routine patrol and one scramble. The patrol was on the usual patrol line, Hornchurch to Biggin Hill. There was a lot of mist near the ground and we had to form up after take-off above this and clouds at 5,000ft. The patrol was uneventful. We were scrambled in the afternoon and as soon as we were in the air we heard the Controller vectoring Angel Squadron (46) on to 17 bombers. We joined in the chase but neither squadron saw anything (and we secretly think the 17 bombers were a myth). The reservoirs around London were shining blood red through the haze. We flew around a bit on patrol and then pancaked. I really thought we were going to have a picnic with unescorted bombers like the September days.

Friday, October 18th

There was visibility of 25 yards owing to fog all morning – notwithstanding we were brought to readiness at dawn – quite crazy.

It cleared up after lunch and we did a routine patrol at 15,000ft over south London above cloud. We were meant to be with 46 Squadron but we had to climb through 8,000ft of cloud. Everything went haywire and the Controller put the cap on it by keeping us up two hours. Sergeant Bouquillard force-landed through lack of petrol.

I am sleeping in the Operations Room now as after the recent bombing we have seriously begun to disperse pilots. Ops have been completely evacuated now so it's very quiet and comfortable.

I cannot go to Uncle Alfred and Uncle Murray's [Alfred Buxton's brother, an engineer, killed in the same air raid][1] funeral tomorrow as there are already too many on leave – I'm the only Section leader in 'B' Flight on this station.

At about this date in October, on a Friday, George wrote to his sister Mary:

Thanks so much for all your letters, which I ought to have answered years ago. I was so sorry I couldn't get over to Holland when you were at home, but that Friday happened to be an extremely busy day. I hope to get a week's leave in about a week from now. It will be grand to get home for a bit and find out anew what an ordinary existence is like! How wretched to hear that Mummie has not been well and that Weiner didn't report well on her health. What did he say? I imagine 'Take things easier.'

I'm so glad to hear that you've been evacuated from London. Although there's some discomfort, I suppose it's grand to be away from the inferno of bombs and guns. We have the nightly bombardment here and usually the odd bomb fairly near. We had a mine actually on the aerodrome the other day, but the gallant Navy removed it safely. Though we go up often, we haven't had any really good scraps for about 10 days. As to my bag about which you are so insistent! I have 4½ Huns to my account as 'destroyed' (2½ bombers and 2 fighters). The ½ means that two of us brought it down together.

Added to this I have three 'probably destroyed' and six 'damaged'. This bag is for your information only. Please don't write home about it or tell the cousins etc, as the most fantastic stories are already going round about me!! I mean this and I only tell you on condition you keep it to yourself!!! I suppose it sounds as if we are having a grand time – well I suppose we are really – I'm realising an ambition, but it's a bit tough to see fellows wiped off one by one. There are only four officers in the squadron, myself included, who have come through September absolutely unscathed, and of the five officers, myself again included, who were at Cranwell together, I am the only survivor. Two of the other four are dead, and two wounded. But it's remarkable how hardened one gets to people not coming back. Normally this warfare is thrilling, and a successful scrap puts one on top of the world – but I won't deny it has its frightening moments, though having survived a frightening moment is also exhilarating!

About knitting for the winter – I would like very much a pair of thick woollen socks – longer than

[1] *They were together at Church House, Great Smith Street, Westminster, on 14 October, planning a translation of the Bible for Abyssinia. Alfred was father of Lional (killed at Salerno in 1943) and Susan, who spent their school holidays with the Barclays.*

socks are usually, but shorter than stockings! It's getting infernally cold at 25,000 feet!

Phyll's address is Stewkley Vicarage, Nr Leighton Buzzard, Bedfordshire. [Phyll Parsons, later Mrs A. Shaw, a friend from Cambridge, referred to in the diary for 17 November.]

Do try and meet her some time – though I've not the faintest idea how far apart Leighton Buzzard and Oxford are! I'm sure she would love to see a face she knows. I'll try and get to you on the weekend of Oct 26th, but I don't promise anything. What station in London does one go to for Oxford? I'm beginning to look forward to that day already and who is this mysterious fairy princess you've got tucked up your sleeve for me?!!

It will be grand to get a bit of shooting when and if I get home – and here's to Oct 26th!

Must stop, and go to bed – we come to readiness at 6:05am tomorrow morning!
Best love George
PS Do write again soon!

Saturday, October 19th

I had a slight accident in the squadron van in the dark last night – a Ford 8 and I had a brush on the perimeter track of the aerodrome – little damage done.

The morning was very foggy, but in the late afternoon every cloud vanished. We saw condensation trails over London, but were not scrambled on their account. We went up later on a convoy patrol off Harwich. I had a good look at Gt Holland on the way out, and the mudflats around Horsey and the Naze.

We patrolled the convoy for about an hour uneventfully. I had to take the lead from Keith Lofts as his R/T went u/s. We came back in the dusk, and as there was a considerable haze I spent some anxious moments lest the squadron should be caught in the dark owing to my bad navigation.

Sunday, October 20th

Fog in the morning so we had a good breakfast in the Mess. It cleared completely in the afternoon and we carried out a stooge patrol south of Maidstone. We had a good view of the French coast (including the Somme Estuary) and the Isle of Wight. No enemy aircraft sighted.

Messerschmitt Bf109E, 'White 13', flown by Unteroffizier Arno Zimmermann of 7/JG54, was severely damaged in combat over Kent by RAF fighters and belly-landed on the shingle at Lydd on 27 October. (*TopFoto*)

Crossey and Lewis (centre), Neil in Balaclava, Mills in background
reading a magazine, at 249's sandbagged dispersal, North Weald.

Monday, October 21st

A very cloudy day today and lots of single Huns. I
went off with Sergeant Mills. We went all over the
eastern counties in cloud from 2,000 to 12,000ft. We
didn't see anything but it was good fun and excellent
I/F practice.

Butch and I walked round the wood by dispersal
with Robbie's 12-bore (Robbie = Flying Officer
Robinson, RFC, Interrogation Officer). It was
marvellous to get away into the woods; though
only 300 yards from the Hurricanes, we were in a
different world.

Tuesday, October 22nd

Wing Commander Beamish has got the DFC, and
very well deserved too.

Fog all morning but a fine afternoon. We
scrambled at about 2:45pm and patrolled
Hornchurch at 20,000ft. We saw smoke trails and
thought they were high Messerschmitt 109s. One
came down to attack us and I warned the squadron
but it turned out to be a Spitfire. How I wished
he had been a 109 as I was all ready for him. Pilot
Officer Tommy Thompson force-landed, probably
due to his oil freezing up owing to leaving his
radiator open.

There was a complete schemozzle owing to
Butch's radio going u/s. Sergeant Beard took the
lead, as I was weaving, and lost himself in a cloudless
sky. So I brought four guys and myself home and left
Beard and Co to his own devices. I'm glad I've got
some leave coming along – I'm getting so intolerant
of the shortcomings of the new pilots, etc.

Wednesday, October 23rd

Nothing all day – foul fog, etc. My old GN-C is
now GN-L in 'B' Flight. I'm glad to stick to my old
machine. Ginger Neil broadcast last night about Sept
15th's fights. But we missed him, unfortunately.

Monday, November 4th

I returned from 10 days' leave today. I've had a grand

Flight Lieutenant Tommy Thompson DFC

An Me110 down in the Channel. *(Topfoto)*

time and an excellent change – shooting at home and Higham and staying the weekend at Oxford to see Mary [his younger sister, who was working in MI5 at the time]. But all the same it's very good to be back with the squadron. I've missed one or two scraps and the aerodrome has been bombed by Me109s. The squadron did a spectacular take-off amidst the bombs. Unfortunately one of 257's pilots was killed when his aircraft was hit by a bomb. It's very sad to find that Bill Millington, DFC, is missing after chasing some 109s out over the Channel. It just shows it never pays. Bill is a great loss – he was a grand fellow, one of the most likeable in the squadron.[1]

Tuesday, November 5th

Since I have a very stiff neck I went to Sick Quarters to have some radiant heat.

In the afternoon I went to a flick in Epping with Robbie (Flying Officer Robinson, Interrogation Officer).

Wednesday, November 6th

257 Squadron moved to Martlesham today and 46 Squadron moved here because Stapleford is u/s having no runways. So in future we shall work with 46.

My first flight since leave! It was just as if I'd never flown a fighter before and I had the same thrill as when I first flew a Spitfire. [On 12 June, when he

[1]*Pilot Officer William Henry Millington, DFC, of Edwardstown, South Australia, missing in action on 30 October 1940. Commemorated on the Runnymede Memorial.*

RECOMMENDATIONS FOR HONOURS AND AWARDS 17 AVR.

Christian Names: Richard, George, Arthur   Surname: BARCLAY

Rank: Flying Pilot Officer   Official No: 74661

Nationality: British   Unit: No.249 Squadron

Command: Fighter   Group: 11 Group

The above named officer has flown on innumerable sorties with this Squadron since the squadron moved to the front line. He has proved himself a very able section leader and has destroyed four and a half enemy aircraft and probably six others. He has also damaged four.
He flies with admirable coolness and at all times shows a fearless keenness for the destruction of the enemy.

State what recognition is recommended: D.F.C.

State what employment held or how employed: Section Leader 249 Squadron.

Signature of Commanding Officer

...F.V.Beamish.... Wing Commander.

Date: 8th November, 1940   Unit: R.A.F. Station, North Weald

Covering remarks of Air Officer Commanding or senior officer

Covering remarks of Air Officer Commanding-in-Chief

George was recommended for the Distinguished Flying Cross (DFC) by his station commander, Wing Commander Victor Beamish, on 8 November 1940. The recommendation was approved by the AOC No 11 Group, Air Vice-Marshal Keith Park and by Air Chief Marshal Sir Hugh Dowding, Commander-in-Chief, RAF Fighter Command.

REMARKS OF THE AIR OFFICER COMMANDING.

Pilot Officer R.G.A. BARCLAY.

This gallant young officer has fought in many combats. He has proved himself to be a very able Section Leader. He has combined admirable coolness and outstanding courage with a great keenness for the destruction of the enemy. He has personally destroyed 4½ enemy aircraft and probably destroyed a further six and damaged four. I strongly recommend him for the Immediate Award of the DISTINGUISHED FLYING CROSS.

K. R. Park
Air Vice-Marshal

8th November, 1940.   Commanding, No. 11 Group

REMARKS OF THE AIR OFFICER COMMANDING-IN-CHIEF.

Approved. H.C.T. Dowding. ACM.

Date. 11th November 1940.   Headquarters, Fighter Command.

was at No 5 OTU, Aston Down]. When I went on leave I felt the Hurricane was out of date – when I came back I felt it was the only thing worth flying!

The aerodrome is extremely soggy and there were four Hurricanes up on their noses in bomb-hole subsidences, etc, at the same time.

Thursday, November 7th

Bill Millington introduced a new pet to the squadron before I went on leave – Wilfred, the white duck. Bill got him to satisfy Butch's craving for a duck! Wilfred is a great character – comparatively tame – he spends most of his time 'up the creek', *ie* in the ditch round the aerodrome.

We were informed this morning that 249 has been appointed the Gold Coast Squadron, *ie* the squadron paid for by the Gold Coast! No 257 was the Burma Squadron. We hope the GC will sponsor us with nuggets of gold!

I went up in the morning to try and intercept a lone Hun. I saw a streamer and climbed up hard. I saw the trail cease and a black dot descend vertically. I was just able to keep it in sight but it turned out to be a Hurricane (46 Squadron) which had just attacked a Me110 at 31,000ft and damaged it. The 110 was last seen south of London with both engines smoking.

I returned to North Weald and saw the squadron scrambling below me, so I joined up with them. We went to patrol a convoy off the Thames Estuary. We flew around a bit at 14,000ft and then saw the convoy being bombed heavily with a cruiser firing with every gun she could muster, but we couldn't see any enemy aircraft anywhere, so we dived down and I saw a burst of machine-gun fire and then three 109s. I dived and did a beam attack on one – no result. I saw five 109s at about 2,000ft streaking for home and, pulling the plug, gave chase. I caught them and had a dog-fight with one. Eventually he went into a climb and I saw that his engine had stopped. Whoopee! But then I saw five more 109s between me and the shore, also going home and therefore coming towards me head-on. I gave one of them a burst from below and in front. The whole formation split up and turning I gave the same 109 another burst. He slowed down to about 140mph and

smoking slightly he went on – waggling his wings as he went. I couldn't deliver the *coup de grâce* as I was out of ammo. So two 'probably destroyed' it had to be!

I was then 25 miles east of Margate so I lost no time in getting home since I had no ammo. We had no loss and got about four destroyed and four probables. Ginger got three – two 109s and one Ju87. Thompson saw 15 87s going home in formation!

In the evening we did a patrol at 15,000ft on the Maidstone patrol line. The Wing Commander was flying No 4 in the first section. He flew off to investigate something in his usual way and in returning to formation he cut off Ginger's tail, Ginger flying No 1 of the second section. We were glad to hear later that Ginger had baled out OK. The Wing Commander had force-landed OK. We had our doubts about Ginger as he spun from 15,000ft to the clouds at 6,000ft without getting out.

Friday, November 8th

I went up in the morning to chase a lone raider, but was immediately brought back, so I did some aerobatics. It was a wonderful morning and it reminded me of the carefree flying in the CUAS.

Later we did a stooge patrol for 1hr 50min. We all got bored stiff as we knew there was nothing about.

The third trip was more exciting. We were just south of the Thames when we saw some ships around Sheerness letting fly with all their guns, and bombs dropping in the water near them. But the enemy aircraft were obviously below us and were not to be seen. No 46 Squadron leading did not see the ack-ack so in desperation Butch led us down in a dive. But it was then too late! We saw nothing.

Saturday, November 9th

I shot at Easneye[1] today. Great fun – 97 pheasants. I shot well for me at pheasants but disgraced myself at the sundry partridge drives!

Sunday, November 10th

No flying – very poor weather. Butch spent the day trying to shoot starlings, rooks and sparrows with Robbie's 12-bore, from the door of the dispersal hut!

---

[1] *The estate near Ware, Hertfordshire, belonging to Harry Buxton; also the home of George's grandmother.*

The ditch round the aerodrome at North Weald was where Wilfred the duck spent most of his time.

The meeting of Wilfred and Pipsqueak, co-ordinated by Sergeant 'Titch' Palliser, Flying Officer Cassidy and Flying Officer Dickie Wynn.

Wilfred the duck tries to fly, encouraged by Sergeant Parish. When George was killed, Parish cycled a considerable distance to offer his personal condolences to the Barclay family.

Every time he let fly we all jumped about a foot off our chairs. It was stopped in the end in favour of preserving our nerves!

Monday, November 11th

In the morning we were scrambled too late and saw some high 109s away above us fleeing down the Estuary. I expect they had successfully bombed London.

In the afternoon we did a convoy patrol in pretty bad weather. We found an enormous Hun seaplane (Heinkel 59 – span 97ft), low on the water. It did steep turns to the right while we tried to shoot it down. It turned so sharply that a stern attack turned into a head-on attack. I got its port motor, and it had to do its turns to the left, turning against its dead engine. Eventually Pat Wells, who has now returned to the squadron, set the port float on fire (there is a petrol tank there) and the enemy aircraft landed perfectly into wind. It gradually burnt until suddenly the petrol tanks went up and covered it and the sea around with burning petrol. I think all the crew were dead or badly wounded.

Meanwhile Butch shot down an old Ju86 which fell into the sea like a torch. Meanwhile, 40 Italians were being shot up 40 miles north of us: 13 were destroyed – some of them were fighters [Fiat CR.42s] looking like Gladiators. I wish we had got into them. I dived low over Gt Holland on our way home. The weather was bad and it took us some time to find North Weald.

Tuesday, November 12th

Most noteworthy from my point of view – November 12th I was awarded the DFC.[1] This morning the Wing Commander announced it. I don't feel I deserve a medal, and I feel still less like the dashing type one imagines wins medals! I have also been made a Flying Officer, as I've done a year's war service as a Pilot Officer.

Wednesday, November 13th

Sewing, sewing, sewing – DFC ribbons and Flying Officer stripes on to my tunics! We didn't do much flying today – there was cloud at about 4,000ft. We did one patrol over Kent and chased one Blenheim! Ginger made me very angry by saying that he almost shot at it – there was no question of its identity. Ginger has been awarded a bar to his DFC. He has done very well and has about 12–13 confirmed victories. He always seems to see his opponents crash, which I seldom seem to do. Why? Does he shoot straighter and therefore knock out the enemy aircraft outright?

Thursday, November 14th

We did a convoy patrol outside the Estuary today. Two 109s suddenly appeared at our own height of about 18,000ft. We split up and dived after them – one climbed away out of reach, the other dived and about six people followed it. I won the race to reach it first and approached from astern firing from 200 yards inwards. My throttle stuck fully open so I overhauled the 109 very rapidly at about 7,000ft. I fired until I had to break away for fear of hitting the enemy aircraft, and then turned in again and did a quarter attack. As I fired glycol and black smoke came out – very satisfactorily as I deliberately aimed at one radiator.

Other Hurricanes fired and the enemy aircraft turned inland and tried to force-land near Manston aerodrome. Just as he was at tree top height Sergeant Smyth shot at the enemy aircraft. It flew straight into some trees and crashed in flames.

On returning Butch tore a terrific strip off Sergeant Smyth about his unsportsmanship, etc, and we all heartily agreed. I was given the 109 to my credit by the squadron as it was useless for everyone to put in a combat report. Flight Lieutenant Burnett of 46 Squadron apparently joined in the mêlée and claimed a share in the 109. It was quite ridiculous of him as there were six of our Hurricanes dealing with enemy aircraft. A 249 pilot ought to have had the other ½ Hun!

Friday, November 15th

Hearing of the bombing of Coventry last night[2] we are inclined to think that perhaps Sergeant Smyth's action yesterday wasn't so bad after all.

---

[1] This was eventually presented to him by King George VI on 11 March 1941 – two days before Buckingham Palace was bombed and when George was still limping from the injuries received when he had been shot down on 29 November.

[2] Coventry was attacked on the night of 14 November by 437 enemy aircraft; about 380 people were killed and 800 seriously injured.

Today we had to post six pilots as we had too many. This is unfortunate as we shall not now be able to take so much leave this winter.

We did two long patrols (too long) on the Maidstone patrol line today. We feel we were made stooges of today. We landed short of fuel very fed up and angry. (See cutting about 'Nick's' VC).[1]

Saturday, November 16th

We did one patrol over Dover at 20,000ft this morning. Butch's radio packed up so I had to lead the squadron. We flew over Dover at 20,000ft watching six 109s trying to lure us out over the Channel. I realised the difficulties of leading a squadron at that height; a Hurricane squadron at 20,000ft cannot climb except extremely slowly and in a straight line – as soon as the squadron turns it loses height or at any rate does not gain any. I got rather slow on one turn and imagined the whole squadron spinning off the turn behind me, but when we got back everyone was OK and just remarked that I was a bit on the slow side.

This evening some of us went to see a Dornier 17 that crashed owing to ack-ack last night – there was just a large crater, still smouldering, full of bits and pieces with bits and clods of earth strewn around for hundreds of yards. There were bits of German everywhere, but so mangled that it wasn't as gruesome as one would have thought – the toes of one foot rather put me off, but in the failing light it didn't look human.

Sunday, November 17th

We did one patrol at 9:00am over convoys in the Thames Estuary. We saw some high 109s leaving streamers but they were too high and showed no signs of coming down.

In the afternoon I motored to Sherfield where I spent a grand 48 hours. I rode on Peggoty with Phyll (on Magnette) – it was very good to ride again. I drove Phyll up to Watford on Tuesday morning and then returned to North Weald greatly refreshed by the breath of country air. I returned to find the squadron fog-bound at Martlesham so there was no flying to be done.

Wednesday, November 20th

We did no flying at all today.

Thursday, November 21st

I did a convoy patrol with Sergeant Mills. We saw nothing though there were meant to be a few odd Huns about.

Friday, November 22nd

I got up at 6:00am and as I left the Battle HQ where I sleep, a Hun went over. I heard a whistle and bang, bang! Two bombs and then a third heavy one further away. I got in the car and drove off to Higham for 48 hours.

A splendid holiday! Father came for Friday night and Saturday and Mum and Mary for Saturday lunch. We got 140 pheasants on Friday and 114 on Saturday. We had a couple of bottles of fizz on Saturday night as Theodore[2] insisted on celebrating my DFC.

Sunday, November 24th

Even after 48 hours it's good to be back with the squadron.

I drove back in the morning and tried to come back on the state, but everyone was happy where they were so I stayed off the state till –

Monday, November 25th

Fog all day. I went to see a flick in London with Hopalong Cassidy (Flying Officer Cassidy, late of 25 Squadron). We didn't see any of the really badly bombed parts, just scattered damage everywhere.

Tuesday, November 26th

We did a convoy patrol in the afternoon in brilliant sun over about four convoys 15 miles east of Harwich. Suddenly the destroyer escort put up an ack-ack barrage and we saw two Me109s above us. They attacked Red Section (I never saw such cheek!) and we all gave chase. I was just gaining well on one about 400 yards dead astern when some idiot shouted, 'Messerschmitts behind – look out, look out,

---

[1] *Awarded to Flight Lieutenant J.B. Nicolson for shooting down an Me110 over Southampton while his own aircraft was in flames.*

[2] *T.D. Barclay, a first cousin and a director of Barclays Bank. He had inherited Higham from their mutual uncle Robin Barclay – also of the Bank.*

look out!' There was nothing for it but to see if there was anything behind, shooting from behind – to cut an annoying story short, it lost the 109 for me, but of course it is quite ridiculous to ignore something behind one when one is flying a dead straight course.

Wednesday, November 27th

I did a weather test in the morning and climbed up through cloud to 8,000ft where there was brilliant sunshine. We were scrambled just before tea – Keith Lofts' wireless was u/s, so I led. We climbed up to 16,000ft over the Thames Estuary and saw sundry groups of Me109s above us, and the position was rather ticklish as we were meant to be gaining height while these 109s sat above in the sun. Eventually the 109s went home without attacking and we returned to North Weald. My directional gyro was u/s which made flying on the vectors considerably more difficult.

Thursday, November 28th

We patrolled over Kent in brilliant sun with very high ice clouds. Lots of 109s played about very high above us in the sun. I saw two do a head-on attack at each other – one turned, spun and then climbed after the other. We knew circumstances were ideal for the Huns to pounce on any straggler and sure enough I heard a shout – looked round and saw a long vertical trail of white smoke and then a little white blob far below – a parachute. I tried to think who it might be and came to the conclusion it was Pat Wells. Rotten luck as he was in hospital as a result of Sept 7th for some weeks. This time we hear he is in the same hospital as before with burns on face and legs and dislocated shoulder.

Friday, November 29th

I was shot down today – a most novel experience. The squadron was scrambled for a patrol and I took Davidson as my No 2, to chase a Hun up Debden way, but we rejoined the squadron as the Hun was too far away. Later the two of us went off again after a streamer coming in over Dover.

I spoke to Squadron Leader Roberts (a Controller) on November 28th as to how much of our R/T the Hun picks up. So when I said this time, 'Have sighted streamer and bandit' I was interested to see that in a minute or two the Hun turned and went out again over the Channel.

We were vectored after Huns for a time at about 22,000ft then told, 'One enemy believed a 109 near you.' Some minutes afterwards we were told to rejoin the squadron and Davidson, who had been weaving behind, came back into formation. I was told to look to the north-west over Maidstone for the rest of the squadron. Suddenly four explosions down on my right-hand side – I realised they were cannon shells and as I whipped into a left-hand turn over Davidson two more explosions and something hit me hard in the right leg but didn't hurt. I felt waves of hot air and the Hurricane went into a spin from which I couldn't recover, so I decided to bale out. All this of course in a couple of seconds. Back with the roof, straps undone and lean out and push with feet on dashboard – no result – back into cockpit, undo oxygen bayonet connection and try again. This time I'm out straightaway and fell forward over the leading edge missing the propeller by inches!

As I leant out over the side I heard a burst of machine-gun fire – was it aimed for me or Davidson? Or was it Davidson aiming for the Hun? As I fell out and down on my back one of my boots fell off, apparently to me falling upwards as I left it behind. [It was subsequently found by a Kentish farmer and returned to George.] I began to spin to the left as I lay on my back, ever faster until it became unpleasant. Meanwhile I felt for the ripcord with both hands. As soon as I found it I was quite happy and settled down to the novel sensation of dropping through space. But the spin had become unpleasantly fast to the left so I put out my right arm and gradually slowed up. I tried to turn on to my back but was quite helpless, I suppose because there was nothing to push against. I eventually succeeded by drawing up my legs and I slowly rolled over but couldn't see the ground owing to the wind in my eyes.

Meanwhile I saw my Hurricane spinning furiously directly above me and as I watched a large puff of white smoke shot out of it as if there had been an explosion inside. But I was so enjoying myself nothing seemed to matter in the least.

I began to feel I had delayed the drop quite long enough so I pulled the ripcord with both hands and hung on to it like grim death. (The pilot who drops his ripcord is said to have been 'windy' and I expect it would take a long time to live down!)

The parachute streamed out between my feet and there was a small jerk followed immediately by a pretty severe jerk, which I imagine caused me to do a complete somersault, and my second boot came off, and then there I was, dangling in complete silence at about 2,000ft. Immediately my fall was broken my Hurricane flashed past quite near and 'spun in' directly underneath, bursting into flames. I immediately realised my drift would take me away from the wreck. I was pretty low by now and the ground began to come up quicker and quicker. I made a feeble attempt to swing round and land facing drift, but as there was no swing I decided to let well alone and just waited for the bang, which was not too bad. I landed in an apple orchard, my 'chute settling down on a small apple tree.

The usual crowd came running up and put me in a car. I was taken to Pembury Hospital [Tunbridge Wells] in high spirits and very excited. Nasty hole in ankle, whence came nose of cannon-shell; few holes in calf and thigh and right elbow. Operation in evening! I baled out at about 12:00 o'clock and delayed the drop about 18–20,000ft, *ie* just under four miles! Thus I joined the Caterpillar Club!

Mrs Dorothy Barclay, George's mother, recalled that her son's parachute descent was seen by a relative living near Pembury Hospital, Miss Christina Barclay, whose two old maids brought her out to see the airman. When Miss Barclay learnt who he was, she invited Mrs Barclay and her youngest son Richard to stay – which they did for George's 21st birthday on 7 December, bringing a birthday cake and presents with them.[1]

[1] *See George's letter to his sister Mary, dated 9 December, on page 88.*

Recovery and Back to Operations

George Barclay, awarded the DFC on 12 November 1940 and shot down and wounded on 29 November, was in hospital for six weeks – first at Pembury Hospital, Tunbridge Wells, Kent; then at the RAF Hospital, Ely, Cambridgeshire; finally at the RAF Officers' Hospital, Torquay, Devon.

The citation for his DFC award said that he had shown 'admirable coolness and courage in combat. His keenness and determination have enabled him to destroy at least four enemy aircraft.' In fact, his score during the battle was five e/a damaged, six probably destroyed and five destroyed.

While at Pembury he wrote cheerfully to his sister Mary on 9 December 1940, two days after his 21st birthday:

Thank you a thousand times for the shower of presents, letters, telegrams, etc – especially for the grand cigarette case – it is, as you know, exactly what I want. I hear you will have it engraved for me, but may I keep it and look at it and use it until I see you next? I am v. much better – the stitches came out of my arm this morning and only my little finger has yet to return to normal. My leg has quite settled down now and I suppose it's just a question now of giving it a few weeks to heal. And above all I'm now really feeling well myself. I'm afraid I won't be home for Christmas but I might see you in January. We had an amusing 21st party here – Mum, Aunt Chris, Richard and self. Everyone has been extra very good to me – Mum especially and Far – I've had some lovely presents – gold links from Chas [his elder brother Charles] – £50 and ring from Mum and Far – leather holdall from Buxtons as well as lots of cheques.
  Best love George
  Thanks a million.

George in a wheelchair with his legs wrapped in a blanket, and his godson Leo in a pram, with brother Charlie and family members during the cold winter of 1940–41.

Then he wrote again on 21 December, after she had visited him:

My dearest Mary,

It was grand to see you on Thursday – thank you so much for making such a long trek to see me. I did so enjoy gassing to you; I wish it could have been for longer! I hope you got back OK. I thought of you trying to get a place on the bus when I heard the Jerry bombers over that evening.

I am now back in the general men's ward, as they have taken my room for a very ill patient who shouts in delirium and keeps everyone awake. It's bearable now that I'm well, but it's no fun talking to visitors with an audience of Tommies, yokels etc! But thank heavens I'm going to the Studds[1] for Christmas – it will be fun. I think after Christmas I shall start agitating to move to an RAF hospital or convalescent place.

Thank you so much for the book – Fun in Bed – it causes much amusement, but you mustn't spend all your hard-earned cash on books for me as I have really got lots to amuse me!

Thanks so much for the £2. I enclose a cheque.
Yours with love, George

PS A happy Xmas if this reaches you in time! Mum left your woolly boots with me but I stupidly forgot to give them to you. I'm so sorry.

After he had gone to Ely he wrote again, on 20 January 1941:

Dearest Mar,

I am quite delighted with the pullover – people remark on it frequently and it is much admired. It is quite the nicest I have had knitted for me. Thank you so very much for knitting it for me.

I'll tell you what has been happening to me lately – I went to the Eric Studds again from Pembury for two days before I left Pembury. They were very good to me. Eric lent me a ciné camera to take some pictures of the squadron when I get back. When

I returned to hospital I was suddenly told I was leaving and would probably be going home next day. Of course I was delighted. An RAF MO came to see me and he arranged for me to drive home in an enormous 40hp Buick plus MTC driver! It was a very comfortable means of travelling and I looked in at North Weald on the way home. It was grand to see 'the boys' again and made me champ to be back again.

It was marvellous to get home. I don't know if I have ever appreciated it quite so much. Pembury was all very well, but I was sick of the company of the Tommies, though they were mostly excellent fellows, and the food was lousy. I found Mummie not at all well with violent pains. She had the doctor and he gave her an examination. He found it was a kind of rheumatism. After massage at the hospital I'm glad to say Mummie was much better and said she felt a different person.

There had been a Junkers 88 on the lawn for the Spitfire Fund. The lawn was worse than a ploughed field. Richard went back to Gresham's quite happily – a two-day bus journey![2]

I'm afraid I shall not be at home for your leave, as I came here after six days at home to have my plaster changed[3] and to let the RAF look at me. This hospital is a dream after Pembury. I thought I would be going to one nearer you at Halton near Aylesbury, but this is a nicer hospital. It is good to be with RAF pilots again. Most of the wounded officers here are bomber boys and it's good to hear their point of view. I may go home or to Torquay (RAF convalescent hospital) after this.

I had a letter from Dick Osborn to say he was going on an operational squadron and he was sorry he hadn't been able to take you out.

Best love and thanks a 1,000,000 for the grand pullover.
George.

Then when he was at Torquay, convalescing, he wrote again to Mary on 4 March 1941 to tell her about a visit he'd

---

[1] *Sir Eric Studd of Limpsfield, Surrey, one of his mother's cousins.*

[2] *Gresham's School, Holt, Norfolk, which had been evacuated to Newquay, Cornwall.*

[3] *The cure then used for a large flesh wound was to encase the limb in plaster; rotting of the area around the wound initiated the healing process. The Barclay family still have the head of the 20mm cannon shell dug out of George's ankle. The elasticity of his Achilles tendon had held it – just, for the tendon was nearly severed.*

Buckingham Palace. 1529

Admit one to witness the Investiture.

Claredon.

Lord Chamberlain.

'Admit one to witness the Investiture.' This is one of the admission tickets given to members of the Barclay family when George received his DFC in person from King George VI at Buckingham Palace on 11 March 1941. Two days later the palace was bombed.

In January 1941, when he was well enough to leave Pembury Hospital, George visited his cousins at Limpsfield in Surrey. He is seen here out for a walk with cousin Lady Stephanie and her daughter Buffy Studd.

had from his cousin Lionel – who was with him at Stowe and at Cambridge, and was later to lose his life at Salerno in 1943:

> *Dearest Mary,*
> *Thanks so much for your letter and news. I'm sorry you have been in bed such a lot, but you seem to be having a good holiday as well. We had great fun when Susan, Jean,[1] and Lionel came over for the afternoon. We went and lunched at the Grand Hotel and gossiped afterwards, until Lion had to catch a train. We saw him off and then I took Sue and Jean to a flick and then on to tea at the Imperial!*
>
> *Lion has grown at least 1½ inches, but he's the same old Lionel – I don't know why Sue tells you he's formidable.*
>
> *This is a grand spot really, though one spends far too much boudle. I shall be bankrupt soon at this rate. There are lots of fellows I know here which makes life very well worth living. ...*
>
> *The leg goes on slowly – it is better, but it takes such an awful long time to heal. They say another six weeks to go yet.*
>
> *I'm sorry this is such a terrible mess. I'm struggling with an awful old 'J' nib.*
>
> *The sweater is much admired, whenever the talk switches to the subject of clothes. Everyone remarks on what a nice and sensible cigarette case I have.*
>
> *I am just starting the* Forsyte Saga *– I'm wondering whether I shall ever finish it, though people say one can't put it down once one gets well into it.*
>
> *There is lots of talent here and we put on plays, dances, and concerts – all of them usually a great success.*
>
> *I must stop and take a very charming VAD to a flick!*
> *With best love,*
> *George*

When he was fit again, what was to be done with George? The fighter situation had changed; the Battle of Britain had been won and lost and RAF Fighter Command was now going on to the offensive.

[1] *Daughter of Murray Buxton and cousin of Susan and Lionel.*

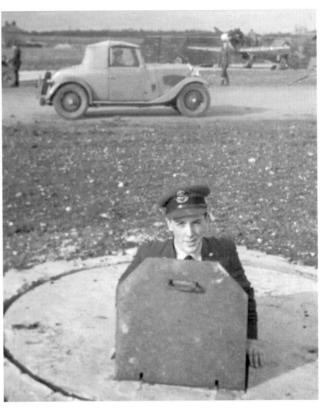

George with his parents, Dorothy and Gilbert, at Buckingham Palace.

Not taking things too seriously! George at RAF Debden, where he instructed on No 52 Operational Training Unit from May to August 1941.

North Weald 1941. No 249 Squadron pilots with their Hurricanes. From left: Mills, unknown Australian, G.C.C. Palliser, Davidson, A. Lewis, R.A. Barton, Lohmeyer, T. Crossey, P.H.V. Wells, Wynn, A.R.F. Thompson, Cassidy, Woolmer (intelligence officer), T.F. Neil, unknown.

John Grandy (with thumbs in his breast pockets), and to his right in the picture Tommy Thompson and George.

Taking it easy outside the dispersal hut, 52 OTU Debden.

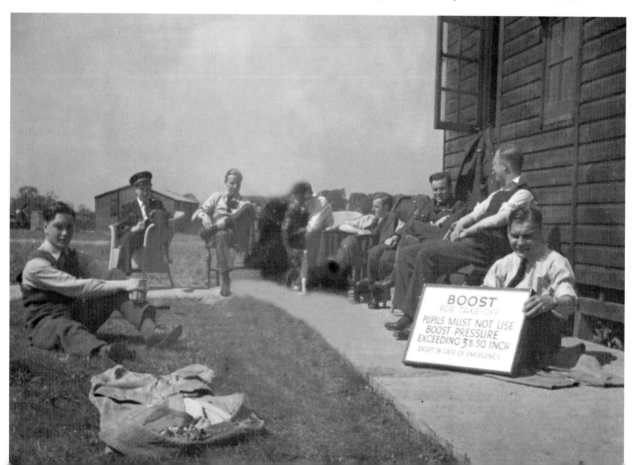

First he went back to No 249 Squadron at North Weald and on 26 March 1941 flew his beloved Hurricane, GN-C, again. For the rest of that month and until 21 April he flew around, re-familiarising himself with fighter exercises – aerobatics, mock interceptions, air firing and formation – and drew the familiar pencilled patterns of fighter formations in his log book; but towards the end of April left North Weald for good. He had been posted to No 52 Operational Training Unit (OTU) at Debden, Essex, from 7 May 1941 for flying instructor duties. The chief flying instructor there (later that year to return to operational flying on Spitfires at Coltishall) was Wing Commander John Grandy, his former CO on No 249 Squadron.

No 52 OTU had Hurricanes, Masters and Battles; its task was to train new generations of fighter pilots. But it is clear, from a letter which George wrote to his sister Mary on 23 May 1941 (for her birthday) that he had one thought in mind – how to get back on operations himself:

Dearest Mary,
Very many happy returns of the day – I hope it's fine and you can find some suitable way of celebrating, such as riding or picnicking at Trimingham[1] – but alas! your beastly brother has stolen the green car. I do hope it doesn't stop you going wherever you want to on your birthday.

I so enjoyed my rides when last at home, that I then and there decided to give you some rides as a birthday present – a very dull sort of suggestion as you have no present to unwrap, and pulling a note out of an envelope sounds so like a tip! But actually I am giving you a ride or two, not a note!

I hope all goes well with you – and that Father is better and Mummie is getting some sleep. The car is a tremendous boon here.

I went to see Aunt Rhoda the other day – she was flourishing and has made the cottage very nice indeed by adding on one or two rooms. The baby farm at 'Gastons' was most amusing – a complete babel as all the children shouted at the top of their voices. We walked round the garden – the first time for me for years. I hope to go over to Brent Pelham one day to see what is left of the Puckeridge pack.

I flew to Halton yesterday, had a full medical board, and am now an operational pilot again – whoopee!

Please tell Father I am enquiring about the value of the Vauxhall – BUT (1) what year is it (2) how many thousand miles has it done (3) what are its present defects?

I hope to see Patience in Cambridge some time – Love and once again the happiest of birthdays.
George.

News of the posting he wanted came in a telegram from 52 OTU on 2 August 1941 (he was on leave at the time) asking him to report to No 11 Group Headquarters. His posting was to No 611 – the West Lancashire Auxiliary Air Force Squadron – which was at Hornchurch with Spitfire VBs; from 4 August 1941 he was promoted to Flight Lieutenant and joined the squadron as a flight commander. Its ORB for 3 August 1941 recorded:

Posting: Flight Lieutenant Richard George Arthur Barclay, DFC, who is one of the CO (Squadron Leader E.H. Thomas)'s ex-pupils,[2] posted as 'A' Flight Commander. He has been instructing for some months and is very glad to be back on operational flying.

He hadn't flown Spitfires operationally and the squadron ORB for 10 August 1941 comments:

'No more flying except for some air testing of aircraft and F/L Barclay busily chalking up his 25 hours' Spitfire flying, the stipulated time he must complete before he leads his flight operationally.'

Already his log book is full of notes in neat, enthusiastic handwriting, with pencil sketches of squadron formations; and some of his obvious enthusiasm spills over into an undated letter he wrote to Mary at this time:

My dearest Mary,
Thanks for your p.c. It really is time I wrote you a line of some sort! I am afraid I can't manage next weekend at Oxford, but I might well fly over on the Sunday if the weather is fine.

---

[1] A small Norfolk estate near Cromer belonging to Arthur Buxton, a cousin; it was a favourite place for relaxation and rough shooting, and contained a small bungalow on high ground with beautiful views of the sea.

[2] At Cranwell. Richard Barclay recalls that his brother was 'immensely proud to be posted to one of the famous Auxiliary squadrons'.

As you see from this address I have changed my job. I am now back in an operational squadron of the latest Spitfires. It is delightful to be away from the training racket and back in the friendly operational atmosphere. We employ ourselves in sweeping the skies over France mainly – a new and different form of warfare to the one I am used to. I have a flight on my own now, which is grand, because it is the first unit one definitely commands – so Flight Lieutenant on letters, please! I knew the other Flight Commander in this squadron (611 Auxiliary Squadron) previously at Debden and the CO was at one time my instructor at Cranwell! I also know people in the other squadrons here. I had a grand time at Smoo[1] and caught some large trout with which I was quite delighted – true I missed a day or two, but I was lucky to get as long as I did.

> *I hope life goes well with you.*
> *With best love*
> *George*

On 17 August 1941 the No 611 Squadron ORB notes: 'George Barclay is now operational and is straining at the leash to get out and have a crack with the squadron'; and his first opportunity came on 18 August, when the Hornchurch Wing – Nos 54, 403 (Canadian) and 611 Squadrons – gave high escort cover to Blenheims bombing Marquise. His operational career on these offensive sweeps ('circuses') and 'rhubarbs' (low-level flights over France) was to be short – only just over a month before he found himself down in a field in northern France on 20 September. But in that short time he threw himself energetically into the fighter offensive role on which his squadron was employed. His fighting spirit was soon very much in evidence, as the ORB for 19 August records in a note on Circus 81:

> ... 403 Squadron got two destroyed and six damaged and we were unsuccessful, being baulked by a thick bank of cloud below into which the e/a dived, though not before Smithy [Flight Lieutenant Duncan Smith, a New Zealander who visited the Barclay family at

Cromer], George Barclay, Ken Campbell and Spud Hayter all had squirts without being able to observe results.

George himself described this operation thus (the whole of his log book's right-hand pages now are covered with descriptive notes):[2]

> High independent cover wing to Blenheims bombing Gosnay near Béthune. Crossed coast at 28–31,000ft in condensation trail layer. Dived on many 109s silhouetted far below against cloud – they as usual wouldn't stay to fight. Flying No 2 on Wingco [Wing Commander D.C. Stapleton, DFC] had long-range squirt with Smithy at 109F. No result. 603 and 403 got five between them – lost one.

Again, for 21 August the squadron ORB and George's own words tell the same story, with slight variations in detail. The official chronicler notes:

> After a hurried lunch we came to: Circus 84, began with conference at 603 and we then took off at 1305hr acting as Escort Cover to five Blenheims who were to repeat the morning's attack on Chocques. We saw more flak[3] than ever before, which caused great discomfort to all concerned, but only saw three 109s at which George Barclay and Sergeant Ingram had a squirt which caused the [censored] to dive some 17,000ft which we hope broke his ear-drums if nothing else.

In his account, George says that the:

> Wing was high escort cover at 22–30,000ft to six Blenheims in an abortive attempt to bomb factory at Chocques near Béthune. 611 bottom squadron led by Wing Commander Stapleton. I was Charlie 2 on the CO. Owing to ten-tenths cloud [complete cloud cover] we turned back at St Omer. Saw 109s below on way in, but had to stick with bombers. Pecked at by 109s in sun on way home. Saw aircraft dive straight into sea off Gravelines.

---

[1] *On the north coast of Sutherland; the Buxton family had a house there for fishing and shooting. Mary (by now Mrs P.H. Bosanquet) says, 'How he got there is a mystery!'*

[2] *Being a single-engined pilot meant that he only used normally the second column of figures to record his flying times, leaving plenty of space for unofficial comments!*

[3] *Jargon (abbreviated from the German word* fliegerabwehrkanone) *for anti-aircraft ground fire.*

Hornchurch, early 1942. The man on the right is Wilfred 'Smithy' Duncan Smith, DFC, who became firm friends with George. Smithy spent convalescent leave with George and his parents at their home in Cromer.

Later the same day, again escorted by the Hornchurch Spitfires, the Blenheims had another go at this target, No 611 being (as George records):

> ... escort cover at 20,000ft to six Blenheims bombing Chocques – which they did excellently. Saw 109s above against cloud. Heavy flak, dead accurate for height. 403 lost CO [Squadron Leader Morris] and Sergeant pilot. I shot up a 109F with yellow nose that jumped Charlie section.[1] I was No 2 to Pilot Officer Smith.

This was a war of attrition, tempting the Luftwaffe to fight and to possible losses; but it was costly also to the RAF fighter squadrons.

There was occasional recreation: on 26 August George flew over to West Malling, Kent, with Flight Lieutenant David Scott-Maiden, DFC, of 603 Squadron to have lunch with some of the friends they had made during OTU days at Aston Down – Hugh Percy, Roddie Nocker and Desmond Hughes.[2] But that same day, late in the afternoon, both he and Scott-Maiden were operating. As 611's ORB describes it:

> Circus 87... put on at 1720hr after we had been at readiness since dawn. ... We were middle squadron in Target Support Wing in attack on St Omer aerodrome and saw more 109s than for a long time past – 120+ was on the board at Ops. ... We couldn't come to grips at all but George Barclay and Sergeant Gray were jumped on coming out at Gravelines by four Me109Fs with the result that Sergeant Gray has not yet returned – a great pity as he was a real good lad.

George's own account differs in two details – the times of the operation and the number of 109s plotted. Nor did he know exactly what had happened to Sergeant Gray: 'Wing high cover 27,000ft [he wrote in his log book] to six Blenheims bombing St Omer. 54 Squadron have replaced 403 Canadian Squadron.[3] Flew as Charlie 1. Got jumped by four Me109Fs but eluded them and returned over Gravelines in cloud and saw a 109F destroyed by Flight Lieutenant David Scott-Maiden, DFC, crash into the drink. Many 109s – 160+ plotted. Annoying not to get a shot. Sergeant Gray, my No 2, missing – probably jumped by the same ones as I. 17:05–19:35hr.'

---

[1] *Normally the squadron flew in three sections of four aircraft each – Charlie (left), Red (centre) and Blue (right).*

[2] *Retired from the RAF as Air Vice-Marshal F.D. Hughes, CB, CBE, DSO, DFC, MA. He was with George Barclay in Cambridge UAS and remembers with affection his happy personality.*

[3] *On 25 August the former had returned from Martlesham and the latter left Hornchurch to go to Debden.*

Next day (27 August) George had another narrow shave – for quite different reasons, including being airborne for 2½ hours, as he himself recorded:

Wing + 403 Squadron provided escort cover to nine Blenheims bombing Lille. I flew Charlie 1 at 25,000ft. Blenheims' navigation was non-existent and they led us towards Amiens. We passed Lens and came out over Lille, and east of Dunkirk. Accurate flak. Saw barrage balloon in sea and thought it was a dinghy. Landed Manston with five gallons' petrol.[1] 611 followed correct route – rest of beehive went to Amiens! 07:00–09:30hrs.[2] 603 and 56 Squadrons lost one pilot each. Squadron Leader Louden (603) shot up, but OK except for a few splinters.

On 29 August he did his best to 'fix' two pilots down in the sea – again having to land at Manston because he was nearly out of fuel:

Wing high independent cover to six Blenheims bombing Hazebrouck. Flew Charlie 1; squadron led by Wing Commander Stapleton, DFC, at 28,000ft in condensation trail layer. Cloud up to 30,000ft except over France, where it was clear. Saw two blokes bale out in sea 10–15 miles south-east of Dover. Got fix for them on R/T – attracted attention of rescue launch and orbited until Lysander arrived. Landed Manston short of petrol. 06:25–08:40hrs. Saw three Me109s behind and above dive down on unidentified Spitfire.

Each day almost, someone failed to return from an operation. In his log book for 29 August 1941 George noted:

Channel escort, 1hr 25min. Squadron led by Flight Lieutenant Hayter escorted two MTBs in Straits of Dover at 1,000ft. Boats looking for Wing Commander Gillan, DSO, DFC,[3] reported missing from previous sweep. I led Blue section. Patrol uneventful and Wing Commander Gillan not found. 11:00–12:30hrs.

Each day, too, the squadron was across the Channel, keeping up the fighter offensive, either escorting naval vessels or providing cover for the Blenheim bombers. Often things failed to work out as planned. On 30 August George recorded in his log book: 'Squadron led by Squadron Leader Thomas ordered to rendezvous Manston with three Blenheims to bomb tanker off Ostend. We proceeded towards Ostend at 0ft as we couldn't find Blenheims. Operation cancelled as Blenheims never took off.' Again early in the morning of 31 August, when things not only failed to work out as planned but he nearly ran out of fuel again, after 1hr 45min flying. 'Wing patrolled two destroyers and eight MTBs (he noted) at 10,000ft, 30 miles south of Dungeness, placed there to attract enemy dive-bombers, but this object was not achieved. As Blue 1 I landed with five gallons of petrol.' That afternoon when the wing was again escorting Blenheims, one of the squadrons lost an experienced pilot and George himself nearly got into trouble:

Escort cover wing to 12 Blenheims bombing Lille. Wing Commander Stapleton, DFC, led 611. As Charlie 1 I got isolated over Lille with Charlie 2 (Sergeant Ormiston). Weaved our way back and caught bombers ten miles inland from French coast. Very accurate flak, 15,000ft. High 109s seen, but not attacked by them. 54 Squadron lost Flight Lieutenant Mottram.

No 611's Spitfire VBs bore the code letters FY – and George usually flew in FY-K. On 31 August, after the convoy patrol and offensive sweep (a total of 3hr 45min flying) he did a short air test in a new FY-K with a de Havilland propeller, 'as old FY-K was too slow with Rotol airscrew', he noted in his log book. The DH propeller was metal, with longer blades than the wooden Rotol ones. The test flight brought his day's flying to 4hr, and in August as a whole he did 47hr 40min.

September was to be George Barclay's last month of operational flying over Europe; he came down in northern France on the 20th and his next operations were to be in the Western Desert, over El Alamein in July 1942 – but before that time a lot was to happen to him.

---

[1] *Spitfire VB carried 85 imp. gallons without an overload tank.*

[2] *Total time from Hornchurch. He landed at Manston – an emergency airfield near Ramsgate – after 1hr 50min flying.*

[3] *Flying from North Weald. On 10 February 1938 he had set up an Edinburgh–London record in a Hurricane, covering the 327 miles' distance in 48 minutes at an average ground speed of 408.75mph.*

For No 611 Squadron, September began much as August had ended; in the early morning of the 2nd the Hornchurch Wing (in George's words)

escorted three Blenheims at sea level to bomb tanker off Dunkirk. 611 looked after 242 Squadron (four-cannon Hurricane IIs), who had to beat up the flak ships; 54 looked after bombers; 603 independent. Blenheims all went home early and only half 242 found the enemy shipping. Very poor show! Intense flak from Dunkirk – could see it throwing up sheets of water. Led Charlie section. 08:10–09:30hrs.

That afternoon, the squadron was up again with the Wing, plus their neighbours at North Weald, on a fighter sweep which produced no results. George describes it succinctly: '611, 54 and two North Weald squadrons [Nos 111 and 222 – Spitfires] carried out sweep – Mardyck, St Omer, Hardelot – at 27,500ft. Wonderful visibility – no ack-ack, no 109s. A good afternoon jaunt. Charlie 1. 13:34–17:10hrs.'

But on 4 September, when 611 formed part of an escort for Blenheims, it was a different matter. The ORB records that

... the squadron took off on Circus 93 at 15:35hrs, being an attack on Mazingarbe by 12 Blenheims with the Wing acting as escort cover. Just before reaching St Omer, with the squadron flying at 27,500ft, a wing of 109s was intercepted and the squadron engaged in a general dog-fight. The CO, Flight Lieutenant Barclay, Pilot Officer Reeves, Pilot Officer Gardner and Sergeants Leigh, Ormiston and Evans all had squirts but Sergeants Leigh and Ormiston were the only ones to whom it was possible to allocate casualties.

George with the sergeants of his Flight (611 Squadron) at Hornchurch in September 1941, not long before he was shot down over France. From left, seated: Flying Officer Clive Mellersh, Intelligence Officer; Sergeant 'Tubby' Townsend; George Barclay, OC 'A' Flight; Flying Officer Appleton, Adjutant; Squadron Leader E.H. Thomas, Commanding Officer. Standing: Sergeants Turlington, Wright, Ormston and Evans. The metal panel with cross has been cut from a downed Dornier Do215, shot down in North Wales on a reconnaissance flight to Liverpool, and used by the squadron as a scoreboard for enemy aircraft they had destroyed.

George's own account adds some more details:

> Wing high escort to 12 Blenheims bombing
> Mazingarbe power station, south of Béthune.
> On crossing French coast at Mardyck, wing was
> intercepted by wing of 109Fs, slightly higher, with
> four black crosses on undersides of wings. Mêlée
> took place – had two short squirts. Everyone came
> back in ones and twos. I found yellow Hun chute
> and Hun ten miles north of Gravelines in sea. Flight
> Lieutenant Prevot (Belgian), attached 'A' Flight, 611,
> and Pilot Officer Roeper Bosch (Dutch) landed
> shot up at Manston. Sergeants Ormiston and Leigh,
> DFM, each destroyed one Me. 54 lost two pilots –
> one 'Streak' Harris. Cloud down on Channel and
> Kent hindered rescue work. Too much natter on
> R/T. 15:35–16:55hrs.

Between that date and 19–20 September, when George
Barclay flew his last two operations with a UK-based
fighter squadron, he had several short practice flights. On
7 September No 611 did a 'spoof sweep' – in George's
words: 'Practice sweep formation in Channel from
Beachy Head to North Foreland. 200+ Me 109s took off
in France, thinking we were a sweep. Charlie 1. 3,000ft.
15:15–16:40hrs.' In other words, radar returns from the
formation deceived the Luftwaffe into thinking a sweep
was on its way, and they rose in strength to meet it.

George cannot resist, now, putting a little description
of almost every flight into his log book. On 8 September,
when doing an hour's formation cloud flying:
'Scenery just like Japanese painting. Lots of smoke.
08:40–09:40hrs.' In another squadron formation on
11 September, this time foreshortened to 40 minutes:
'Climb to 30,500ft and cloud penetration by 15° method.
Chased Beaufighter over south coast. Came home early
with unserviceable engine and R/T – noise like a motorbike. 14:50–15:30hrs.' In the evening of that day, when
the Hornchurch squadrons made an offensive sweep:
'Wing swept Channel at 20,000ft from Calais to Dunkirk.
No enemy activity seen. Grand sunset in cloud and haze.
Dusk landing. 18:15–19:40hrs.'

In a letter to his sister Mary on 14 September 1941,
about a week before he came down in France, George
summed up his operational career at that time:

> *Life at Hornchurch is very good. There are lots of very*
> *good blokes here, not only in 611 Squadron but in*
> *the others here as well. These sweeps are a new sort*
> *of fighting to me – always against Messerschmitt 109*
> *fighters, never bombers – and over enemy territory*
> *instead of Kent. Last autumn you felt very brave if*
> *you went two miles out into the Channel off Dover;*
> *now when you reach the French coast on your way*
> *home you feel you are almost back at Hornchurch*
> *– very dangerous as one tends to relax and then*
> *get shot into the drink! I often come back over the*
> *Goodwins – you'd be amazed at the number of ships*
> *sticking out of the water there and in the Thames*
> *Estuary. We haven't had much to do in the last ten*
> *days as the weather has been poor and we've had*
> *some afternoons off. I have been to the Big City once*
> *or twice with the boys and had a gay evening. There*
> *are some nice WAAF officers here, and some of us have*
> *had some good mixed foursomes of tennis and golf.*

On his last eight flights with No 611 Squadron George
used his favourite Spitfire, FY-K. On 12 September he did
20 minutes' aerobatics; on the 13th, practising deflection
attacks, he 'had a dog-fight with CO then thoroughly beat
up two Tomahawks[1] over Bishop's Stortford'; on the 14th
there was co-operation with the local gunners – 'best
bit of flying for a long time, beating up the Hornchurch
defences' – and a weather test; on the 15th and 16th,
cloud flying and a dog-fight. Then on 19 September the
squadron ORB records:

> Dull morning with cloud was spent in Barrow
> Deep[2] patrols over one of the largest convoys seen
> there for a long time. In the last patrol before lunch
> George Barclay and Sergeant Jenner saw four bombs
> dropped near the stern of one of the ships in convoy,
> but as their R/T was unserviceable they couldn't find
> the Hun, who escaped in the cloud.

---

[1] *Curtiss Tomahawks, American single-engined fighters used in limited numbers by the RAF, superseded by more successful
Kittyhawks and Packard Merlin-engined Warhawks, used by Middle East (Desert Air Force) squadrons.*
[2] *An area of the North Sea off the Maplin Sands, extending northwards to opposite Clacton and southwards to opposite Southend.*

George's log book entry for that morning simply records one hour's Rhubarb with Wing Commander Corner, AFC, at 8,000ft and 30 minutes' flying to Manston 'to refuel for Rhubarb with Squadron Leader Thomas.'

This was to be George's last completed operation in 1941. The No 611 Squadron ORB says briefly: 'Squadron Leader Thomas and Flight Lieutenant Barclay took part in a Rhubarb during which they severely shot up a flak ship in a Dutch island harbour.' The Barclay log book description is longer and more graphic:

> Left Manston and flew to Dunkirk. Chased two Tomahawks thinking they were 109s. Continued to Zeebrugge, Flushing and Hook of Holland. Saw two enemy aerodromes, shot at by Bofors. Beat up flak ship off Walcheren with good results. Lots of green tracer! Landed at Hornchurch. Carried out with Squadron Leader Thomas.

On 20 September 1941, when George Barclay took off from Hornchurch with the Wing in mid-afternoon and an hour later found himself in the middle of a French field, there are two detailed accounts of what happened – in the No 611 Squadron ORB and in George's log book. The ORB records:

> Circus 100A began at 14:50hrs. We were Close Escort for the first time to three Blenheims attacking Hazebrouck and we only had North Weald [squadrons 111 and 222] about us. Two other Circuses operated at the same time against Rouen and Abbeville. Small numbers of 109s nibbled at the Wing during the whole trip and Roeper Bosch got jumped just after the target and had a squirt at one of three 109s but couldn't quite claim a damaged. Sergeant Ingram got a damaged off Gris Nez, which might be turned to probable if his camera has worked satisfactorily. George Barclay and Sergeant Ingram were jumped by five 109s just before reaching the coast at Mardyck on way home and Sergeant Ormiston was plugged well and truly in the tail, fuselage and magazine in starboard wing. ... George Barclay has not returned but Spud Hayter is pretty certain it was his Spitfire he saw begin smoking immediately the 109s dived and he circled round as if to get on the tails of the enemy aircraft and then glided back into France. Our thoughts were

very much with him for a safe landing as he was one of the best flight commanders a squadron could possibly have, and his cheery personality will be much missed at dispersal.

George himself thus described his last flight with No 611 Squadron:

> Took off Hornchurch 15:00hrs to escort three Blenheims to bomb Hazebrouck. Our first close escort job. 611 were middle squadron of close escort wing. Wingco Stapleton led squadron, Tommy led Charlie, Spud Hayter led Blue. I flew Red 3 on Wingco. Over St Omer attacked by 109Fs. While shooting at one 109F two 303 bullets struck my FY-K. Engine packed up. Tried to get home on shot-up engine. Target practice for 109s. Force-landed at Buyschoeure, north-east of St Omer, after breaking high-tension cables. Ran like a rabbit!

The rest of that day, and the following days and weeks, were to be recorded in the diary George Barclay kept of his evasion of the Germans, helped by many French friends in the organisation which aided Allied pilots, and his eventual escape into Spain, and thence his return home from Gibraltar.

On 21 September 1941, the day after George failed to return to Hornchurch, the CO of No 611 Squadron, Squadron Leader E.H. Thomas, wrote to the Reverend G.A. Barclay at The Vicarage, Cromer:

> *I wish to express deepest sympathy with you with regard to your son being reported as Missing.*
>
> *Your son had been with this Squadron as Flight Commander of 'A' Flight for six weeks and he had already greatly endeared himself to all ranks. He led his flight with great courage, skill and enthusiasm and his firmness and rigid adherence to duty, both in the air and on the ground, made him a particularly valuable member of the Squadron. He was very popular in the Officers' Mess and his cheerful personality will be greatly missed.*
>
> *On the afternoon of 20th September 1941, the Squadron was escorting bombers in operations over enemy-occupied France and on the way back your son's No 2 was damaged by enemy action*

The telegram sent to Cromer Vicarage by the adjutant of No 611 Squadron informing the Barclays that George had been reported missing.

and fell out of formation. When he regained his position, he noticed that your son was not with him and he did not return from the flight. Although every enquiry has been made, there has – as yet – been no further trace of him. There was no wireless message which might give a clue to the reason of your son's failure to return. There is, on these flights, a possibility that one's aircraft is damaged and that a forced landing in enemy-occupied territory is made, which results in being made a prisoner of war. Should the Air Ministry or I receive any further news it will be immediately communicated to you.

Your son was one of my pupils at Cranwell soon after the outbreak of war, and since then I have formed the highest opinion of him in every respect. He proved himself to be a very gallant fighter pilot.

The whole Squadron, the Officers' Mess and I feel his loss very greatly and would like to express profound regrets to you.

On the day after Squadron Leader Thomas had written to Cromer, George Barclay's elder brother Charles, then a Lieutenant in the Royal Norfolk Regiment, visited No 611 Squadron and described the poignant experience in a long letter of 23 September to his parents:

I do hope Far arrived all right and did not have too bad a journey.

I have so much to report that I shall try and put it all down in the sequence that it took place. We have not rung you up today, because I could not possibly tell you all about it on the telephone – it would take too long, and I can write it more clearly than talking on the 'phone.

Well, I arrived at the Aerodrome at about one o'clock. I found it was not the main entrance where I was, and the Mess and Offices were the other side of the 'drome – about two miles away. Luckily, there was a very nice Corporal in charge of the Guard, who put an Airman at my disposal as a Guide.

We got a lift in a bus and eventually arrived at the Mess. I found the Adjutant, who was most frightfully nice (Flying Officer Appleton). He gave me a drink – although it was my lunch I was in need of, far more! I told him what I had come for and he was very pleased, as it is so easy for things to get lost.

There is a Committee of Adjustment to whom they are supposed to send all belongings, but he said personal belongings – such as guns and cameras – are so often sent there and never seen again that they always try and send as little as possible. He also said how frightfully sorry they all were, as George was such a favourite.

I did not see the CO at all and his letter has not yet arrived, but the Adjutant told me that the CO was so very keen on George and thought very highly of him.

All George's belongings had been taken to the Adjutant's Office, so I didn't see his room at all – presumably it was being occupied by somebody else.

We got the car from the Mess and went along to the Adj's Office. He showed me his Log Book – which of course they have to keep, and actually, there was very little in it, except just what planes he had flown each day, where to and with whom, etc. The chief thing I did notice in it were reports from his various COs, which all said he was above average.

The Adj then explained that they would have to keep his Service Clothing and toilet things to send up to the Committee, but that I could take the rest. So, I have brought away all his civilian clothing, correspondence, gun, rod, cameras, tennis racquet, etc. I had to leave several films that had not yet been developed, but they will develop them and send them on to you. Also, he had to send the Committee everything dealing with financial matters.

When everything had been loaded into the car, he took me to George's Flight Office, in his Dispersal Hut. The Wing was just going off on operations (ie, the two Squadrons of Spitfires), but unfortunately it was cancelled at the last minute. The Flight Hut was an ordinary wooden Army but on the perimeter of the 'drome – one large room with beds, a table and chairs in it – the walls covered with various maps and pictures from mags, etc.

Then, there was one little room, which was G's Office – with all the Flight's Orders and time-tables, etc, all in G's handwriting. Apparently, he was the only Officer in the Flight. I did just meet the Officer who had taken his place, but he didn't have very much to say – of course he may have only just been posted there and not known G at all.[1]

Just before leaving I saw G's Number 2, who struck me as being particularly nice. He was a Sergeant and I had quite a good talk with him. He emphasized to me again and again how terribly sorry they were, as they were all so fond of G and he was so popular in the Squadron. He showed me on the map where they were going.

They had crossed the Coast, just west of—— and were making for——. When they were about 10 miles inland – somewhere round about——[2] he and G were 'weaving' together (flying towards each other and away again). Their Wing was the bottom layer, so to speak, at 15,000ft – with the two other layers above them, of fighters. The No 2 suddenly felt his plane rock and thought an AA shell had burst between them, but suddenly realised that it was an Me109 on his tail that was firing at him. He took evasive action and when he had regained formation could not see George. When they eventually got home he found that the Me must have opened fire at extreme range – and with only machine guns and not cannon, as none of the bullets penetrated his plane – even as far as the armour plating.

Of course enquiries were made, but no-one at all had seen what happened to G. and no-one at all had seen any Spitfire go down, or even any plane at all catch fire. His theory was that a lucky bullet from the Me must have hit some vital part of G's engine and he emphasized very strongly indeed that he considered G must have either made a forced landing or parachute jump. He did not seem to consider that he might have been killed at all. It all took place apparently during Saturday afternoon.

Just before I left, the Adj told me that G made such a good Flight Commander because he was a stickler for detail and was very particular that his Flight should not get into any bad habits. For instance, he was always very particular that his Flight turned out their pockets before taking off. They all said he seemed to be in good spirits before he took off.

PS The Adj said that it would be several weeks before they got any news, but they would hear first and would pass it on directly they heard to you.

[1] The No 611 Squadron ORB for 22 September 1941 records: '... Posting: Flight Lieutenant Kenneth Coryston Powell (37868) posted from 603 Squadron as Flight Commander of "A" Flight.'

[2] These three names were obliterated by the censor.

Another letter, which reached the Vicar of Cromer, was from a fellow-clergyman, a Royal Air Force padre, the Reverend S.W. Betts,[1] who wrote from Hornchurch on 23 September:

As Chaplain to this Station, I felt I would like to express my deepest sympathy with you and your family in your great anxiety over your son, George.

It seems that we must just go on praying through these difficult days of waiting – hoping for good news of him.

He and his Squadron have put up a wonderful show. You must justly feel proud.

I am not making this point just for the sake of making it when I say that George, with his openness of character and charming manner won his way to the hearts of most of us in the comparatively short time he was here. I believe his faith is in the right object, his heart in the right place.

Last Sunday evening[2] a few of his friends gathered in our little camp Church to offer a prayer for him.

Through these anxious days may God himself richly comfort you and your family. You have not been forgotten in the Prayers that have gone up from this Station.

Then on 26 September Wing Commander John Grandy, who had commanded George Barclay's squadron, No 249, during the Battle of Britain, wrote to Mrs Barclay from Aston Down:

Thank you for your letter about George, forwarded to me from Debden yesterday. Funnily enough, it was only yesterday morning that I heard through other sources that he was missing.

I have just spoken on the telephone to Group Captain Broadhurst, commanding Hornchurch. He tells me that George was leading his Flight over Northern France and, more or less, just disappeared. His number two, that is, the pilot who flies next to him, returned with his aircraft rather

badly shot up. It may sound strange to you that he did not see what happened to George, but you will understand that on these shows one's eyes are all over the sky and it is easy to miss such an incident.

The only thing they conclude at Hornchurch is that as nothing was heard from him over the wireless, he may have had his set hit and perhaps his aircraft was so damaged that he had to land in France or bale out.

I told Group Captain Broadhurst that I had heard from you and he asked me to tell you how very sorry indeed were Air Vice-Marshal Leigh-Mallory, the AOC 11 Group – as well as himself and everyone at Hornchurch – and how very much George was missed by them.

It was only the other day that I was talking to Group Captain Beamish (he used to be our CO at N Weald and is now on the Staff of 11 Group) and he was saying that George had been earmarked as one of our future Squadron Commanders.

As you know, George is a very great friend of mine and, apart from personal feelings, I admire him tremendously as being such a fine type of officer and fighter pilot. We had a grand time together last year in 249.

These missing cases are always difficult – it is impossible to give an opinion. A man may be taken prisoner or attempt to evade capture, or escape and it is sometimes many weeks before news gets through.

I will, of course, write as soon as I hear anything.

PS Please don't hesitate to let me know if there is anything at all I can do in any way.

Then on 29 September the No 611 Squadron intelligence officer, Flying Officer Clive Mellersh, who had been one of the party with whom George dined out in London just before returning to Hornchurch from his last leave, wrote to Mrs Barclay:

I feel I should like to write you a little personal letter about George.

I am the Intelligence Officer for 611 Squadron and am completely devoted to it and the boys who come

---

[1] *Later Dean of Rochester and previously (1956–66) the Archbishop of Canterbury's Episcopal Representative with the Armed Forces, Bishop Betts was a Royal Air Force chaplain from 1938 to 1947. He had met George Barclay's father.*

[2] *The day following the Saturday afternoon when George came down in France.*

into it, and do all that is in my power to get to know them intimately.

Before George came, we had been having rather an unsettled time in "A" Flight, owing to the Flight Commander being rather an unsettling personality, and then George arrived – and from the moment I met him I realised our troubles were over.

I have had a good deal to do with handling men, but I can honestly say that never in my life have I met such a born leader or a more charming personality.

When George came into Dispersal Hut on a chill morning, it was just as if the sun had suddenly come out and one felt a better man in every way for being in his presence.

He was good enough to give me his friendship right from the start and we used to do everything together in our spare time, even though I am nearly 20 years older than he, and the weeks we had together I shall always count among the happiest I have ever spent.

I can only say that I found George pure gold through and through and everyone with whom he came in contact was bound to be enriched.

When he did not return from the sweep on the 20th, I must confess I was knocked completely endways and felt that the sun, moon and stars had gone from the Universe and I had lost the best friend it has ever been my privilege to have.

I had a talk with the Padre, and the next day we held a little Service in Chapel, which has helped me enormously and I think George would have been glad we did so.

I do hope you won't think from this letter that I think the dear old boy has passed over – far from it. No! I think he has more than a sporting chance, so please don't give up hope if you do not hear anything definite for some considerable time.

He may be a prisoner, in which case you should get news inside a month from the Red Cross. Or he may have succeeded in escaping when he landed, and in that case we shan't get any news till he suddenly walks in amongst us in 3 or 4 months' time, but whatever happens, I thought you would like to know just how much he meant to all of us and how tremendously we miss him.

The words of Clive Mellersh about succeeding in escaping and not getting 'any news till he suddenly walks in amongst us in three or four months' time', generous and optimistic in spirit when they were written, also proved to be uncannily prophetic and accurate – as George Barclay himself demonstrated in his account, in diary and note form, of his successful evasion of German capture and his return home through France and Spain, aided by many brave men and women who risked their lives to protect British and Allied airmen and soldiers.

Flying Officer Clive Mellersh, No 601 Squadron Intelligence Officer at Debden.

France and Spain: September 1941

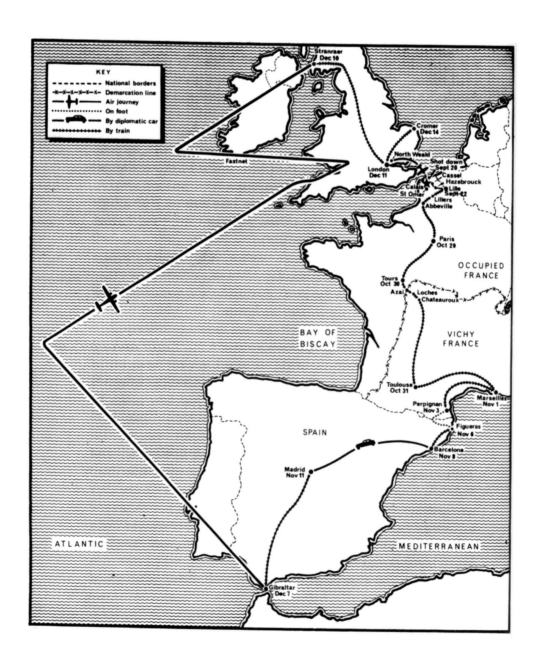

In September 1941 I was commanding 'A' Flight, No 611 (AAF) Squadron, stationed at Hornchurch. The squadron was then under the command of S/L Eric H. Thomas. Hornchurch was commanded by Group Captain Harry Broadhurst, DSO, DFC, AFC. The wing consisted of Nos 611, 603 (AAF) and 54 Squadrons.

Tuesday, September 16th

The weather being bad at that time and no sweeps having been carried out over north-east France for some days, I asked for three days' leave at a moment's notice. It was granted so I drove to Trimingham, where the family was staying for a short holiday, in Rome's [wife of his brother Charles] Ford 8. All the family were at home except for Ann and family and Charles and family. I had some shooting with G.A.B. and R.F.B. [his father and younger brother] as well as Arthur Buxton.[1] Convoys were bombed each night off Happisburgh, and as I left on Sept 18th to drive with Mary to London a large tanker came drifting ashore in flames, torpedoed by an E-boat. While on leave I visited the bank in Cromer and, finding I had a slight overdraft for the first time in my life, sold a few savings to get rid of it, telling the manager that an overdraft was a worry and generally shooting a shocking line about the uncertainty of my present job! So, having put my house in order, I drove to London, dropped Mary in her taxi, and went to see a theatre show with Flight Lieutenant W.G.G. Duncan Smith, DFC (603 Squadron – ex-611 Squadron), Flying Officer Clive Mellersh, 611's Intelligence Officer, and two WAAF officers from Hornchurch. We dined at the Mirabelle restaurant and returned to Hornchurch, taking with us six partridges I had brought from Cromer. I told the WAAFs to cook them and ask us to dinner in their mess to eat them. They agreed and suggested Wednesday, September 24th.

Friday, September 19th

Next day I discovered that there had been several costly sweeps in my absence and Squadron Leader (Fanny) Orton, DFC, CO of 54 Squadron, was missing. Squadron Leader David Scott-Maiden took command of 54 Squadron. I said to the Wing Commander Flying, Wing Commander Eric Stapleton, DFC, that I was sorry I had missed all the fun. He remarked 'never mind, there's much more to come' and my, my, was he right!

The weather was bad, so I flew up to Duxford to see Squadron Leader Hanks, DFC, OC 56 Squadron, to ask if there was any news of Flight Lieutenant Taffy Higginson, DFM, who had been shot down from North Weald on one of the first daylight sweeps over France. Prosser Hanks would only say that he thought Taffy would be home soon, which amazed me as I thought he had been bumped off.[2] I returned to Hornchurch for lunch and got talking about being taken prisoner of war. I said to Broadie [Group Captain Broadhurst, later Air Chief Marshal Sir Harry Broadhurst, DSO, DFC, AFC] that I imagined it must be the worst fate imaginable and he agreed. I said I would not be taken prisoner if I could possibly help it, if I was shot down in France!

That afternoon I went on a 'rhubarb' [low-level flights over France] operation with Tommy. We flew to Manston and refuelled and set course for Ostend – just off Ostend I sighted two aircraft that looked like Messerschmitt 109s. I gave chase and called up Tommy. We caught up with the aircraft and to our great disappointment found they were Tomahawks doing the same thing as we were! We stooged on up the coast past Zeebrugge and then past the Dutch islands. We crossed the coast of one of these islands near two aerodromes and were fired at by light ack-ack. We could see nothing worth beating up so we came out again and found a flak ship about a mile from the coast. Tommy flew inland of it and we attacked in echelon port in a steep dive. I saw Tommy's cannon fire exploding on the ship and all around it, and then opened fire myself. I seemed to be diving down the middle of a cone of green tracer from the flak ship. I saw my stuff hitting the ship

---

[1] *Owner of the Trimingham estate – from the bungalow on which the convoys could be seen battling against aircraft by day, and against aircraft and E-boats at night.*

[2] *In fact, he got back home after many hair-raising adventures. See* The Way Back: The Story of Lieutenant Commander Pat O'Leary, GC, DSO, RN *by Vincent Brome (Cassell, 1957).*

and sea and then broke away taking violent evasive action. My aircraft was not hit and I last saw the flak ship surrounded by a small cloud of steam. We returned in a straight line to Hornchurch.

Saturday, September 20th

The next day the weather cleared by lunch time and the Wing took off on Circus 100A [codename given to escort of Blenheims] as close escort wing to three Blenheims to bomb Hazebrouck marshalling yards. This was a diversionary operation for Circus 100 to bomb a target in the Abbeville district. No 603 Squadron were close escort squadron to the bombers, 611 were middle squadron 1,000ft above and behind the bombers, and 54 were above and behind us. In order to have a better view of what was going on, Wing Commander Stapleton, DFC, elected to lead us, so that Squadron Leader Thomas led Charlie Section, and Flight Lieutenant Spud Hayter Blue Section, being the senior Flight Commander. I therefore flew No 3 on Wingco, with Sergeant Ormiston as my No 2. We rendezvoused with our babies at Manston at about 3:00pm and climbed up towards the French coast in fours, line astern. Reaching the coast, we split into pairs with each aircraft weaving. The weather was magnificent and quite cloudless.

When over St Omer district I saw half a dozen Me109Fs diving down behind the squadron. I gave a sighting report, but as I learnt after my return to this country, my R/T had packed up, so that no further message was received from me. The 109s, with the speed they had collected in their dive, rapidly overtook us. I watched them and took appropriate evasive action as they closed into range. I watched a Spit down on my right being shot at and taking very little notice. He was probably my No 2 as I learnt later that he was asleep at the time, got shot up and came home saying he had been hit by light flak! The 109 behind this fellow pulled up past me and passed about 50 yards to my right. I steadied up and had a quick burst of cannons and machine guns, but saw no result – at the same time two 303 bullets hit my aircraft. I heard them – plonk, plonk! – and immediately took evasive action. The 109s either pulled up above us or dived vertically down to ground level, as are their usual tactics.

I noticed I was straggling behind the formation and so tried to catch up, immediately noticing that I had no revs, in other words my engine was just wind-milling in the slipstream. I saw a hole in my port wing root which was one bullet, the other must have hit some part of my engine. I saw the bombers pulling away above in the distance, and juggled with the controls. I found that by throttling back and then opening the throttle half an inch I could get a few revs out of the engine. By this time the six 109s had woken up to the fact that I was straggling and proceeded to do line astern quarter attacks – as each one closed the range I turned into him and they all missed. I could see the hose pipes of tracer cannon and machine-gun ammo passing underneath me.

They came back in a head-on attack but were easy to foil. I realised that it was a mug's game and so dived down to ground level in an aileron turn to try and get back. One 109 followed me and settled comfortably on my tail. I took slight evasive action whenever he fired and he missed; but I nearly hit some high tension cables and hoped that the Hun would do the same more successfully, but he didn't. By this time my speed was very low and I was stalling whenever I took evasive action. I used my last speed in avoiding the 109's fire and turned back towards the south.

I was immediately confronted again by the high tension cables – I had no speed to fly over them so flew between two trees underneath them. I missed most of the cables but hit one with more sag than the others – there was a flash and bang and the cable wrapped round the nose and then dropped. I put the flaps down and made a normal wheels-up landing in a very large field. The IFF [identification – friend or foe] detonated when I hit the cables. I was quite happy that the squadron knew what had happened as on the way down I called up Wingco and told him that my engine had cut out, but as already stated my R/T had packed up – to the squadron I had simply vanished into thin air.

I sat in the cockpit of poor old FY-K and pretended to be dead while the 109 circled around at 150ft. It was the first time I had heard the noise a 109 makes – a mixture of a Spitfire's whistle, some stones in a tin can and a harsh grinding sound. It circled about three times and then flew off south-west.

I got out, leaving my flying kit in the aeroplane and began to run eastwards;[1] a French worker in the field about 50 yards from my aeroplane never even looked up throughout the crash. I have never felt so lost – everything seemed so utterly hopeless; so I destroyed the code card and hopped it quickly. I ran to the east for this reason – Sergeant Phillips of 54 Squadron, a French Canadian, was shot down earlier in the year and escaped back to this country via Spain. I had heard that he had walked about the streets of Lille and seen the 'Vs' on the walls. So I struck out down sun in the same direction that Phillips had taken, scattering small pieces of code card like a small-scale paper chase!

I expected there would be Huns everywhere and so I peeped round hedges before turning corners and bolted flat out across open spaces so as not to be caught in the open. It occurred to me that it was ridiculous to run about France in full uniform, so I turned the tunic inside out, thus showing the lining to the sleeves, and put my trousers over my flying boots. I deposited my collar and tie in a hedge. There seemed to be a great many tame partridges in France as I continually put up coveys almost at my feet. I ran until I felt sick and then ran again approximately parallel to a farm track, waving to some Frenchmen, who waved back, and to others who took no notice. I came to a French peasant family in the fields who looked amazed when I said I was a British pilot and immediately offered me a job in the fields working with them. But it was far too risky a proposition as I had no identity card and the Hun was bound to look for me and check up on the locality. However, I asked for some civilian clothes, and immediately the old woman went off to get me some. She returned with an old coat and black trousers. I was just going to put these on when she cried, 'Run, run! They are coming with dogs.' I ran, hid the clothes in a ditch and went on running.

I was getting very footsore from running in flying boots and it was a very hot afternoon, so I slowed down and walked across a field about 60 yards from the track. In the middle I heard a car coming along slowly. I couldn't do anything about it so I just stood there trying to establish the mastery of mind over matter by thinking myself into a Frenchman! It worked! A car with two Hun officers in it went past quite slowly but they took no notice of me, so I continued to run, a considerably shaken man! I ran at about the same speed as a Frenchman meandering along the track on a bicycle. I kept hiding as he went past, but then I would climb over the hedge and almost fell into his arms the other side; so I thought I would give him a rest from these surprises and walked up to a largish farm house's back door, knocked, and walked in. Two middle-aged women were gossiping and they didn't know what to make of me. I asked for some water which they gave me, and then two dogs began barking furiously in the front yard. They both shouted – 'Run away! Quick! They are here with dogs.' Once again I ran. Personally I don't think I was ever chased with dogs, as if I had been I should have been caught.

I ran on and came to a village. I walked up to the first cottage and knocked at the back door.

'*Bon jour, Madame, je suis aviateur anglais – voulez vous m'aider, s'il vous plait des habits civils?*'[2]

But the two old women were windy and their menfolk were out in the fields so I moved on to the next house, again no help, but no hostility. So I said, 'Well, who will help me? I quite understand that you cannot.' Immediately I was told to go and see Madame Ourse[3] in a house on the main road through the village. I walked down the track and climbed over a fence into the back garden. I was confronted by two equally dirty doors. I knocked and opened one, only to shut it again immediately to keep the swarm of rabbits inside from getting out!

I knocked on the next door and it was opened by a stout, shortish woman, who blinked at me and said, 'Well?'

'Madame Ourse?'

'*Oui.*'

'*Je suis aviateur,* etc.' This was becoming my travelling salesman's slogan. I was at once taken into a room behind Madame's clean but empty

---

[1] *He later told his brother Richard that he had attempted to set fire to the aircraft, but without success.*

[2] *'Hello, I am an English pilot, would you please help me with civilian clothes?'*

[3] *Her actual name was spelt Madame Leurs.*

grocer's shop. Two children came in and gaped and I hoped Madame Ourse had sufficient control over her offspring to make them keep their mouths shut. Madame produced a bottle of red wine, for which I was very grateful, it being a very hot day. I took off my uniform and told Madame Ourse to destroy it. I kept the wings, gong ribbon and a couple of buttons for future identification as well as my identity discs which hung round my neck. I had turned out my pockets at Hornchurch, so I only had my pipe and tobacco pouch and the 500 francs that we were all carrying. I was given some blue worker's overalls, and a good pair of boots in exchange for my flying boots. I asked Madame where she thought I ought to go. She told me to follow her daughter to the curé's house. I thanked her profusely and kissed her on both cheeks *à la française!* She was quite overcome and muttered '*charmant, charmant*'[1] several times! As I left the house she pressed 1,000 francs into my hand. Not knowing what was in store for me I took them willingly.

I followed a hundred yards behind the ten-year-old daughter up the main road and then up a turning off to the left towards the church. We went to a house and I hid in a hedge while the girl looked for the curé. They suddenly returned and I tried to look as if I hadn't been hiding! The curé was a jovial rotund individual who took me into his house and brought out some wine and biscuits. In two minutes about six people seemed to have collected from nowhere. I asked what to do with myself and where I was anyway. Out came a very old map. I was in the village of Nordpeen, west of Cassel, and I had crashed in the vicinity of Buyschoeure, north-east of Clairmarais aerodrome. After much talking and periodical scares when everybody hushed everyone else, the curé decided I ought to go to a doctor in Cassel – on asking how to get there, the curé said he would provide someone to take me.

Eventually I started out past the very Roman Catholic churchyard, following a small girl of ten or eleven on her fairy cycle! I dirtied my boots to make it look as if I had been working all day, and consoled myself with the thought of how pleasant it was to be able to walk in the country out of uniform on a lovely evening. A French workman on his way home on a bicycle loitered up the road and attached himself to me. '*Vous êtes l'aviateur anglais, hein?*'[2] I could hardly understand what he jabbered about but eventually passed his house and he left me with a glum '*bonne chance*'.[3] After a few minutes I saw a Hun coming down the road on a bicycle; he loitered along and looked at me as he went past. I looked at him as casually as my hammering pulse would let me, and he passed on. I am sure that one immediately arouses suspicion, if, having passed some Huns or gendarmes, one looks back over one's shoulder at them.

We walked on and on, stopping in a much shelled village (Zuytpeen, I think) to blow up a tyre for my guide. Eventually as it was getting dark we climbed up the hill into Cassel. We passed a couple of Hun sentries outside the local army HQ and then came across a patrol of two Huns with rifles. They took no notice of us, though of course I imagined everyone must be looking at me and seeing that I was not French. We passed through the town and then got hopelessly lost looking for the doctor's house.

Eventually after carrying the little girl's bicycle some way across country we came back into the town and the girl asked the way at two houses while I hid in the ditch and watched heavy Hun army lorries going past.

At last we got to the doctor's house and rang the bell – a girl answered the door, and my guide said that '*ce monsieur*' wished to see the doctor urgently.

'Why? It's after hours.'

I said in my school boy *j'ai-la-plume-de-ma-tante*[4] French, 'I want to speak to him personally quickly.'

We were admitted to the waiting room. The walls were covered with crude and supposedly amusing medical drawings – intended, no doubt, to instil mystery and fear into the simple Frenchman! The doctor swept into the room and shook hands warmly

[1] *Charming, charming.*

[2] *'You are the English pilot, ey?'*

[3] *Good luck.*

[4] *I have the pen of my aunt.*

– 'Splendid – no wounds, quite all right? Well, you can't stay here, go to Monsieur Ghorice.[1] He'll fix you up.' We were ushered out again into the dark. After asking the way twice we found the house and amidst the barking and snarling of three dogs walked up the short drive. We were admitted by a jovial fellow of about thirty-five who at once produced his wife and family, who were presented formally. The house was quite a large detached one in its own small garden. It had about four bedrooms, as well as several living rooms, but it was almost entirely unfurnished and the family only used three rooms. It was my first experience of French dirt. I was told that Maurice Ghorice was a Cassel garage proprietor, but the German bombing and shelling had flattened the garage, and he had been lent this house.

Maurice Ghoris: the man who helped George escape through Occupied France.

[1] *His actual name was spelt Maurice Ghoris.*

Maurice produced some brown bread and paté (a concoction with garlic rather like a mixture of brawn and meat paste) and some French beer – very gassy and tasting of not very much. I was not very hungry but I had just sat down at the kitchen table, which was cluttered up with bottles, shoes and other household necessities, when there was a banging at a door. I thought I had had it and stood up to greet the Hun 'It's all right,' said Maurice, and opened the door. A larder was revealed out of which walked a tame sheep. 'I'm not allowed to have it by the Boche,' Maurice explained, 'so I keep it here.' He was absolutely flat out against the Hun and pro-British. If the Boche made another law to be added to the already long list of restrictions, Maurice did his best to disobey it. He wanted some carrier pigeons and was always asking why our bombers didn't drop him some! He also wanted the bomber boys to drop him a '*post émiteur*' (wireless transmitting set). Whenever he saw a parachute coming down he got on his bicycle and, taking some mufti in a sack, proceeded to the spot where he thought the parachute would land. He would then get the pilot out of uniform and well away from his aircraft before the Huns arrived. One day he found a pilot with a head wound. He was just going to whip off his uniform when some Huns arrived and he discovered that the pilot was a Hun too! The latter died half an hour later. He also told me the story of some Huns who saw a 'chute coming down so opened up with machine guns so that the pilot should have no chance of escape. When they got to the pilot they found that they had shot one of their own boys. The French rocked with laughter, so the Hun CO forced the burgermeister to issue an edict to the effect that it was a British pilot and not a Hun.

After supper, Madame was sent to sleep with the four children, and I was offered half the large double bed – a large mattress on the ground which from the dust and dirt looked as if it had not been moved for about six months. (Perhaps you think I am being extremely finicky – well, perhaps I am, but I am trying to present a true picture.) Maurice wound about six towels round his underclothes and went to bed very much like an over-nappied child! I slept well, for I was very tired. We had the youngest child in a cot in the room and apart from a few wild outbursts from him the night was undisturbed.

George dressed in civilian clothing.

Sunday, September 21st

Maurice went off very early in the morning to Lille to contact people he knew in the organisation and to get some better clothes for me. It was a lovely day. In the morning the children went off to church. I lay on my bed most of the day and read an English book left by the troops in the retreat to Dunkirk in June 1940. During the day I heard two sweeps go over and caught sight of wings glinting in the sun. Quite a lot of ack-ack was put up a few miles away – the French didn't like it and retreated from the windows. I heard cannon and machine-gun fire and a few weeks later met Sergeant Patrick Bell, ex-602 Squadron, who was shot down that day, Sunday, September 21st. On that day I came out in a plague of spots on my hands and face – it was probably the change of air and diet! Several other blokes I met had the same symptoms when they first got to France. The lavatory in this house was my

first introduction to the horrors of French sanitary arrangements, though the flies were not too bad.

Maurice Ghorice, sometimes known as Nel or Joseph in his pro-British work, returned in the evening. He said that the train had had to be diverted round Hazebrouck due to the damage done by our recent bombings there. He also said the whole area was talking about me and the doings of the Huns. Three hostages had been taken in the village of Nordpeen, including the jovial curé; all bicycles in the area were commandeered for the search, and the area round my aeroplane and Nordpeen was searched by troops with dogs. This search went on for three days. Maurice said the three hostages would have a fortnight's prison and would then be let out, but I could never discover what actually happened to them.

I went out into the garden with Maurice at dusk, and he showed me a bare patch behind the house where a British Tommy was buried – killed in the Cassel fighting. There is a British cemetery in Cassel – I have a photograph of it; it seems to be well kept – not by the Huns, I imagine.

Maurice asked whether I wanted to go to Lille late that night and get there just before curfew (11pm) or go on Monday morning. I didn't know which was the better as regards safety as I had no identity card, so told him to decide. We agreed to take our time and go the next morning. Maurice fitted me up with some shoes which I could get on but were too small. I regretted not having got a good fit later on. I think the acquisition of comfortable footwear is one of the first essentials of escape. With the shoes and a blue suit Maurice had bought from Lille I looked pretty smart.

That evening was spent talking of the next morning's journey. The French seemed to have an idea that one would give in unless one received constant encouragement! I heard the first 'aeroplane' stories that night. They are all the same – an aeroplane is coming to pick you up next Tuesday – next Sunday, etc, to take you to England! It is not always an aeroplane – it may be a destroyer or a submarine. It is all sheer fiction, but I met two pilots who actually went to an appointed rendezvous to wait for the mythical *Fortresse volante!*[1] It is always

[1] *Flying Fortress.*

a *fortresse volante* – the name has caught the French imagination. Later I heard a story of an army captain and a Tommy who actually rendezvoused with an aeroplane which took them direct to Stalag XII or some other *Kriegsgefangenelager*.[1] Good counter-espionage on the part of the Hun if it is true.

Maurice was very keen that if I got back I should send a message over the wireless – something like 'Hullo Nel; *la famille de George est en bonne santé*'.[2] But when I did get home it was not allowed. Most of the French houses I stayed in listened to the news from England – '*Les Informations*'. It was strictly forbidden but they would turn it on very loud, jamming and all – even in districts where wirelesses were banned. A maid gave away one family – who were put in prison for four months. When they came out they said, '*Sale collaborateuse – elle sera pendue.*'[3] If the French carry out their threats of hanging after the war, half the country '*sera pendu*'.

Monday, September 22nd

The next morning Maurice, his 14-year-old daughter and I set out at about 7 o'clock to the station – I should think it was about three miles. We skirted round Cassel, because the search was still on, and then walked down the main road, passing a large country house taken over by the Huns. We passed a spot where Maurice said two German tanks had been burnt in the Cassel fighting, and then about half a mile further on came across a British light tank in the ditch. It had several holes in it – and was all rusted up.

We passed a very heavily shelled estaminet[4] at a cross-roads which the British had held. Here Maurice bought a paper for me to read in the train and so avoid conversation. In trains, if you want to avoid awkward moments, either appear engrossed in the paper or pretend to be asleep. Both are a strain but well worth while. The papers are completely German-controlled. They make amusing reading – every day we lose phenomenal numbers of ships and aeroplanes and every day somewhere in England is

reported to have been heavily bombed. The French don't believe a word of it, and are always making such remarks as 'England was annihilated six months ago according to the papers – why haven't the Huns won the war?' As we passed through the streets near the station the houses of the local *collaborateurs* were pointed out to me, as well as a small factory working for the Huns.

It was in Cassel that I first saw the victory 'Vs' on the walls.

When the first crop occurred the Boche was furious and made the local schoolmaster send out the schoolchildren to wipe them off.

They got rid of them but only for one night as a second crop appeared – so the schoolmaster was sent to a concentration camp. Then the Hun had the idea of adopting the 'V' for his own use so he painted a small white 'V' with a swastika under it on all his transport vehicles and large ones on walls in towns, the whole device being surrounded with laurel leaves. The French retaliated by obliterating the swastika and substituting a croix de Lorraine inside the 'V'. There was then no doubt as to whose victory was intended by the 'Vs' as the croix de Lorraine is General de Gaulle's symbol. France is therefore littered with the two kinds of 'Vs'.

We eventually arrived at the station – I think the station's name was Bavancore. There was a Hun sentry on guard so we nipped into the station café and had a cognac. The station staff, who seemed to spend their time doing the same, were all talking about the British pilot who had vanished two days before, but they jabbered so fast that I could not understand what they were saying. Maurice went and bought the tickets, and escorted me to the stationmaster's office, where I was introduced to the young stationmaster, an ardent *camarade*.[5] I stayed there until the train came in, when he conducted me to the carriage where Maurice and daughter were already installed and bade me farewell as if he was saying goodbye to a close friend. I read

[1] *Prisoner-of-war camp.*

[2] *George's family are in good health.*

[3] *'Collaborator – she will be hanged.'*

[4] *A small French café selling alcoholic drinks.*

[5] *Friend.*

the paper and had periodical ganders at the Huns in the carriage – they looked the same as English Tommies except for their uniforms. The journey to Hazebrouck, where we had to change, was uneventful – except that I nearly had a fit whenever the ticket collector came through the carriage, as one check-up on identity cards and I was stuck in up to the neck.

Hazebrouck, September 22nd

At Hazebrouck we had 40 minutes to wait. We agreed not to know each other on the platform in case of trouble. I strolled around and surveyed our bomb damage – a large shed had been hit but very well cleaned up. I was later informed that a large number of locomotives in it had been written off, also a troop train had been blown sky high and many Huns killed. The old house near the station had been knocked down. My interest soon flagged, but I was concerned lest the boys should come and bomb Hazebrouck while I was on the platform! I was standing there trying to look natural when a Hun army officer came and stood 5–10 yards away. He looked at me and beckoned over a Hun railway official who looked rather like a commissionaire in his uniform. They talked a bit and then the railway official came straight over to me and planted himself about a couple of feet plumb behind me.

I thought it was a case of now or never, so ambled up to an old French couple and said, '*Il fait du brouillard, n'est ce pas?*'[1] The French love chatting when travelling and so they talked away without noticing my accent. I tried to put the odd *oui* and *non* in the appropriate places in the conversation. This seemed to allay the Huns' suspicions and they moved off – the train came in and in we got.[2]

The journey on to Lille was uneventful – we passed a large aerodrome (Bondues) but could see nothing in the mist. As we came into the suburbs of Lille we passed an enormous factory – one of the Kuhlman plants making chemicals – which Maurice informed me had never been hit by bombs – a useful bit of information.

We got out at La Madeleine, a station in the suburbs of Lille, to avoid a possible check on identity cards at Lille main station. We walked up the road and caught a train into the main part of Lille. This train was very crowded and we were jammed amongst some Hun soldiers – I got quite a kick out of travelling in such close proximity to my would-be capturers! We got out of the train by the main railway station and walked up to a square where there were cameramen taking photos of passers-by – in about five minutes I was furnished with three pretty pictures for an identity card! We walked on and visited a Monsieur Pugeot who had a bicycle shop, but we were quickly hustled out of

---

[1] '*It's foggy, isn't it?*'

[2] *This incident was described – though with some difference in detail – by A.J. Evans in his book* Escape and Liberation 1940–1945 *(Hodder & Stoughton, 1945; quoted with permission):*

'*The biggest danger for Barclay lay in his appearance. He was a tall, fine-looking fellow, and even in French clothes could hardly avoid being conspicuous, for there were few healthy young men left in France in those days. As he stood on the platform waiting for his train a German officer with his batman came and stood a few yards away. This at first did not disturb Barclay in the least, but soon he noticed, out of the corner of his eye, the German looking at him repeatedly and suspiciously. Barclay did his best to appear unconcerned, but when suddenly the German turned to his batman and, indicating Barclay, whispered something, it was obvious that action had to be taken, and taken quickly – but what? He turned slowly and glanced round him. At that moment a group of old market women with baskets on their arms clattered noisily on to the platform. Without a moment's hesitation Barclay gave a cry of joy and rushed towards them. He threw his arms round the first old woman and whispered, as he kissed her,* Aidez moi, je suis aviateur Anglais. *In a flash she not only grasped the situation, accepting the terrible risk, but acted as though she had been in the Comedie Française all her life. She went off into a spout of French – they all shook him by the hand – they all kissed him – they welcomed him home. The German recalled his batman (who had by then moved round behind Barclay) and got into his reserved carriage. Barclay got into a carriage with the old woman and was safe. I know of no better example than this of spontaneous skill on the part of an evader, and of courage and quickness of brain (which is the heritage of the French) on the part of those peasants. Barclay was an outstandingly good escaper; cautious, bold and intelligent.*'

there by Madame P. because they were under the eye of the Gestapo as their son was a talkative type of about 15 and had given something away. While walking about the town I wore an arm band that dubbed me as a railway official in order to allay any possible suspicions. I was very doubtful as to its use, as it would only have complicated matters if a railway official had spoken to me, but as the stationmaster at Bavancore (?) had lent it to me, I felt I ought to wear it. Maurice returned it when he went back.

We went and had a drink at a café to use up time until the rendezvous that Maurice had arranged the day before. We went to keep this rendezvous in a church, but as the agent was late we had to go on saying our prayers for an incredibly long time – eventually a woman, who claimed she was Irish, came in and gave us the password – 'The Duke of Wellington'. She spoke a few words of English with a bad French accent to make me reply and prove my identity, then a man came in and joined the party. I gave the Irishwoman a photo and she went off to get me an identity card. Maurice and I then followed the man about half a mile to a café, where we were taken upstairs and given a drink by the manageress and her daughter. The Irish woman turned up again with my photo stuck on an identity card and properly stamped – there is a tremendous racket in forged identity card stamps. We filled in the necessary particulars, then bent the card in all directions and rubbed cigarette ash into it to make it look old. From then on I became Georges, Maurice, Barrois, of 195 Rue de Solférino, Lille. I was born at Bergaes near Dunkirk, because all the records were destroyed there in the evacuation!

The Irishwoman was still not convinced of my identity, as the Gestapo had been trying to get a German through this organisation to see how it was done. I showed my identity discs – they meant nothing to them.

The Irishwoman asked me how the guns of a Spitfire were fired. I told her about the button one turned from 'safe' to 'fire', that there were eight guns usually, etc. But she had been told by someone before and was hopelessly muddled. I took the offensive and asked her why, if she was Irish, she spoke English with such a French accent. She said she was only half Irish and had lived in France the

greater part of her life. Finally she was satisfied and left. I did not see her again. Maurice and daughter left to get the evening train back to Cassel. I thanked them as warmly as I could, but they seemed very pleased to have been able to help. Maurice kept my wings and buttons as souvenirs. There was a tremendous noise outside and an old Junkers 52 flew over at about 500ft, heading east – the only 52 I have ever seen.

When the party had broken up, André, the fiancé of the daughter of the house, arrived. He was a lively fellow of 21 who worked in a bicycle factory which turned out bicycles for the Hun. The mother (I can't remember the family name) was a short, kindly woman, the daughter a plain, plump girl of 20. We had a very large dinner – everything was laid on in my honour – apéritifs galore before the meal and bottles of red wine with the meal, which consisted of vegetable soup followed by meat, chips and salad. We talked mostly of the war. André expressed the opinion that France was quite all right under the Hun – they behaved themselves and all this talk of atrocities and killings was so much bunkum. They preferred to own their own country but if they had to be invaded, well, the Hun was as good as anyone else. He said he sometimes went out with Hun soldiers and liked it. He seemed quite drugged with their propaganda about the new order and how they were flat out to help France. I shared Andre's bed with him – he lived in a room at the top of the house next door to a cupboard full of rabbits. I did not have a very comfortable night as it was a small bed and anyway I still had a plague of spots.

Tuesday, September 23rd
The next day I spent reading German and French magazines and got rather bored. A Heinkel 111 with yellow wing tips flew over the town once or twice during the day at about 1,000ft. Once again shared André's bed. I went to bed before he did and suddenly a gendarme began shouting in the streets below and a light was shone on my window. What I could have done wrong I couldn't imagine so I just lay there and hoped the noise wasn't meant for me. It transpired that it was not. The dame in a flat next door was breaking the blackout regulations and was being hauled over the coals.

Wednesday, September 24th

The next morning a man called for me in a car – we drove through Lille back to a house quite near La Madeleine station, where Maurice and I had arrived in Lille. We went in and said a quick how-do-you-do to the owner and when my guide had talked a little business, left quickly, as there were two German officers billeted there. We parked the car in a side street and then walked on to another house, belonging to a Madame Deram, a Belgian whose husband is a prisoner of war. As soon as Madame Deram arrived the fellow who had brought me went away, as he was a factory director and didn't want to compromise himself. That was one of the most remarkable things about the whole show – no one knew what anyone else was doing, who they were, or where they lived, so that it was impossible for one man to give away everyone.

Madame Deram was about 30–35 and had a son of 13, named Marcel. When I arrived Madame was just going shopping so I played with Marcel's Meccano and showed him how to make various things he wanted to make. This Meccano was the only amusement he had and so he was constantly going out and playing with the other boys in the street, much to his mother's annoyance, as she didn't trust his tongue an inch. The two of them used to have tremendous fights – they ended by Marcel going to bed in tears – the mother used to shout at him at the top of her voice 'I'll kill you' and rush at him seizing any old bottle and brandishing it above her head. She was sending Marcel to a boarding school in about ten days' time.

They were very afraid that the Gestapo was on their tail and I imagine this accounted to a large extent for their frayed tempers. I heard later that the Gestapo did search the house a few days after I had left but the birds had already flown. Marcel went to school, Madame Deram crossed into Unoccupied France.

One of the first things I noticed on entering the house was a photograph of Taffy Higginson on the mantelpiece. I was astounded. Apparently he had stayed 12 days in the house after he was shot down. What a coincidence that I enquired after him at Duxford only five days before! The photo was a good one. He had cut off most of his enormous moustache. I heard that he had been wounded in the shoulder by cannon splinters. He got down to the Spanish border but was taken by the French before he got across. Unfortunately he had a forged French identity card on him and stated that he was French – a great mistake. He was had up before a judge, witnesses were produced to say that he had associated with Communists and saboteurs and he was sentenced to two years' imprisonment. He was very ill in prison and got sent to the internment camp at St Hippolyte near Nîmes by the American Consul on a plea of ill health. I was given a copy of the photograph which was sent to his wife when I got back.[1]

Madame Deram supplied me with a clean shirt and a smarter suit than that I had been wearing, and also some shaving tackle, which I hung on to and brought home. She had one English book, _Sorrell and Son_, [a novel by Warwick Deeping] so I spent the day reading and enjoyed the diversion. A Heinkel 111 with yellow wing tips droned over the town at about 1,000ft several times during the day. In the afternoon a Monsieur Fernand Salingue from Lillers arrived with some meat for Madame Deram. He lived in the country and could supplement rations through the black market. The amounts of the French rations or _ravitaillements_ are about the same as ours, with this great difference – bread is rationed to 300 grammes per day. Anyone with an appetite eats more than this. The French who live in the country have a large black market and a lot of bartering goes on. They work on the principle that the larger the black market the less food for the Hun; and they manage to get on alright as far as food is concerned. The town dwellers are not so well off, unless they have friends in the country who will risk bringing them extra rations. There are all sorts of restrictions forbidding people to carry vegetables, etc, from place to place.

Fernand Salingue's home in the country seemed to be a more favourable situation for me – there was more food and less danger of a swoop by the Gestapo – also he told me I could go out sometimes there, which I certainly could not do in Lille. So it was agreed that he would return the next day and escort me to Lillers. I

[1] _See earlier footnote on the story of his escape on page 105._

The traitor Harold 'Paul' Cole.

was very pleased as Marcel and Madame Deram were working themselves into a new pitch of fury. I spent the afternoon trying to quell the riot by playing with Marcel's Meccano, playing games with the dog, Kirsch, and talking to a French schoolgirl named Bete who looked grown up, but still wore short skirts and socks and was keen on music and the piano.

Thursday, September 25th

Fernand did not arrive the next day, which I spent reading *Sorrell and Son* and got profoundly bored. Madame Deram was always talking about Monsieur Paul, an Englishman who I gathered was the mainstay of the organisation getting bodies out of France. Everyone seemed to look up to him, he had a great hold over the Frenchmen who knew him, owing to his fearlessness and the splendid work he was doing. I was to meet him later on.[1]

Friday, September 26th

Next morning Fernand arrived – he had some things to do in Lille, so we arranged to meet him at the station at about 1 o'clock. I packed my brown paper parcel of shaving kit and a spare shirt, and Madame Deram, Bete and I walked to the station. Fernand arrived just before the train left. He had just enough time to buy me a newspaper, so that I could appear engrossed and so avoid conversation.

The journey was uneventful – we travelled with some Hun troops and other French civilians, and so I industriously read the ersatz news. We passed La Bassée aerodrome, where I saw about half a dozen dummy Junkers 87 dive bombers, and a Heinkel 111. We changed trains at Béthune and got into the same carriage as some friends of Fernand's, so when we got to Fouquereuil we got out with the friends and walked to their house. There I was fêted by two old women and their two plump daughters as well as other small children. We drank a bottle of wine and I was given two tins of sardines for the journey. Before we left one old woman took me into the next room and gave me 100 francs. I remonstrated but had to give in and accept it, but I had to kiss one of the plump daughters goodbye! We caught a train on from Fouquereuil and arrived at Lillers without incident. We went to a brasserie opposite the station and had a quick beer. I was left in charge of the barman who had an English step-brother, while Fernand went and did something in the town. We then walked to Burbure from Lillers, about a mile. Fernand was waylaid by a friend on the way. I was introduced and the man never twigged who I was. He thought I was a pupil from the state school where Fernand was a master. The buildings of the school were taken over by the Hun, and we walked by the sentry, a most ferocious-looking ruffian, and listened to the Boche playing accordions and singing inside.

We walked up the Route Nationale and Fernand took two turnips from a field and put them in his bag for his rabbits. He was always doing this. The Salingues' house was one of the first on the left as

---

[1] *This was Harold 'Paul' Cole, who 'achieved the distinction of working for the British, French, Germans and Americans' and was shot just after the war. He is referred to frequently in* The Way Back. *See also, for more detail,* In Trust and Treason, *by Gordon Young (Studio Vista, London, 1959), and* Letting the Side Down, *by Sean Murphy (Sutton, 2005).*

'We went to a brasserie opposite the station and had a quick beer', George wrote in his diary on 26 September 1941. Fernand Salingue outside the said brasserie – Hotel du Commerce – in Lillers.

you approach Burbure, just opposite the sign on the side of the road with the name of the village on it. During the walk I saw the first signs of the French fifth column that had betrayed the country – huge white arrows painted on the roads, walls and fences to show the oncoming Hun the way to go.

The house was quite small – a front drawing-room-cum-study, a back dining-kitchen, a front bedroom upstairs for the family and a back bedroom-cum-storeroom where I slept. All

modern conveniences were absent, or primitively represented in the small back yard.

I was welcomed by Madame Salingue and the six-year-old Jean.

Madame was a typical working Frenchwoman of about 28–30. She taught in the kindergarten of the local school. Jean was very spoilt, like Marcel in Lille and most other French children I met. His parents had very little clue on how to bring him up and at times I felt very sorry for him. He did exactly what he liked, but occasionally his parents ticked him off once. He then continued to do whatever he had been ticked off for. He was very cute and knew he could get away with it, and his parents rarely insisted on his obeying. But suddenly his parents would jump on him for some quite trivial thing, make him kneel in the corner with his hands held above his head and smack his legs. There was then a scene of fury and shouting of expletives – *sale gasse*, etc – accompanied by Jean's crying. After about three minutes all was forgiven and there was much kissing all round. Jean would then know he had won his battle though slightly wounded in action, and continue what he was doing before!

I was given a very friendly welcome. Immediately we arrived Madame cooked us two eggs and chips each. Apparently that is what the troops always asked for before Dunkirk. Burbure had had quite a large number of British troops billeted there, and wherever I went I was shown photos of them. The French liked them very much.

This is as far as George himself recorded his journey in diary form. But he made detailed notes – on which the subsequent account has been based – and their neatness can be seen from the photograph below.

'A back bedroom-cum-storeroom where I slept.' The room where George stayed – chez Salingues.

CHAPTER FIVE

Down the Line and Back to the UK

Albert-Marie Guérisse G.C, alias Pat O'Leary.

On 10 October, while George was still with the Salingues, three members of the crew of a No 9 Squadron Wellington, which had been shot down, arrived there. They were Squadron Leader Henry Bufton and Sergeants William Crampton and Kenneth Read. Other arrivals on that day were Sergeant Patrick Bell and Pilot Officer Alex Nitelet of No 609 Squadron. All of them – and Pilot Officer Oscar Coen, an American pilot of No 71 'Eagle' Squadron whom George met on 26 September – are mentioned in *The Way Back: The Story of Lieut-Commander Pat O'Leary, GC, DSO, RN.*[1]

O'Leary, a Belgian whose real name was Albert-Marie Guérisse, took over the escape organisation started in Marseilles by the then Captain Ian Garrow, Seaforth Highlanders, himself an evader from northern France. (Garrow was caught and imprisoned in November 1941.) O'Leary, a man of incomparable courage, was the heart and brains of the Organisation which passed men down 'the Line' into Vichy France and then into Spain. In one passage the book described the situation in the autumn of 1941:

> Presently every week men were coming down the "Line". Sometimes they were soldiers left over from the days of Dunkirk; sometimes crashed pilots; sometimes Resistance men for whom the chase had become too hot.
>
> In October 1941, Sergeant Patrick Bell, Sergeant William Crampton, Flight Lieutenant Barclay and Sergeant Kenneth Read were all spirited out of Occupied France to Marseille, over the Spanish border and away. Pilot Officer Oscar Coen, of the American Eagle Squadron, also "passed through", giving an account of his adventures in slang

[1] *By Vincent Brome (Cassell, 1957).*

American, which richly rewarded his rescuers. He was the first of scores of American pilots. More important for the moment was the appearance of Pilot Officer Alex Nitelet, of 609 (Belgian) Squadron, RAF. Outnumbered in his Spitfire, he had shot down one German plane, and then himself suffered a series of direct hits, one bullet gouging away part of his right eye. He managed to crash land and found himself in the Fauquembergues area, near the village of Renty. In great agony he was eventually picked up by Norbert Fillerin, a man already active for the Organisation in the St Omer region. The legend of the Fillerin family was to become famous. Tall, blond, tough, Fillerin found a doctor, Dr Delpierre, who treated Nitelet's eye, took him into his home and at great risk nursed him back to health.

From Fillerin, Nitelet was passed down the underground chain to Didery, then working with yet another key man, the Abbé Carpentier at Abbeville. Carpentier provided forged papers which carried Nitelet, now totally blind in one eye, down to Le Petit Poucet, a bar on the Boulevard Dugommier in Marseille.

This had become the receiving centre where "parcels" had to prove their identity before going into hiding. From Le Petit Poucet, Nitelet passed into the hands of Louis Nouveau, and remained in hiding under treatment from Dr Rodocanachi for ten days. Presently he, too, took the train from Marseille along the coast to Arles, Montpellier, Perpignan, and Banyuls, to be smuggled over the frontier by Spanish Republican guides en route to England, destined to play a bigger part in the developing Organisation than he then knew.

Fernand Salingue (right) and André Reveillon, his neighbour, who in 1942 warned Salingue that the Gestapo were searching for him, allowing him to narrowly escape arrest.

George Barclay stayed with the Salingues, in their small red-brick house on the Route Nationale at the edge of Burbure, for 13 days. At the back was a little garden, which his room looked out upon and in which he played with young Jean. It was possible to walk through it to a path that led to other houses in the village. He went out quite a lot, either on foot or by bicycle, and spent much of his time listening to the radio. M Fernand Salingue and his wife Elisa helped to save the lives of 152 Allied airmen and soldiers during the war. In 1942 Fernand only just escaped arrest by the Gestapo, as his friend and neighbour André Reveillon warned him of their coming. He first went to Toulouse and then to Albi, Département du Tarn, in southern France, serving in the Resistance there until August 1944.

Elisa Salingue was arrested by the Gestapo and taken to Lille for interrogation, then released *faute de preuve* – on lack of evidence – on 15 May 1942. She was allowed to live in Burbure with her son Jean, under Gestapo surveillance. She served for more than three years in the RIF. The Salingues are Honorary Members of the RAF Escaping Society and Fernand's many decorations include Chevalier de la Legion d'Honneur and Croix de Guerre with palm. Fernand Salingue writes of those days:

I met Flight Lieutenant George Barclay on Wednesday, 24 September 1941, in La Madeleine 1 Lille, at No 57 Avenue Bernadette, where he had arrived on the 22nd. I was struck by his appearance:

tall, dark-haired, with sharp and mischievous eyes. I was surprised to see such a young RAF officer. From the beginning there was a natural confidence between George and myself. There is no doubt that this handsome young man was the archetype of the hero of the Battle of Britain. My English was pretty bad, but I managed to converse with George, who could speak a little French. Shot down on September 20, he had a single aim: to get back to Britain as quickly as possible, to fly again. His eyes sparkled when I promised him that he would soon leave La Madeleine for Lillers–Burbure, a necessary step towards Abbeville, before getting to Paris, thanks to Abbé Carpentier. When he heard that beyond Abbeville he wouldn't be in the forbidden sector any more, immense happiness could be seen in his face and he slapped me on the shoulder. He took his pipe out of his pocket, filled it with tobacco, and lit it with his lighter. He said, "My pipe, my lighter and my scarf bring me good luck."

Mme Deram, whom I had known for several months, offered us some coffee or tea, and I promised George that I would take him with me the next day. Joy spread over his face again, he looked at me and put his hands on my shoulders and said several times "Ah, Fernand, Fernand!" I left him then after a long handshake.

I called for him two days later at about 10 o'clock. We decided to take the train for Lillers, via La Bassée, Béthune and Fouquereuil. Just before the train left I met George at the station in Lille and gave him a newspaper I had just bought, so that he should look occupied during the journey. The train was full of civilians and German soldiers. George smoked his pipe and looked around him at the travellers, the soldiers, the aircraft near La Bassée – he watched everything very closely. Sometimes George looked at me and his eyes laughed at the idea of our fellow passengers not knowing that an RAF officer was sitting by them! One of the German soldiers offered us a cigarette which I refused, because I never smoked, but George accepted it and offered his lighter to his neighbour!! In Béthune we had to wait for the train which would take us to Lillers, via Fouquereuil, where we had to wait for about an hour and a half. We left the station and visited friends of mine – M and Mme Fleury Guilbert. They gave us a

very warm welcome, and George often talked to me about it. We arrived in Lillers about seven o'clock in the evening; German soldiers were on duty on the platform, but George didn't seem to take any notice of them. He was very confident in his good luck and that he would fly again.

From the station we went to the Hôtel du Commerce. The owner, an Englishman, John Croft, married to a Frenchwoman, had been arrested and sent to East Prussia. When we entered, Gaston, John Croft's brother-in-law, showed us into the dining-room and brought us a cool beer, then a second one and some jam sandwiches. I had to leave to buy a few things, and George stayed. Gaston, while serving civilians and German soldiers, passed George, gave him a slap on the shoulders and said, "All right? Another beer?" ... After sunset, we left Lillers for the house where I lived, in Mensecq on the dividing-line between Lillers and Burbure (the house was in Lillers and the garage in Burbure). I showed George the Institut Anatole France where I taught French, history and geography. He was very interested to hear that three-quarters of the school had been occupied by enemy troops and the dormitories transformed into a hospital for injured Luftwaffe pilots. As I told him that during the Battle of Britain the dormitories were full and some of the pilots, refusing to fly again, had been taken by lorries to an unknown place, he said, "I want to get back to my Hurricane, or my Spitfire, to fly again and shoot down other aircraft."

We walked to the house – about a mile – where Mme Salingue and my son Jean were waiting for us. On the way, we met a friend – M Lemille – and I introduced George as one of my new pupils, George enjoying the joke. We got home about half-past eight and we were welcomed by Mme Salingue. Jean was happy to have a friend and playmate. George felt at home at once. He was a young brother for us and it was the same for George who told us about his family, his father and mother, his brothers and sisters whom he dearly loved. We understood very quickly that he loved his country too. During that first evening he was happy to listen to the BBC. George slept in the room next to ours, on the first floor. From the window he could see the garden and fields, and the mines of Auchel.

After that first night, George told us he had slept very well and that he felt much more secure than he had in La Madeleine. He liked the country! We asked him whether he liked an English or a Continental breakfast with coffee, milk and bread. He replied "Like you, Elisa, and like you, Fernand!" That direct and friendly answer proved that George already belonged to our family. (Now, 33 years after, we still consider him to). Mme Salingue and Jean left for school in Burbure. I didn't have school on Saturday; I gave my 20 weekly lessons from Monday to Wednesday, to have some time left for my "private activities".

Seeing that I had two bikes, George said he'd like to have a ride. It was market day in Lillers, so we went there. It was a good opportunity for George to study the army: military convoys on the main road (N16), soldiers, feldgendarmes on duty at crossroads, sentries at the entrance to the Institut Anatole

Squadron Leader Bufton, 'Poupette', Jean Salingue and George Barclay. Poupette was the daughter of Mme Giséle Reveillon, and George taught Jean and Poupette how to make paper aeroplanes during his time living with Fernand and Elisa Salingue. Squadron Leader Bufton also stayed with the Salingues and later he and George reached Spain together.

France, where the Nazi flag and the Red Cross one could be seen, civilians and soldiers in the market, ammunition lorries parking on Place Jean Jaurès and watched by soldiers with Alsatian dogs.

George badly wanted to have a beer in a French pub, so we went to the Café-Français. Happily drinking his beer, George looked with a smile at four German warrant officers playing billiards. We went back home for lunch and had soup, steak and chips, and cheese, beer and coffee. In the afternoon, George looked at the books we had, and was happy and surprised to find some English novels: *Three Men in a Boat*, *Rip van Winkle*, *The Cricket on the Hearth*, *Travels with a Donkey in the Cevennes*. He read those books while we were at school.

On Sundays, we visited our families in Robecq or Allouagne. George's presence didn't change anything. On September 28th, he met my father, my sisters and my nieces. He came with me to the churchyard in Robecq, where my mother had been buried ten days before. I introduced George as a cousin to some of the villagers we met on the way. He played with Jean and his little cousins.

On the following Sunday, we visited my parents-in-law in Allouagne, and George enjoyed looking at the rabbits bred by my father-in-law. On the way back between Allouagne and Burbure, we went to the graves of three RAF aircrew shot down after bombing the Kuhlman factories in Chocques, on 21 May 1941. George stayed there a long time and was struck by the many bunches of flowers brought by local people although this had been forbidden by the Kommandatur in Béthune. The crew[1] was Sergeant Maurice Jackson, pilot, Sergeant Joseph Donovan, observer and Sergeant Tudor Beattie, wireless operator.

How did George spend the time when he was alone? He read a lot: French or German newspapers and magazines, English novels, history books (especially chapters about dictatorships – Hitler and Mussolini), geography books and an atlas – but only maps of Britain, France, Germany and Spain interested him. He often told us, looking at them, that British aircraft would destroy the Nazi army! He believed in the RAF. He often imagined how he would get back to Britain. I had explained to him he would go through Abbeville, Paris, Tours, Toulouse, Marseille or Perpignan and Barcelona to Gibraltar. His eyes sparkled when we talked about it, he slapped his knees or putting his arms on our shoulders kissed us.

From Burbure, other members of the RAF – Sergeant Larry Robillard, of the RCAF, shot down near Burbure in July 1941; Sergeant Douglas Barker, shot down in August 1941, near St Omer; and Pilot Officer A.L. Winskill, [later Air Commodore A.L. Winskill, CVO, CBE, DFC, AE, Captain of the Queen's Flight] shot down over Calais in summer 1941, who got a new identity as Achille Leblanc – had got back home safely, and George was confident. (British and Scottish soldiers had also got back home safely too, for instance: Frank Rowe, Arthur Fraser, H.C. Simmons and James Mowatt.)

After dinner, when he had listened to the BBC, George liked learning some French idioms and teaching us some English ones, for example:

'Please enter – come in.'
'Make yourself at home.'
'Would you like a cup of tea?'

'Have another biscuit.'
'I have enjoyed your company very much indeed.'

George played a lot with Jean and his playmate "Poupette", the daughter of Mme Giséle Reveillon. He taught them how to draw aircraft on paper and cut them out and throw them through the air. You could see the RAF aircraft and those of the Luftwaffe. Often a Spitfire or a Hurricane bumped into a Heinkel 111 or a Junkers. Of course, the British types always won! George also built tanks and ships out of cardboard or wood.

He liked riding and walking a lot. But it was dangerous because of the controls, and so Jean helped us. He always rode ahead of us and if he saw a control he got off his bike and pretended to repair something. Then we took another route or rode back. When we walked, Jean played with his ball or his hoop. So we met a lot of German soldiers, but none of them realised he had met a hero of the Battle of Britain! (General Von Stulpnagel, Militär-befehlshaber in France, had promised 10,000 francs reward for the capture of a crew. The men who helped RAF pilots were executed and the women sent to KK.[2])

George always helped with the housework; he laid the table and dried up. At five o'clock every day he made tea and toast.

When aircraft flew over, nothing could stop George running into the yard or the garden, following them with his eyes or recognising them from their sound. His hands in his pockets, he looked furiously at the Luftwaffe aircraft, pledging himself to shoot down more of them. Smiling, he waved to the RAF ones, wishing he was flying one of them.

It was a big surprise and joy for George when on Friday, 10th October, or Saturday the 11th, at nightfall, I came back from Lille with seven British servicemen, among them Squadron Leader Harry Bufton (of 9 Squadron) and two members of his Wellington bomber crew shot down near Douai, on their way back from Cologne, Warrant Officer K.B. Read and Sergeant William Crampton. George and Harry knew each other; they had learnt to fly together. They hugged each other, both deeply

---

[1] *Of a Blenheim IV of No 110 Squadron, from RAF Wattisham, which had been attacked and shot down by five Me109s while on a 'Circus' (fighter-escorted) daylight bombing operation.*

[2] *KK probably refers to a Concentration Camp; Konzentrationslager (KZ).*

George with Jean and Poupette.

The party was very lively and that evening George promised us, "If I get back to England, I'll fly again and I'll try to come and greet you, Jean, Elisa and Fernand, flying close to your house. I'll drop a box of tea or coffee in exchange for what I've drunk here." On Sunday, 12 October, being afraid of a control because we had seen three men looking like members of the Gestapo in front of our house, we decided to leave for Lillers, through the garden and along a country path. I brought them to M and Mme Fardel, whom George and Harry already knew. Two days earlier George had met in Lillers Pilot Officer Oscar Coen of 71 Squadron, an American from Chicago, brought back from Lille.

George and Harry spent their last evening with us on 26 October. George was wearing a new suit and my black *cire* (a sort of mackintosh) and a cap. Harry was wearing a pair of grey trousers with white stripes, a black jacket and a soft hat. Harry and George were deeply moved when they left us. They were at the same time sad to part from us and confident about their future.

Squadron Leader Henry Bufton stayed at the Salingues with George, and later they reached Spain together. Like George, Bufton went back on operations after returning to the UK; he became a distinguished pilot in the Pathfinder Force and was highly decorated, eventually retiring from the RAF as Wing Commander H.E. Bufton, DSO, OBE, DFC, AFC.

For the moment, the two pilots' concern was to get back to the UK; Bufton accepted the situation phlegmatically, George was restless, eager to be on his way. Paul Cole – whom George had previously mentioned as 'M Paul, an Englishman who I gathered was the mainstay of the organisation, getting bodies out of France' – visited them on 11 October. Then the next day they had dinner with friends of the Salingues and 'moved house', to the butcher in Burbure, M Fardel, his wife Henriette and their young son André. Here the two pilots were to stay for 16 days, from 13 to 28 October, because plans for them to go south on the 22nd fell through.

From their bedroom window at the Fardels they could see what George later described in his notes as 'manoeuvres on the green'. In front of the house was a village green, where German soldiers were drilled and where they were also given swimming lessons

moved, and George cried, "Hurrah!" ... They all were hungry and thirsty, and ate ham – brought by Joseph Fardel, a cousin of Elisa and a butcher in Burbure – and chips made by my wife with George's help. George was happy and surprised "to eat so well ... and so near the enemy ...!!"

That evening there were 15 soldiers and pilots with us; seven of them were hidden by friends in Burbure, among them Sergeant Patrick V. Bell of 602 Squadron, flying a Spitfire when shot down near St Omer, in September; Pilot Officer Alexandre Nitelet of 609 Squadron, a Belgian, shot down in May, near Cassel, and badly hurt in the head; Edward Dimes and Joseph Clapham, two British Army (RHA) soldiers.

Joseph Fardel as a soldier in the French Army.

(dry swims), having been told that the Channel which they were to cross to invade England was only three kilometres wide! Barclay and Bufton used to peer over the low window sill at the Germans; on the other side of the bedroom there was another window, and below it a sloping glass roof. Had it been necessary, it would have been possible to make a quick exit that way, down into a little courtyard at the back of the house, then on to a path which led across the fields.

André Fardel, who was a boy at the time, recalls one narrow squeak when the two pilots were there:

One afternoon when George Barclay and Henry Bufton were in their bedroom, my father and mother had a visit from a German officer, who asked them to let him have a room for the night. My mother, frightened and with a pale face, came

to ask me to let our English friends know of it and beg them to keep calm and silent. They opened the window (giving or looking onto the courtyard) so as to have a chance to escape.

The German officer and his orderly arrived about the end of the afternoon.

My father had observed, with good reason, that there is always enough time for some kind of observation when one gets into an unknown place. He had thought of a diversion.

I had moved into a bedroom situated beside the officer's and whilst he was settling down I started playing my accordion. As a matter of fact he congratulated me on it. It was a good thing he couldn't read my thoughts at the time. That evening we ate our supper in silence. I could guess the intense strain in my parents' minds.

At about ten o'clock on my way to bed, I went to visit our friends. My father had warned me to cough before opening the door. Switching the light on, I saw with surprise George Barclay sitting on his bed, tense but smiling. He winked at me and as was his habit rubbed his hand through my hair. Much later I thought that his gesture had not had the same significance. He wanted to reassure me then. I am quite sure that he ate his sandwich with a good appetite that night.

Later on he told my parents that he had especially feared for their lives. However, I think I was the only one who slept that night and (of course) the German officer also, no doubt.

Next day after the officer's departure, there was a complete relaxation and on the following days the funny side of the situation appeared to us, but at the same time alarming.

There was another day, but this time our anxiety was short-lived. We saw German lorries stopping on our communal square – and numerous soldiers got out. Quickly I went up to our friends, who having seen them also were ready to jump into the backyard. Seeing that the soldiers were in no hurry, parading in front of their officers, our anxiety vanished.

They started a mock battle in the streets, firing with blanks. Through the half-open bedroom shutters we watched so close to the fighting. George saw my keen interest and passing his fingers through my hair said something that I did not quite understand.

Joseph Fardel and his wife Henriette Fardel who housed George during his escape through France. George and Harry (Squadron Leader Henry Bufton) stayed with the Fardels for 16 days. George left the Fardels on the day that the Air Ministry officially declared him as missing, presumed dead – one month since he was shot down.

André Fardel – who was just 12 when his parents housed George – standing by the window of his former home that George was prepared to escape through.

"André, it is better for you that the war should always be a game."

And now, those few words, which at the time I had not really caught the meaning of, I like to remember. Very often I imagine with pleasure what the reaction of the German officers would have been if they had known that they were watched by English officers at the time.

The hour of departure – I have forgotten the last preparations.

Henry had a hat and had gone with my father.

George was my friend and I had to take him to a small station where someone had to take care of him. I was feeling very sad. He kissed my mother and asked her: "Mme Fardel, do I look like a Frenchman?"

This question leads to reflection when one has had the luck and the honour of knowing well a man like George Barclay who did not fear death, and did not glory in inflicting it.

It was 29 October when Bufton and Barclay finally left the kindly shelter of the Fardels' home. George had been equipped with a new suit, which arrived on the 21st, the day before they were originally scheduled to leave, and a day on which he had remarked to André: 'Today I am officially dead' – referring to the fact that, as it was a month since he had been shot down, he would have been posted 'missing, presumed killed'.

All those days had been spent in the Pas de Calais;

now was to come the momentous journey south, with the help of the Organisation – to Paris, Marseilles, the Pyrenees and all being well to Madrid, Gibraltar and freedom.

George recorded only fragmentary notes on this part of his escape. Undoubtedly he would have written a full narrative had he had time to do so, based on the notes he made, but after returning home on 11 December 1941 he only had four months in the UK before going to the Middle East, and in that time he got back into flying and took over command of a squadron.

On 29 October he recorded that he 'bicycled to Maries with Fardel and Henry where we picked up the Abbeville train. On board were Paul, Roland (guides), a friend of Roland's, Oscar, Ken, Bill, Joseph, Patrick, Alex and about four other Scottish Tommies. Proceeded to Paris via Abbeville. Help from priest of Abbeville.' The 'priest' was probably the Abbé Carpentier, described by O'Leary as 'a key man' in the Organisation.

From Paris – where, he remarked, they had a good dinner and only just caught the train – they went to Tours; the party was now seven, plus Roland and Roland's friend, plus Paul and six soldiers – 16 in all.

In his notes, George says 'P meets girl' – this was Suzanne Warenghem (later to marry Paul Cole), who accompanied the party to Marseilles. Her poignant story is told in *In Trust and Treason*, by Gordon Young (Studio Vista, 1959), who recounts that this was 'the largest single party of men whom Suzanne had helped on their way to freedom in a single group' and that it included Squadron Leader H.E. Bufton, Flight Lieutenant R.G.A. Barclay, Warrant Officer Read, Sergeants Bell and Crampton and eight Army other ranks.

In Tours he went to a cinema, then there was a two-hour train journey to Azai, where they had to cross the demarcation line between Occupied and Vichy-controlled France.

On the night of 30–31 October they crossed the line and made for Loches, an operation not without its excitement, judging from the breathless notes which George made:

Walk by CDF [presumably *chemin de fer* – the railway line]; bolt into woods when car came – bad. Bridge – patrol in café – rowed across by man on whom they were billeted. N [Nitelet, the Belgian pilot] muffled oar.

Knife; gun; contents of bags. Dogs barking. Moonlight – saw patrols. ... Bad fitting shoes. Haystack – very cold sleep. Farm barn – hay, bread, chocolate – cold, shaking, shivers. Blisters – watching signposts. End of tether at station. One hour wait – train – clean up.

The train took them from Loches to Chateauroux, where they had lunch and were given tickets for Toulouse, which they reached on a crowded train; then an overnight journey (31 October–1 November) to Marseilles, not without its risks:

Wait in station to get tickets – danger from gendarmes looking at us. Raining. Crush on platform – rush for seats. Henry and I with soldiers who talked of two spies on train and platform. Pretended to sleep. Talk English in sleep. Burnt-up country in morning. Arrive Marseilles – 8am?

For two days they stayed in Marseilles, at the flat of Louis Nouveau, with its 'lovely view', as George remembered. This view is quoted in *The Way Back*, by Vincent Brome: 'If Nouveau's flat was surprising, with its fine proportions, objets d'art and sweeping window giving a wonderful view over the Old Port, Nouveau himself was even more remarkable. ...' There he met Pat O'Leary and other members of the Organisation – a meeting not without incident, as he cryptically recorded in his notes: 'Argument with Belge over Paul. Meet O'L and others. Swollen hand in fight. Slept on floor. Changed shoes and doctored feet. Left behind tinned food.'

On 3 November Barclay, Bufton, Patrick Bell, William Crampton, Ken Read and Alex Nitelet set off for Perpignan, where they were accommodated in the Hotel du Loge, and on the night of 5–6 November taken by car to the foot of the Pyrenees, from where they walked 15–20 miles and crossed from France into Spain.

George's monosyllabic sentences in his notes indicate vividly what this involved:[1]

Walk. Vines. Hills. Guide. Stops. Not too fast over hills. Wind, blown off feet. Very cold. Moonlight, run over top 3,000ft. Shoes off; tear up identity cards. [George's had been given to him in Lille.] Sleep in leaves. View down to Figueras. Valley resting for day. Very cold.

---

[1] *See the description in* The Way Back, *pp. 64–66.*

During the cold, moonlit night of 6–7 November they walked about 20 miles by the outskirts of Figueras, and the following day rested in a field of maize; then the next night they went into Figueras – George suffering from violent pains and tummy trouble, as a result of the heat and the cold and drinking bad water – and hopped on a goods train bound for Barcelona, which they reached despite being caught in a van by the guard.

It was four o'clock in the morning when they arrived there, and George's monosyllabic notes recorded vividly the tenseness of their situation: 'Out offside of track. Walk on line. Clean shoes. Walk to café. Large lighted streets. No black-out. Café au lait. Taxi to consul.' George's sister Mary remembers him describing the anxious wait – still 'on the run' – from four o'clock in the morning up to about ten in the café, until the consulate opened.

At the British Consulate, where they must have been used to bedraggled groups of Servicemen arriving out of the night, Barclay and Bufton were directed to a house owned by people called Dorchy. There they were given fresh clothes, had a bath and 'slept like a log'. Gratefully, George remembered: 'Nice couple and dog. Cakes – fancy cream ones! Sleep.'

Private & confidential

Barcelona!! now Madrid
10th November, 1941.

My darling Mummie and Far,

No doubt by now you've heard that I am still in the land of the living, and anyway this letter confirms the fact! I am afraid your anxiety must have been great while I was comparatively enjoying a European tour - but I couldn't possibly let you know before. I am very well and quite whole - no wounds or even bruises. I do hope I shall find the same of you when I return shortly. I don't know how shortly - but expect in time for Christmas is a safe bet. I cannot tell you anything about my doings now, but I have seen the "V"s on the walls in France, I have heard and seen hundreds of huns singing their hymn of hate, and I've walked past other huns who were looking for me! Pretty dim on their part! Though I find that given the right clothes and my idiots expression so often used in charades I can pass for an imbecile school boy, without taking a correspondence course!

I am with very nice English people now and enjoying a needed rest and regular existence. I wish I could pot some of this sun for you! I shall move on soon, so it is impossible for you to write me for the moment.

I hope all the family are well- I'm afraid I can't write more - and anyway someone is waiting for this letter.

All my love,

George

A letter George sent home to his parents from Barcelona, 10 November 1941.

On 10 November, the second day he and Bufton were at the house, they went to a cinema in the evening and Sergeant Payton arrived. Next day, the three of them journeyed to Madrid by diplomatic cars with Bill Crampton, Ken Read, Alex Nitelet and Patrick Bell; the British Embassy there was to be their last stop in Spain before going on to Gibraltar and from there – hopefully – reaching home. The Ambassador, Sir Samuel Hoare, later Viscount Templewood, was Ambassador Extraordinary on Special Mission to Spain, 1940–44, and was also a distant relative of the Barclay family. He described some of the problems his Embassy had in dealing with evaders and escapees in *Ambassador on Special Mission*.[1]

A register entitled: 'RAF Personnel. Escapees Passing through Spain' has as its first, second and third entries under 'B':

Madrid			arr	dep
BUFTON, Sqn Ldr	33223		11/11/41	7/12/41
BARCLAY, F/Lt	74661		11/11/41	7/12/41
In Barcelona (Chancery ref 33/302/41)				
BELL, Sgt	915544		11/11/41	7/12/41
In Barcelona 8/11 (Chancery ref 33/302/41)				

[1] *Collins, 1946.*

George Barclay – through the Pyrenees
Richard Barclay

It has been pointed out to me that the story in George's diary rather trails off after he joined the Salingue family in Burbure on 26 September 1941. Thereafter the book relies on his very brief daily summaries. Why was this? At first I imagined that George simply did not have the time to write up his escape in full during the period he was in England; from 10 December 1941 to his departure for the Middle East on 10 April 1942, owing to his duties in passing on his experiences to assist future evaders, and then his appointment as Squadron Leader of 601 Squadron, which was to travel out to the Middle East by sea under his command. I just wonder now if he had become aware of Harold [Paul] Cole's betrayal of the Pat O'Leary Line at the very time that George had been in Marseilles (1–3 November), leaving him at a loss as to how to report truthfully on what had happened, or what amendments he needed to make to what he had already written. It seems probable that his first reaction was to defend Cole – hence the mention of a fight in Louis Nouveau's flat and a 'swollen hand' – was it his own hand or O'Leary's as reported by Airey Neave.

Unfortunately I am not in a position to add much detail to the record in the book, but accounts of similar crossings of the Pyrenees to George's have appeared in a number of books. Probably the best-known ones are Airey Neave's *They Have Their Exits* and *Saturday at MI9*. Nevertheless, I will record what little I do remember from conversations with George at Christmas 1941 – now more than 70 years ago!

It seems likely that O'Leary and Garrow were anxious to get rid of their 'parcels' as soon as possible, and George and five others were sent off to Perpignan on 3 November, where he and five other evaders stayed at the Hotel du Loge for two nights. On the evening of 5 November, they were taken by car to the foot of the eastern end of the Pyrenees, where they joined a party guided by a Spanish smuggler. This method of leading escapers from Nazi Europe across the Spanish frontier had been set up by none other than Nabor Gulbenkien, under the direction of Donald Darling (code name 'Sunday') of MI9. The rate of reward to the smugglers for a safe crossing was £20 for a soldier and £40 for an officer!

The climb in darkness, extreme cold and high winds on lonely, barely perceptible, tracks was very demanding for men who were mostly in torn clothes and ill-fitting shoes, all suffering from long-term under-nourishment. Keeping in touch with each other and just keeping going taxed them to the full in a 20-mile scramble at heights of up to 3,000 feet, but they managed it. Once over the frontier they were in danger of arrest by Spanish frontier guards, and they all feared the conditions in Spanish prisons, which were even worse than under the Germans or the French. Furthermore, the Spanish authorities often failed to advise national representatives in Madrid of escapers they were holding; in some cases, escapers were condemned to many years of imprisonment for illegally entering the country.

During the day of 6 November, George and Squadron Leader Bufton hid up by themselves in high pastures, the party having been split up into ones and twos for the sake of safety. They tried to rest and replenish their energy, despite feeling desperately cold and hungry. Their object for the following night was to walk another 20 miles to the railhead at Figueres. It was still very cold and stormy and they were both suffering from tummy troubles caused by chills or drinking tainted water. George told me that sometime during this period a guard stopped them, but to their surprise another Spaniard appeared and negotiated at length to enable them to go on. Apparently the price was a fountain pen! Presumably the guard could not risk being discovered with unexplained cash, but a fountain pen could be 'cashed' at a safer time in the future.

The mysterious Spaniard was, I imagine, one of a chain of agents established by the British to look out for their nationals entering Spain, and no doubt similar assistance was provided to enable George and Bufton to unofficially board a goods train, which took them about 80 miles to the outskirts of Barcelona on the night of 7 November. There, at 4:00am, they slipped off the truck on the 'off side' of the railway line and followed the line into central Barcelona. They took to the well-lit streets but had to avoid patrolling police at all costs. Fortunately, they found a back-street café open, and made a cup or two of coffee last until they reckoned the British Consulate would be open. Then they nipped up the street and into the Consulate – at last they were *safe*.

For two nights they were housed extremely comfortably with a British family called Dorchy. One wonders how they had money for the café and how welcoming accommodation was available. Was this all through the chain of agents established by Gulbenkien and Darling?

It was not straightforward for the Consulate, and later the Embassy, to accommodate illegal entrants, particularly as the Ambassador, George's cousin Sam Hoare, had the overriding task of preventing Franco joining forces with his German and Italian fascist allies who had assisted him so heavily in the recent Civil War. If Franco had dropped his neutrality, not only would the escape route have been lost, but probably Gibraltar as well. At least Lady Hoare was able to send George's mother a message by a roundabout route to say that George was 'well and in high spirits'.

At the Embassy, where he was to be from 11 November to 7 December, things were obviously difficult with the influx of airmen and soldiers. George noted: 'Embassy disappointing. Appalling conditions. Prisoners.' On the 13th the Ambassador gave a sherry party for the escapees, an event which somehow jarred with George, who referred disdainfully to 'Sammy Hoare and cocktail party'.

It must have been trying to have to hang about in Madrid before getting through to Gibraltar and the last hop for home; inevitably, nerves were strained, there were some quarrels which erupted into fights, there were comings and goings, and there were social recreations.

In his chronology of these days in the Spanish capital George recorded some of the events, for example on 15 November: 'Lunch with Wing Commander Jimmy Dixon. Party at El Mason with Jimmy, Henry and Squadron Leader Vincer. Dinner party in Madrid.' Then, on the following day: 'Cinema – *The Lady Vanishes*.'

On the 19th there was a reunion for them with Pilot Officer Oscar Coen, the American, who arrived with Ted Dimes, Richard Parkinson, and Sergeants Campbell and Ives. (Coen was also in a party escorted by Suzanne Warenghem.) The Embassy's accommodation must have been getting crowded.

Inevitably some of its temporary residents, because of the hardships and unusual diets to which they had been subjected in preceding weeks, became ill. George noted on 22 November: 'Crampton got diphtheria.' The understanding with the Spanish authorities was that evaders who were ill could be evacuated; the others had to be escorted to Gibraltar by the police as undesirables to be expelled from Spain. Crampton's diphtheria was apparently not serious enough to prevent his homeward progress, for on the 24th 'Bill Crampton went to Gibraltar.'

Nor did a similar illness impede Sergeant Payton. On 28 November George noted: 'Payton got diphtheria, Ken Read – kidney chill.' Then on the 29th: 'Payton went to Gibraltar.'

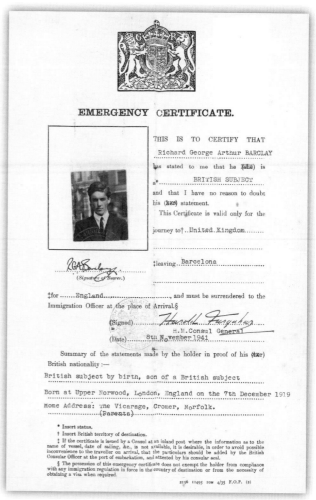

A letter from the Foreign Office informing the Barclays that George had arrived safely in Madrid on 14 November 1941.

George had to obtain an 'Emergency Certificate' in order to travel from Barcelona to the UK as the only identification he could carry as an airman was his identity tags, which he no longer had.

On the last day of November 1941 George saw two films, *Nurse Cavell*, recalling a poignant episode in the First World War, and *Target for Tonight*, a documentary depicting the early days of the RAF Bomber Command offensive against Germany. He was to have only a week more in Spain before the long-awaited return home, a week which seems to have been agreeably filled.

On 2 December the Embassy gave a party for the escapees; next day there was a sherry party, and on 5 and 6 December respectively George recorded: 'Lunch with Captain Hilgarth, Naval Attaché. Party at El Mason with Vincer, Henry, Jimmy Dixon.' Then on 7 December, his 22nd birthday: 'Left Madrid by train for Gibraltar in evening with Spanish detective, Babington Smith, Alex, Henry, Pat, Ken, Oscar and many soldiers.'

They arrived in Gibraltar at 4:30am on the morning of 8 December and George was billeted at the Bristol Hotel – 'freedom!' he ecstatically recorded. His happiness was reflected in a telegram to his family: 'Safe Gibraltar Hope see you soon Love and best wishes for Xmas Letter received Feeling very pleased with life.' No doubt he was supposed to wait his turn for a flight to the UK, but he happened to encounter a Catalina flying-boat pilot he knew, Flying Officer Edwards, and (unofficially) arranged to fly back with him as 'third pilot'.

The Catalina took off from Gibraltar at 16:15hrs on 9 December on the longest flight George made in the whole of his RAF career – 18 hours – reaching Stranraer at 10:15hrs on 10 December. In his log book, against what was to be the last entry for 1941, he vividly

POST OFFICE TELEGRAM

Charges to pay — s. — d.

RECEIVED

Prefix. Time handed in. Office of Origin and Service Instructions. Words.

10.35 LONDON TELEX 31

From

THE REV GA BARCLAY THE VICARAGE CROMER-NORFOLK

= FROM AIRMINISTRY KINGSWAY –

P 6339 10/12 INFORMATION JUST RECEIVED STATES

YOUR SON ACTING FLIGHT LIEUTENANT RICHARD GEORGE

ARTHUR BARCLAY DFC HAS REACHED ENGLAND TODAY =

1800 +

For free... btful words telephone "TELEGRAMS ENQUIRY" or call, with this form at office of delivery. Other enquiries should be accompanied by this form and if possible, the envelope

The Post Office telegram sent on 10 December 1941 informing the Barclays that George had arrived in England.

described it: 'Almost stowed away. Sausages and mash above the clouds! Crew of ten and one survivor of the *Ark Royal*.[1] Gib – Scillies – Fastnet Rock – Stranraer. Home sweet home!'

His sister Mary recalls George's description of this flight – how he had to join the aircraft at the very last moment before take-off, how he acted as 'chef' en route, was reported by radio to Stranraer as an 'unofficial passenger', and was placed under arrest at gunpoint after the Catalina landed, until he had identified himself.

At 23:00hrs that day George left Stranraer for London by train, which got him in at 10:30hrs the following morning, 11 December, when a telegram was delivered to the Reverend G.A. Barclay at The Vicarage, Cromer, Norfolk. From the Air Ministry, Kingsway, it read: 'Information just received states your son Acting Flight Lieutenant Richard George Barclay DFC has reached England today.'

In London, George went first to a transit camp, where (his notes record) he was 'interrogated by Flight Lieutenant Grey, Captain Langley, MC, OBE, and Captain Le Brimier. Dinner with Langley.' His interrogation took place on 11 December.

On 12 December he went to the Air Ministry, where amongst others he saw Air Marshal Leigh-Mallory, the AOC No 11 Group; then he went up to Hornchurch, where his great adventure had started on 20 September, and where he must have received a warm welcome on his return.

Next day, he recorded: 'From Hornchurch to 11 Group party with Wing Commander Dawson. Saw Victor B(eamish), Walter C. Gossage, Lewis Way, Archibald Sinclair [later Viscount Thurso, and Air Minister from 11 May 1940 to 28 May 1945], Baldwin, Leslie Howard [the film star with whom George had been involved in making a training film], AOC.' Then, on 14 December 1941: 'To Cromer – home. Everyone at home except Ann and family.'

[1] *Had been sunk by a U-boat near Gibraltar on 14 November 1941.*

George on a shooting expedition after his return from France, with (left to right) his brothers Richard and Charles, nephew Leo and father, 1941.

His sister Mary recalls that when they had a celebration meal at the vicarage, singing the Doxology as grace, George was unable to partake of the food because of his poor physical condition resulting from the previous weeks' privations.

The second chapter of his wartime career had closed happily – after adventures like Othello's account

Of moving accidents by flood and field;

Of hair-breadth 'scapes ...;

Of being taken by the insolent foe.

The third chapter would have for its setting the Middle East theatre, where 1942 was to prove a year of disaster and triumph for the Allies. As the official history puts it: 'The Mediterranean Fleet had heavy losses; Malta was battered almost into helplessness by the enemy's aircraft; the 8th Army was defeated at Gazala; Tobruk fell; the fighting on the "Alamein line" in July 1942 greatly exhausted the British although it put a stop to the enemy's advance.' Yet, from October that year, the Allies took the strategic initiative 'from both ends of the North African seaboard. ... The 8th Army and its supporting Air Forces won the pitched battle of El Alamein and then set out on an anabasis of eighteen hundred miles pointed by battles and actions. ... At the western limit of the theatre the Anglo-American "Torch" expedition, at that time the largest that had ever sailed for a possibly hostile shore, descended from the sea.'[1]

George Barclay was to be involved, as will be seen, in the middle of these great events – when the 8th Army had just consolidated its position at El Alamein, and over its lines where the Desert Air Force and the Luftwaffe daily duelled for air superiority, sparring and probing before the great battle that was to come.

[1] History of the Second World War. The Mediterranean and Middle East, Vol IV. The Destruction of the Axis Forces in Africa, by Major-General I.S.O. Playfair, CB, DSO, MC, and Brigadier C.J.C. Molony, with Captain F.C. Flynn, RN, and Group Captain T.P. Gleave, CBE, (HMSO, 1966)

George at home with family on his return from France. Back row from left: brother Charlie (a Lieutenant in the Royal Norfolk Regiment), George, father Gilbert and brother Richard. Seated from left: Charlie's wife Rome Barclay (née Davidson), mother Dorothy Barclay with Charlie's eldest son Leo on her lap, and sister Mary Barclay, a Land Girl at the time.

Home sweet home. George returned from France in December 1941 after escaping through Occupied France to enjoy four months' leave. George appears here in the clothes he escaped through France wearing.

Journey to El Alamein

George Barclay had been promoted to the war-substantive rank of Flight Lieutenant on 3 October 1941: this confirmed the acting rank he had had since 4 August that year, when he went to command 'A' Flight of No 611 Squadron at Hornchurch. At the beginning of 1942, therefore, after his joyful Christmas reunion with his family, and with the accolade of having evaded the enemy's clutches after being shot down in France added to the distinction he had won in the Battle of Britain, he was ripe for a new posting. Initially, this would be a non-flying post, but he was determined to get back into operational flying.

On 12 January 1942 he went to Headquarters, Fighter Command, at Stanmore, Middlesex, on an attachment (to the Tactics Staff),[1] which lasted barely three weeks. Here, he lectured on his escape. Shortly before leaving there he wrote in a letter to his sister Mary on 28 January:

Life here is not so bad – few flying types and masses of wingless wonders! But good fellows a lot of them. The worst of it is that most of the flying types having a rest here like myself have wives and live out. Nevertheless it is a good rest, and I can get to town a bit. I am so sorry I couldn't meet you and Lion [now 2nd Lieutenant Lionel Buxton, Coldstream Guards]. It was disappointing. I have seen Sue and Lion several times since – both flourishing. I always feel, though, that Lion is treading on thin ice, keeping up a 'society' existence without the cash really necessary – one slip and what might happen. I have felt like this since his motor accident, but I may be quite wrong. I suppose it

is one of the evils of a Guards existence.

I have just been posted to Preston, Lancs. I am to be the Group Tactics Officer – a completely free hand and possibly a Squadron Leader – though it is not certain. Anyway it means that I don't go to the Middle East for a bit longer – for which I am grateful.

On 2 February he moved northwards – to Barton Hall at Preston, Lancashire. This was the HQ of No 9 Group of Fighter Command, responsible for UK air defence from mid-Wales northwards to the Lake District, from the Midlands out into the Irish Sea.

No 9 Group had Spitfires, Hurricanes, Defiants and Beaufighters; George's job was again concerned with fighter tactics, and having nearly four weeks at Preston (to 28 February) he managed to get airborne again – flying himself for the first time since that fateful Spitfire sweep of 20 September the previous year – and his log book started to explode with enthusiastic unofficial notes.

Appropriately, he began again in a Tiger Moth, the RAF basic trainer, flying one from Samlesbury (an airfield near Preston) for 45 minutes on 5 February. Clearly not the only fighter pilot being rehabilitated, he noted with typical candour and compassion:

First flight for a very long time; Moth from 9 Group HQ Flight. Pilot Officer Woodger in other Moth and I had dog fight. His first flight since spending 14½ days in an open boat after being torpedoed on Merchant Shipping Catapult Fighter duties.[2]

---

[1] *Barclay lectured on his escape at Fighter Command HQ.*

[2] *Woodger would have been onboard a CAM-Ship – catapult aircraft merchantmen. Hurricane pilots had an unenviable choice, after being launched for a possible interception, either to ditch in the sea near the convoy, in the hope that they would be picked up, or try to reach land.*

George wearing C Type flying helmet, E Type oxygen mask and intercom set, and Mk IV flying goggles with split lenses and a flip screen to reduce sudden glare from sunlight, 15 March 1942.

Next day he flew a Tiger again, for 35 minutes, with a passenger, Squadron Leader Bancroft, and noted: 'Aerobatics. Quite incredibly cold.' Then on the 10th he had a new experience – a demonstration of AI navigation – airborne interception by radar installed and operated in the aircraft – in a No 68 Squadron Beaufighter II (Rolls-Royce Merlin-engined) flown by a Czech pilot, Flight Lieutenant Vesely. They flew for an hour and three-quarters, from High Ercall in Shropshire to Valley in Anglesey, North Wales, and back.

One hurdle which George had to clear before getting back to operational flying was that of physical fitness, after the discomforts and privations he had endured during his escape through France and Spain. Would he be able to stand the high altitudes, the rapid climbs and steep dives, which were the everyday lot of a fighter pilot?

To find out, he went to RAE Farnborough for decompression chamber tests on 16 and 17 February and – characteristically – recorded these 'flights' in his log book (in pencil). One of the tests in a decompression chamber was to get the 'inmates' to do simple sums in order to see how their reactions were affected by lack of oxygen. Of the first occasion, 45 minutes at 25,000ft without oxygen, he wrote: 'Ten in chamber. All passed out after about 7–10 minutes at 25,000ft. But *mirabile dictu*, I survived OK except that I couldn't remember to add from left or right of the sum first.'

On the next day, when the test was 45 minutes at 38,000ft with oxygen, George wrote:

Some got "bends" [like those suffered by a diver through rapid decompression] – all experienced itching. Turned off my oxygen and passed out after 45 seconds, but never knew I had passed out until told afterwards.

Just over a week later (on 25 February) he had an experience that delighted him – he flew a Hurricane again. This was a Mk I from the Air Fighting Development Unit at Duxford, where he had begun his flying with Cambridge UAS in 1938, and he flew across to Oakington where he experienced something entirely new – a ride in a Stirling, first of the RAF four-engined bombers to enter service. The exercise it was engaged on took place in the Oakington locality, and George noted: 'Fighter attacks and bomber evasive action.

Watched Flight Lieutenant Murray, DFC, DFM, carrying out bomber liaison attacks from the attacked bomber' – adding, with a 'fighter boy's' uninhibited view of the bomber world, 'like flying in a gigantic gin palace!' Then he returned to Duxford in his borrowed mount – 'a very sweet-flying Hurricane I', as he described it.

On 9 March he flew a Hurricane II from Northolt to Farnborough and back, then six days later flew a Spitfire VB again – for the first time since that offensive sweep with No 611 Squadron on the afternoon of 20 September 1941, when he had force-landed in France – and enjoyed himself doing an hour's aerobatics from Kenley, having borrowed the aircraft from No 602 Squadron there. He was clearly getting his hand in again, and on 23 March tried out a type that was new to him – a Hawker Typhoon I.

This aircraft belonged to No 56 Squadron – the squadron which No 249 Squadron, when George was a junior member of it, had relieved at North Weald in September 1940; and the CO, Squadron Leader H.S.L. Dundas, DFC, was by now an old friend. George comments on his 45 minutes' experience in the new type: 'Borrowed one of 56 Squadron's Typhoons (CO, Squadron Leader 'Cocky' Dundas, DFC – Flight Lieutenant Mike Ingle Finch), first squadron to get them. Very fast (412mph) and quite manoeuvrable for their speed, but rather large. Hydraulic pump failed, so spent several minutes pumping undercart and flaps down¹ – rather hectic for first trip!'

Next day (24 March) he flew an Air Fighting Development Unit Hurricane I in a 30-minute ciné gun exercise against a Lysander, the type he had flown at No 1 School of Army Co-operation in June 1940, using a new gyro gunsight. 'Assessed the film with Gunnery Research Unit's new device', he noted in his log book. 'You can tell where your bullets would have gone to a couple of feet.' On the same day he flew in a type of aircraft entirely new to him, a Douglas Boston II nightfighter, on a half-hour night flying test by Squadron Leader Smith of the AFDU.

Clearly he was picking up all the experience he could, in the expectation of joining another squadron. His father, the Reverend G.A. Barclay, later described George's feelings at this time:

After his escape from France and while he was recuperating, he had more than one interesting job, the last of which was "tactics officer" at HQ Fighter Command. It was his special forté. He had lectured upon it and had spent one period after his wounds instructing other pilots [at No 52 OTU in Debden, from May–July 1941]. But he was restless, and agitated to get back into operations. The reason? The chief one was the unrivalled comradeship, quite unobtainable by any other method than that of a common adventure and a common danger, a comradeship in which George "found himself". But there was doubtless the other thought expressed in the words: "It seems to me that if you give yourself to your country you must give your all."

Then within a few days his ambitions started to be realised. On 26 March he was promoted Acting Squadron Leader and two days later had a joyous 80-minute aerobatic session in a Spitfire belonging to his friend Wing Commander David Scott-Maiden at North Weald. This was to be the last time he would ever fly a Spitfire, and the last opportunity he would have of untrammelled manoeuvres in that beautiful aircraft in English skies.

On 4 April 1942 George was posted to command No 601 (County of London) Squadron, Auxiliary Air Force, one of the four original AAF squadrons formed in 1925,[1] which was then based at Digby in Lincolnshire and destined to go out to the Middle East. That day he flew up from Northolt in a Hurricane 'to see 601 Squadron and take over', as he noted in his log book. The 45-minute flight back to Northolt was the last flight he recorded; for some reason, probably because his log book wasn't with him at the time, no record of his third and last tour of fighter operations – in the Western Desert – appears in it.

He officially assumed command of No 601 Squadron on 5 April and there was much to be done before it left for the Middle East on the 10th; but on the 5th George managed to get across to Cromer to see his family. When he reached the vicarage early that evening they were in church, and his father subsequently wrote a moving word-picture of their last reunion:

Full of joy in his new command, though he had less than a week's notice he allowed himself

48 hours at home to say "goodbye". It was Easter Sunday evening. I was celebrating Holy Communion and had just got to the Prayer of Consecration. Charlie[2] had come home for the half day and was with his mother in the chairs just inside the chancel door and opposite me; when the door beside them gently opened and there was George in all his beauty. He hesitated a moment till he saw his mother and then went and knelt down by her. I was almost overcome by emotion; and again when I administered to Dorothy and her two sons, one in khaki and the other in light blue. It was a marvellous and a God-given farewell.

No 601 squadron had fought in the Battles of France and Britain with Hurricanes, joining later in the 1941 offensive; then it was chosen to be the first (and only) Fighter Command squadron to fly Bell Airacobras, the American tricycle-undercarriage fighter with a rear-mounted engine and 20mm cannon firing through the propeller boss. This type proved unsuccessful operationally; there were many accidents and losses of pilots, morale sagged, and it was not until re-equipment with Spitfire VBs and the arrival of a new CO (Squadron Leader J.D. Bisdee, DFC) in March 1942 that squadron spirits were restored.

George noted specifically and proudly in his log book: 'Posted to command 601 County of London Auxiliary Squadron, 4 April 1942, and take them out East.' The squadron ORB recorded on 5 April:

Once more the kitting of new arrivals and squadron personnel took the main part of the day. No 76575 Squadron Leader J.D. Bisdee, DFC, RAFVR/GD[3], relinquished the post of Commanding Officer, and was succeeded by No 74661 Squadron Leader Barclay, DFC, RAFVR/GD, who was posted to the unit from Headquarters, Fighter Command.

Since the squadron had learnt on 24 March that it was destined to go overseas there had been ever-increasing activity at Digby. New personnel were posted in; from the beginning of April preparations

---

[1] The other 'originals' were Nos 600 (City of London), 602 (City of Glasgow) and 603 (City of Edinburgh).

[2] The Barclays' eldest son, later killed at Kohima, Assam, while serving with the Norfolk Regiment.

[3] General Duties, the RAF branch to which aircrew officers belonged

were made for the move, a complete reorganisation being started on the 3rd. On the 9th the ORB recorded: 'A vast amount of administrative work was dealt with in completely clearing the squadron'; and on the 10th:

> Squadron Leader Bisdee, DFC, Second Lieutenant Bartleman, Pilot Officer Pawson, Murray etc were all posted to Digby pending posting overseas on Movement "Newman". Squadron Leader Barclay, DFC, seven officers and 327 men left Digby after a farewell dance which terminated at 2200hr. All ranks were paraded in the squadron hangar, and taken by lorry to Digby railway station. The complete squadron had entrained by approximately 0020hr for the port of embarkation.

The significance of Operation 'Newman' was that the aircrew were to go to the Mediterranean aboard the aircraft carrier USS *Wasp,* and to fly their Spitfires off on 20 April for Malta, subsequently operating from there for two months before going on to Egypt; while the other officers and groundcrew, led by George, went to the Middle East by troopship. Operation 'Newman' originated in a personal request by Prime Minister Churchill to President Roosevelt at the end of March 1942.

Not long after leaving Digby he wrote to his parents:

> *All the last few days have gone well, though there has been a rush for me with such short notice. I am very proud of my men as they have had a lot to put up with and have been commended for their behaviour already! The Adjutant continues to do his excellent work, and everything in the garden is rosy. So cheer up and remember I'll be back before you can say Jack Robinson, as brown as a papoose and as fit as a fiddle – in fact this is probably an excellent thing for my health, like going to take the air at Davos!*
>
> *I am sorry I have told you nothing but of course I cannot do so. This is just to let you know I am in v. good heart and looking forward to new experiences tremendously.*
>
> *Please circulate my letters among our immediate family and ask them to drop me the odd line. Incidentally, it might be a good thing to number your letters to me, so that I know if I am*

> *getting all or some of them. I'll try to do the same with mine.*
>
> *It was a grand 48 hours. Thank you so very much for killing the fatted calf.*

No 601's journey to the Middle East under their new commanding officer was no different in kind from all those made by thousands of troops during the Second World War. They embarked in HMT K.6 (SS *Rangitata*) at Liverpool on 10 April 1942 and had their last glimpse of a receding British Isles at sunset on 15 April when moving out from Gourock. One wonders what George's thoughts were then, and those of the 334 men with him. The numbers involved indicate the logistic problems of moving just one squadron overseas.

In fact there were personnel of five other Spitfire squadrons aboard, including Nos 74, 603 (City of Edinburgh) and 134, whose party numbered 372 – 18 officers and 354 other ranks – and was led by the Acting CO, Flight Lieutenant Neil Cameron, destined to become Chief of the Air Staff and then Chief of the Defence Staff after distinguished operational and post-war careers. Sir Neil recalls how he renewed acquaintance with George aboard the troopship, having first met him at North Weald during the Battle of Britain:

> He was with No 249 Squadron and I was with No 17 (which also had Hurricanes), and though our base was Martlesham Heath we were often ordered down to North Weald or its satellite airfield Stapleford Tawney to operate during the day and be closer to the centre of action.

Sir John Grandy, later the Governor of Gibraltar, who has written the Foreword to this book, commanded No 249:

> Those were exciting days of real comradeship and constant activity, when often seven days a week one rose before dawn and finished usually just after dark, perhaps flying three or four sorties during that time; certainly one was at constant readiness in or around dispersal points, never going far from one's aircraft. Meals were brought out in so-called "hot boxes" and every time the phone bell went one's stomach turned over – what might it be? – "Scramble Dover, Angels Two-five!"

At that time I remember assessing George Barclay (with all the experience of a twenty-year-old) as a very nice chap; and on limited acquaintance he seemed everything a fighter pilot should be – dedicated to flying, always ready to discuss tactics, and more than anxious to stay at "readiness" if there were any chance of getting a sortie against the Luftwaffe attacking his beloved England. It was clear that he had the magic qualities of leadership in good measure.

After the Battle of Britain ended I didn't meet him again until I arrived at Liverpool on 10 April 1942 to board HMT K.6 bound for the Middle East. SS *Rangitata* was a New Zealand refrigerated cargo ship, more used to transporting frozen lamb from Wellington to the UK than to acting as a troopship. Since our meeting at North Weald, George Barclay had been shot down over France and had made a notable escape; I had been in Russia with the

Hurricane Wing (Nos 81 and 134 Squadrons), which went to fly with the Soviet Air Force in and around Murmansk and the Kola Peninsula.

It was clear from the first evening aboard that we were going to have quite an exciting voyage. There was no shortage of personalities in any of the six Spitfire squadrons, and together they gave the OC Troops every indication that though the voyage might be long, it would not be dull. So it proved.

On 6 May the No 134 Squadron ORB was to note:

Crossing the line ceremonies carried out in Flight Lieutenant Cameron's cabin. Helpers included Squadron Leaders Mathers and Barclay, and Wing Commander Darwen. Those initiated included the ship's adjutant – not exactly voluntarily, judging by his costume.

George was promoted to squadron leader at the age of 22 and given command of No 601 Squadron, which he took to the Middle East in May–June 1942. He then took over the battle-weary No 238 Squadron, shooting down three enemy aircraft before he himself was shot down and killed over El Alamein. This picture was taken in Cairo by a street photographer.

The following day's entry added, somewhat pensively;

Repercussions from last night's ceremony took most of the morning, resulting in a threat to close the bar if such goings-on are repeated. This should be a sufficient deterrent until the last night of the voyage.

For two weeks they sailed without incident, through the Atlantic Ocean; then in the early morning of 29 April caught their first glimpse of a foreign land, the green misty shoreline of West Africa at Freetown. Between there and South Africa the convoy had its only excitement and its only loss: on 15 May, three days before they docked in Durban, one of the escorting naval vessels was hit and damaged by a mine and that evening a merchantman was hit and sunk.

For No 601 Squadron the five days they spent in Clarewood Transit Camp, Durban, from 19 to 24 May were a happy respite from wartime Britain and whatever lay ahead for them in the Western Desert; but on the 25th, having said farewell to the new friends they had made and to their hospitable hosts, they re-embarked – this time in HMT *Mauretania,* which moved out of harbour at 17:00hrs. When daylight came on the following day, her passengers realised that she was 'unescorted and alone' (as the squadron ORB noted).

Sir Neil Cameron recalls that during these two voyages, the convoy to Durban, which suffered some casualties in the Bay of Biscay, and the fast 'solo' Cunarder from Durban to Port Suez:

I got to know George Barclay well. The conditions in the two troopships were very cramped, with six officers sharing a small cabin and the "troops" in atrocious conditions in the holds, which had been turned into vast dormitories – though "dormitory" is probably too nice a word to use in the circumstances. Anyone who travelled in this way during wartime will know what it is like to keep those under your command not only sane, but active and employed.

Barclay got to know the NCOs and airmen in his squadron really well, and also was an influence on both these ships for good. He was balanced and calm when others were getting fed-up and bolshie. At the time, I thought it was just his natural leadership qualities coming out in his considerable interest in the welfare of the troops; but I came to realize that

George's letter home from Egypt, 8 June 1942.

S/Ldr R.G.A. Barclay.
601 Squadron R.A.F.   Middle East Force
                        8/6/42.

I have arrived safely in this part of the world, and please note my address. I have had no mail as yet, but hope to receive some soon- it is very erratic. I hope you have had the odd letter and airgraph from me. Life is very interesting but I think the local inhabitants of this town make me want to kick them more than any other race I have met' I am sure I have not met the true Arab yet. We now have to do some patient waiting for a few months to get operational--- very irksome but I have found a job for myself and my boys, who are magnificent. One has to sit down and try to sort out problems of equipment, when one ought to be in the battle-- but patience is a virtue' The pyramids are marvellous and we get lots of sun, so we are quite happy and very fit' I have met an ex C.O. of my Squadron out here who has helped a lot. My best love to you all- do send me airgraphs.

                        signed
                        George

he had a great spiritual strength to support him, which others lacked, when things got difficult. He didn't carry it on his shoulder, but later I heard of his Christian faith – no doubt influenced much by his father, who had been an Army chaplain in the First World War and later the vicar of several parishes in England. One now knows that when George returned home to his father's vicarage after having been shot down and having made his epic escape from France, his family knelt together to give thanks to God – and in doing so, George didn't forget to remind his family to pray for the Germans as well.

On 1 June the Cunarder reached Aden, and that evening entered the Red Sea and reduced speed; the risk of enemy activity was past and No 601 disembarked safely at Port Tewfik, Suez, on 4 June.

Their first real glimpse of Egypt's world of sand, perpetual sunshine and flies came on the train northwards to Geneifa on the Bitter Lake, where they were accommodated in No 39 Camp at the Middle East Pool, a transit stage for units moving into the Middle East theatre. There they had a chance of getting acclimatised, for it was nine days before they received orders (on 14 June) to move to RAF Maryut, near Alexandria, for what the ORB described as 'defence duties' – since 601 was at that stage a fighter squadron without any aircraft. This move, which involved an advance party travelling via Cairo then up the military road to Alexandria and a main party journeying by train, was completed by 18 June; and with the advance party having erected tents, No 601 was 'in business' by the 19th, with orderly room, stores etc successfully operating. But the stay at Maryut was short; on the 21st the squadron was notified that it was to move.

On that date, Tobruk had surrendered and the military situation in the Western Desert was soon to become a desperate one for the Allies, with the 8th Army in retreat towards El Alamein.

No 601 Squadron, latest addition to the Desert Air Force, received instructions on 22 June to move and its preparations were complete by 17:30hrs on that day; then a signal was received cancelling the movement. Instead, the squadron was given instructions to detach a servicing party to Landing Ground (LG) No 12 (Sidi Haneish North,

some 20 miles south-east of Mersa Matruh).

On 23 June a convoy of vehicles arrived at Maryut from Cairo and at 16:00hrs an advance party, led by Squadron Leader Barclay, set off for LG No 12; with him were Flying Officer K.A. Carew-Gibbs the squadron intelligence officer, Pilot Officer L.C. Eagle its engineer officer and 80 airmen. As the convoy travelled through the night it had to disperse three times because of enemy action. Meanwhile, squadron HQ at Maryut had received a surprising telephone message from nearby RAF Aboukir, an airfield just north-east of Alexandria, to say that Squadron Leader Bisdee and eight other pilots had arrived there in their Spitfires from Malta. They reported that, in operations in defence of the besieged island, they had lost three pilots but added another 25 enemy aircraft destroyed to the squadron's operational score.[1]

Now No 601 was ready to become a fighting unit once again; on 25 June its Spitfires rejoined the ground crews at Maryut.

During that afternoon a message came from Squadron Leader Barclay at LG No 13 (Sidi Haneish South) telling the remainder of the squadron to move up there, but at 20:00hrs a signal came giving instructions not to move until further notice. On the following day the squadron's advance party at LG No 12 received orders to evacuate that landing ground and move 60 miles eastwards along the coast, to El Daba. On the same day (26 June) Squadron Leader Barclay was instructed to report to Headquarters, RAF Middle East, in Cairo.

As he set off along the coast road, heading for Alexandria and the turning for the military route to the Egyptian capital, George must have wondered what was in store for him. When he reported to HQ, the blow fell. He was to relinquish command of No 601 Squadron, which he had led out to the Middle East, and to become CO of a Hurricane squadron, No 238. His predecessor at 601, Squadron Leader J.D. Bisdee, who had taken the Spitfires out to Malta, was to resume his former command.

In his subsequent memoir of his son, the Reverend G.A. Barclay wrote:

We had most happy letters from him on board ship. In South Africa for a short time and then in Egypt he enjoyed life to the full and all the experiences of new

[1] *The full story of the squadron's Malta operations is told in* The Flying Sword: The Story of 601 Squadron, *by Tom Moulson (Macdonald, 1964).*

Pictures of No 238 Squadron Hurricane IIBs in the Western Desert are few and far between. This is a rare photograph of the squadron getting airborne.

lands. He was training new pilots[1] and getting the squadron ready for action.

Then suddenly the blow fell. He was transferred to the command of another squadron; a different type of aircraft and different tactics in action. We have heard of the love, one might say devotion, in which he was held by his old squadron and their despair in losing him. He wrote to us: "I was simply furious, but these fellows are grand." An officer who made enquiries for us discovered that someone was needed for a very difficult job. "George was considered exceptional" (the officer's own words) and he was chosen.

The Reverend F. de Jonge, chaplain of No 243 Wing, wrote later to George's father:

He was on this Wing for a short time when 601 Squadron came to us, and he joined our staff while

waiting for his new squadron. It was a very short time, but we very much appreciated having him; he was such a fine and charming young chap. It was just then that he had his big disappointment about 601, which he took in a grand way, as the good Christian he was.

I don't think I need tell you about his tremendous popularity with officers. What I know best is what the ordinary airmen of 601 Squadron thought and still think of him. Only this week some of the airmen at church parade were speaking to me of him and of their real admiration and affection for him. I think that is the biggest tribute a man can have in the Service.

No 601's medical officer, Flight Lieutenant W.B. Thorburn, confirmed the affection in which George was held by the squadron in a letter to Mrs Barclay of 13 October 1942:

I knew George all too short a time, but quite long enough to develop considerable affection and

---

[1] *Certainly not flying training, as 601 had no aircraft at that time.*

admiration for him. His judgement, foresight and breadth of outlook were remarkable in a boy of his age. These qualities combined [with] frankness, honesty and a cheerful temperament made him a delightful companion and a first-rate CO.

He took over the Squadron at a difficult time. We were working madly on our embarkation preparations, and time and tempers were short. He was in charge of the Squadron during those tiresome days of transit, on board ship and in this country when the men were bored, stale and feeling that they were getting nowhere. By his firm and just administration during this period he kept the Squadron a keen and efficient unit. When he left us it was as bitter a blow to us as it was to him. There is no doubt that he was very shamefully treated in this matter. There is no question who would have remained in command if the officers, NCOs and men of the Squadron could have had a say in the matter.

His new Squadron were at a low ebb when he took them over. In a remarkably short time, he pulled them up onto their feet again.

George was posted to command No 238 Squadron with effect from 2 July 1942; it had Hurricane IIBs and was then based at LG No 92, Amiriya, a few miles south of Alexandria.[1] The squadron ORB records that on that date, 'Acting Squadron Leader R.G.A, Barclay, DFC, arrived to take over command of the squadron. Vice Squadron Leader C.J. Mount, DFC.' No 238 had on the same day been transferred from No 243 to No 244 Wing, and on 4 July the latter's OC, Wing Commander R.C. Love, accompanied the AOC-in-C Middle East, Air Chief Marshal Sir Arthur Tedder, when he visited the squadron to talk to its pilots, afterwards inviting them to ask questions. Next day, Squadron Leader Mount left for HQ, RAF Middle East, and George formally took over command of No 238 Squadron.

Why George had been posted to command this squadron was explained in a letter sent to his father on 8 September 1942 from No 11 Group Headquarters at RAF Uxbridge by Group Captain Harry Broadhurst (later Air Chief Marshal Sir Harry Broadhurst, GCB, KBE,

DSO, DFC, AFC) who had been station commander at Hornchurch when George was commanding 'A' Flight of No 611 Squadron there:

I'm so sorry to be so long answering your letter, but to enquire into events overseas takes a long time. I have now elicited all the facts and cross-checked them and they appear to be as follows.

George was CO of No 601 Squadron and was doing exceedingly well with them. No 238 Hurricane Squadron had a disastrous battle with some German fighters and it was necessary to more or less reform them and bolster them up with good and experienced personnel.

George was regarded as exceptional and was of course an experienced Hurricane pilot. He was given the job, therefore, of reforming them and turning them into an efficient squadron.

An inadequate letter by his Wing Commander is nothing to worry about – he may not have known George for long or he may have been a rather inarticulate sort of chap. ...

I can assure you that we in No 11 Group had the greatest admiration for George and we were frightfully fed up when the regulations regarding pilots escaping from Occupied Territories prevented us from having him back. I'm sorry that he should have left Spitfires for Hurricanes, but you will see that there were very good reasons.

You are right to be proud of your son. He was a magnificent fellow and it was an absolute tonic to have him about the place.

Please accept my profound sympathy in your loss, and I hope this letter will relieve you of any anxiety you may have had over his change of squadron.

No word of praise could be too high and I wanted you to know how we all felt.

For Flight Lieutenant Cameron of No 134 Squadron, events had also taken an unexpected turn, as Sir Neil recalls:

When we reached the Western Desert, plans had been changed, as recorded here. George left 601, which

[1] *Mr Clive Mellersh, who as Intelligence Officer with No 611 Squadron at Hornchurch in 1941 came to know George well, has commented that the Hurricanes he was asked to fly in the Middle East were 'really clapped out', but that George 'would never ask anybody to do something he wouldn't do himself'.*

he had nurtured so well, and went to 238 Squadron as CO. I also had the same experience and joined 213 – another Hurricane squadron. RAF fighter pilot casualties were very high, with the Hurricane squadrons being operated at the wrong heights and against the latest mark of Messerschmitt 109 – the 109F. However, George Barclay soon settled down with 238 Squadron, and though we were not on the same desert landing ground (in the first half of July, No 213 were at LG154, south of where No 238 were at LG92, El Amiriya), I heard his voice often on the R/T and knew that his squadron was playing its full part in what was perhaps one of the most testing air battles of the last war.

At this time, the 8th Army was consolidating its position at El Alamein, only about 60 miles from Alexandria; a German–Italian offensive had failed on 2 July and on the 4th Field Marshal Rommel decided to go on to the defensive. The role of the Desert Air Force at this time was to harass the Axis positions, their communications and supply lines, giving the Allies a chance to build up their strength for a counter-offensive. The role of No 238 Squadron was to act as escort to other Hurricane squadrons, particularly No 274 with its 'Hurri-bombers' (carrying two 250lb bombs) and No 6 with its cannon-armed 'tank-buster' IIDs.

On 7 July George led his new squadron into action for the first time, on two patrols over the El Alamein area, both lasting an hour, one in the early morning, the other around midday; on neither was there any incident. Then on 9 July he led a sweep over the same area, lasting 55 minutes; on the 10th an hour's patrol in the morning and a 1hr 20min sortie in the afternoon, when No 238 gave top cover to No 274 Squadron.

Next day, when leading his squadron on an early morning patrol, George had to force-land on the way out at Burgh El Arab (about 20 miles from Amiriya) with engine trouble. He made his way back to base in time to lead another patrol over El Alamein that afternoon.

On this occasion No 238 tangled with the enemy and one Me109 was damaged.

It kept up this daily pressure, with patrols in the afternoon and evening of 12 July (George leading the later one) and two sweeps on the 13th (George leading the morning one, lasting 1hr 15min). Next morning there was contact with the enemy, no 238 Squadron aircraft being lost; and in the evening of that day (14 July) when George led a sweep around the area ten miles south of El Alamein there were no incidents.

He led two patrols on 15 July, one in the early morning and another, lasting an hour and a quarter, around midday. On the second, No 238 ran into trouble, or went looking for it. The compiler of the ORB recorded:

The squadron, led by Squadron Leader Barclay, DFC, patrolled El Alamein and met three Ju88s with fighter escort. The bombers were attacked and one Ju88 was damaged by Flight Lieutenant F. Olver[1] and Sergeant Cordwell, whilst Pilot Officer Nordon damaged a Macchi 202. In the engagement two of our own aircraft were hit. ...

On 16 July, the squadron showed itself even more pugnacious. In the early morning, with the Hurricanes rising up from the dusty square of El Amiriya and coming at the enemy with the sun behind them, 'a patrol over El Alamein resulted in meeting 15 Ju87s ['Stuka' dive bombers] with fighter escort west of El Alamein. The bombers jettisoned their bombs and made for their own territory, hotly pursued. Flight Lieutenant Olver probably destroyed one and damaged another Ju87, whilst Flight Lieutenant D.W. Beedham,[2] Pilot Officers Phelan, Hay, Matthews, Snider and Baker each damaged a Ju87.' This patrol had lasted an hour and 35 minutes.

Later that morning the squadron, led by George, were scrambled to provide top cover to No 1 (SAAF) Squadron over El Alamein. They had been airborne about half an hour when they 'saw four Me109s about 4,000ft below'. The ORB account continues: 'Squadron Leader Barclay led the squadron vertically on to them, himself destroying the last of the four. ... On the journey home Squadron Leader Barclay was attacked by a 109F. Pilot uninjured.'

A force-landing on 11 July, nearly shot down on the 16th; what was to happen next to George?

There was no incident when he led another patrol on the evening of the 16th, lasting an hour and 20 minutes. Then early the following day, No 238 gave top cover to No 274 Squadron, which was patrolling south of

[1] *Who had arrived at the squadron on the same day as George and was appointed 'B' Flight commander.*
[2] *Posted to the squadron on 11 July and appointed 'A' Flight commander.*

Much of Jagdgeschwader 27's (JG27) time in the desert was spent in escorting Stukas. This is a Messerschmitt Bf109E-7 of JG27 escorting a Stuka of 4./StG2 over the desert in May 1942. (*TopFoto*)

George's nemesis. In July 1942, 23-year-old Leutnant Werner Schroer was *Staffelkapitän* of *8./JG27* and in that month he recorded 16 victories in combat over the desert. Schroer survived the war with 114 victories, 61 of which were claimed in North Africa. He died in 1985 aged 67.

Schroer was flying a Bf109F when he shot George down. The Bf109F had a superior performance to the Hurricane which, when combined with the fact that George had only recently returned to operations after a long break, meant that the odds were unfairly loaded against him in combat. This is Schroer's earlier aircraft, a Bf109E-7/Trop, 'Black 8'.

El Alamein, returning to base after 1hr 35min with no incidents to report. George wasn't leading, but it was a different matter when he was, early that afternoon; for 'with 80 Squadron as top cover the squadron patrolled the El Alamein area, sighting 30+ Ju87s with strong fighter escort. The fighters prevented 'A' Flight from attacking but 'B' Flight pursued the bombers and Squadron Leader Barclay and Pilot Officer Gilbert each destroyed a Ju87,

Pilot Officer Oram probably destroyed a Ju87. Sergeant Pilot Robertson damaged a Ju87 and Pilot Officer Waddell damaged an Me109F. Two of our aircraft were damaged.'

On the evening of that day, 17 July 1942, No 238 Squadron led by Squadron Leader Barclay took off from Amiriya at 18:40hrs to patrol the El Alamein area, acting as top cover for No 274 Squadron. The ORB recorded:

At about 19:15hrs 12 enemy aircraft were seen behind flying south. As the squadron turned about they were attacked from all directions and were obliged to adopt defensive tactics. Twelve Ju87s were seen, but the squadron was unable to attack them. ... Squadron Leader Barclay, DFC, failed to return from this operation.[1]

---

[1] *Mr Norman L.R. Franks, who has kept exhaustive records of RAF fighter pilots, states that on 17 July 1942 George 'destroyed a Stuka and later in the day when attacking more Stukas escorted by 109s was shot down and killed. He was claimed by Leutnant Werner Schroer of 111/JG27... one of the most successful German fighter aces in North Africa at that time.' The incident is described in* Fighters over the Desert, *by Christopher Shores and Hans Ring (Neville Spearman Ltd, 1969). Schroer was flying a Me109F, which was much superior in performance to the Hurricane IIB. A similar action only a few weeks earlier when the German desert fighter ace Hans Joachim Marseille 'picked off' his opponents one by one from above is described in Alfred Price's* World War II Fighter Conflict *(Macdonald & Jane's, London, 1976).*

At about the same time that evening, No 213 Squadron, including Flight Lieutenant Cameron, were on their third offensive sweep of the day, and Sir Neil Cameron now recalls:

On 17 July I was airborne with 213 Squadron on a scramble to sweep the south of the El Alamein battlefield and towards the Qattara Depression, when I recognised on the R/T the call-sign of 238 Squadron and knew that they were in action. I picked up George's voice but then everything got very confused, as it usually did in a fighter-to-fighter action of this type. When we landed back we heard that George was missing and a few hours later it was confirmed that he had been killed.

Many of us in my squadron who had come out from Liverpool through Durban to the Western Desert with him had got to know him well. We were used to casualties by then, but a real sense of sadness was with us as we thought of the talent, spirit and potential of George Barclay coming to an end in the sand of El Alamein when so much seemed possible. The pipe, the scarf, the youthful look, the optimistic approach – the spirit and leadership needed to raise morale when things got difficult.

I have often thought about George and wondered what might have become of him if things had been different. At Stowe, his old school, his favourite hymn (I discovered later), set to the glorious melody of *Finlandia* by Sibelius, contained these lines:
'Be still my soul the Lord is on thy side
To guide the future as he has the past.'

George Barclay's future ended at El Alamein on that evening of 17 July 1942 in attacking the King's enemies, leaving many of us who survived with the memory and example of a great leader.

Later a South African chaplain, the Reverend R.D. Lewis, wrote in a letter to George's father:

It happened that on July 17th at about 6.45pm I witnessed an air battle in which a plane was brought down, landing close to me. I will not go into details, but it was fairly obvious that the pilot of this plane was killed before it came to earth. I was able to forward the pilot's wallet and shoulder titles and decoration to HQ.

The Post Office telegram informing the Barclays that their son George had 'lost his life as the result of air operations'. George's father had organised for the Post Master to telephone him before sending such a telegram to the house.

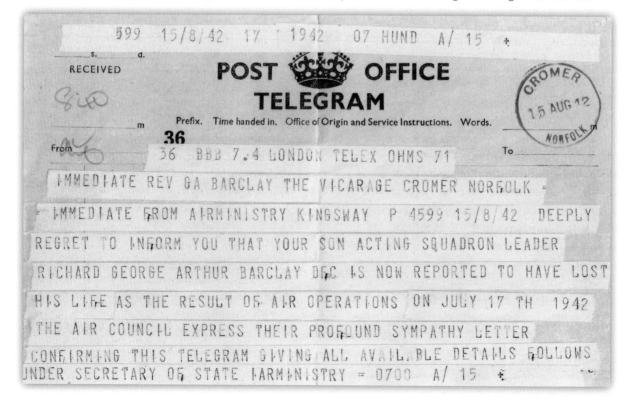

On 22 August 1942 Group Captain John Grandy, who had commanded No 249 Squadron in the Battle of Britain and was now station commander at RAF Duxford, sent the following tribute to *The Times* to be published under the heading 'A Friend Writes':

Acting Squadron Leader R.G.A. Barclay, DFC, RAFVR, was killed on the 17 July 1942 in the Libyan Desert when leading his fighter squadron into action.

George Barclay was the ideal fighter pilot. Fearless, and possessing many original and constructive ideas, his great interest was air fighting, and his one object was to get at the enemy and destroy him.

In two years, he rose from being a young officer in a fighter squadron at home to become a squadron commander in Libya, and this not without setbacks. He was shot down and wounded during the Battle of Britain, and later during his second tour of duty, shot down again over enemy-occupied territory. By his cool courage and aided by his great eagerness to return to continue to fight the enemy, he evaded capture and eventually after overcoming many hazards, succeeded in gaining friendly territory.

After a short rest, undaunted, he volunteered for further active service, and was eventually posted to command a Fighter Squadron in the Middle East.

By his death in action, the country has lost a most gallant Englishman, the Royal Air Force a fearless pilot and invaluable young officer, and those who knew him, an inspiring friend of great charm, delightful manner and infectious personality.

One of the pilots on No 238 Squadron, Pilot Officer W.B. Hay, who had been at Stowe School in the same house as George, wrote to one of his former masters, Mr Humphrey Playford, on 18 October 1942:

Not so very long ago we were given a new CO. Imagine my pleasure and surprise at finding it was none other than George Barclay. He was only with us two weeks before he was missing from an operation. Recently word has come through that his grave has been found. During the two weeks he was with us his leadership was of the highest quality both on the ground and in the air. He shot down

two enemy aircraft in that short time. One of my friends said that although he didn't believe in hero worship he would follow him anywhere because he felt he was giving everything he'd got. Nearly everyone in the ground crews I have talked to has mentioned him at one time or another with real devotion. In short, he made the most tremendous impression on everyone in the squadron which was all the more incredible considering the short period he was with 238. It was a real honour to have been in the same squadron and I was particularly proud in view of the fact that he was not only a Stoic but also a member of Bruce. No word of praise could be too high and I wanted you to know how we all felt.

On 28 October the Senior Chaplain at 1st South African Division Headquarters in Cairo, Major Len Kennedy, who had heard from George Barclay's father, wrote in reply:

Have just received your card of 29 September re your late son, Squadron Leader R.G.A. Barclay. I happen to be senior chaplain attached to Division HQ. I know the spot well where your son crashed, death being instantaneous. I saw the plane coming down; he was then buried where he crashed, but since has been reburied in the main military cemetery which, alas, has greatly increased in size within the last few days owing to this raging battle at present going on. He is in the cemetery now, with hundreds of his gallant comrades. The cemetery, which is situated about a mile west of El Alamein railway station, is very nicely laid out, and looked after by the Graves Registration Unit. Padre Lewis, C of E, who was then attached to the Field Ambulance, performed the ceremony. I understand that he has written to you himself, as regards his personal belongings. Padre Lewis would likely have told you of them. They will be forwarded to you in due course. Whether his signet ring was discovered I cannot say, but owing to the nature of his death, in a crash, it is possible that the ring may not have been found.

I deeply sympathise with you in your tragic loss, which you share with thousands more, including myself who have lost a brilliant nephew in the Far East. "Except a corn of wheat fall into the ground and die, it abideth alone, but if it die, it bringeth

El Alamein War Cemetery today with the Cross of Sacrifice prominent in the background. The wooden grave markers have long since been replaced with the familiar Commonwealth War Graves Commission carved headstones.

forth must fruit; and let us hope, that those who have died, have not done so in vain, that the fruit of their gallant devotion to duty in trying to save mankind, having scorned to save themselves, may bring forth that which this sorrowful world languisheth for – a peace, righteous and lasting."

May God's peace sustain you in your great sorrow; perhaps some day you will get a photograph of the cemetery where your brave boy rests.

It fell to Sandy Barclay-Russell, George Barclay's godfather, in whom he had confided in 1938 about his decision to join Cambridge University Air Squadron, to be the first member of the family to visit his grave at El Alamein and to pay a last affectionate and moving farewell to him there. He wrote to Cromer Vicarage on 7 November 1942:

Yesterday I went to see George's grave. I had been trying to arrange it for some time, but the difficulties are considerable. The Battlefield and Cemetery are closed now, except for very special reasons. However, I got the necessary permit, under the circumstances.

To get the personal side over to begin with, by way of explanation. The young man who I arranged it through Jersey, who I had previously known in Alex, could only let me go on Monday, November 6th. At the last moment I could not go in his car but I hoped for a seat in a truck; this I did not get. The consequent 180 miles of fierce bumping on the steel wheel box of a 15cwt truck did not matter personally, but it made observation or any coherent thought difficult. The whole thing, too, had unfortunately to fit in with Jersey's plans, which again did not lend themselves to either the time at the Cemetery, for which I had hoped, or for getting a really coherent picture to send home.

We started at 7:30am in a UDF [Union Defence Force] truck, with a very pleasant UDF Major, and about eight South African ORs with me in the back. It was raining like a tremendous April shower in England, only more persistent and heavier rain. As usual it took ages getting out of Alex on the Western Desert side, through those long miles of dockland and the spit of land which is hemmed in by the sea and lagoon on either side. The harbour looked grand, and with the great storm clouds behind Cruisers and the great ships of all kinds in rich colour, was most imposing. Alex has been a proud place all through this war, and unlike most of the Middle East remains so now. I last went out along this road nearly three years ago to see the camouflage defences at El Alamein and beyond.[1] There seemed little chance of their being used then and my host said "One thing I hope to God is that we never have to fight on this line, it's more or less a sham; anything could go through it like blotting paper."

The road is very different now. As George would have known it, it was like all the army roads in the desert, one mass of packed transport, a mixture of glare, heat, sweat, and choking dust, of battered but desert-worthy trucks with their sand-mats and attached equipment in light desert camouflage.[2] Now the road was our own.

The Western Desert near the sea is not of course desert in the proper sense of the word, used here, as the hinterland is, or the Sinai, Transjordan, or Iraqi deserts. It has life and charm, and a salting everywhere – the clumps being in places almost touching – of desert tussocks – not much camel thorn, mostly tough leafed bosses of grey-green growth, from six inches high upwards, and it can be cultivated. Here and there one passes delightful untidy patches of green, with the still more, almost fantastic, untidiness and irregularity of grovelets of date palms. The ramshackle squalor of native houses (not tents) and broken-down ruins. There is always the feeling of decay. Today, however, with the rain, everything was fresh and the colours for a change beautifully soft, bright and gay.

About thirty miles out there is the famous turning to Burgh El Arab,[3] and then one begins to come to the old assembly areas with the dotted remains of old camps and the semblance of tracks, which led off to them. For some way one passes down a broad wadi with the hard stone ridge rising a hundred or more feet to one's left, and the great rolling sand dune cast up by the sea on the right, curving over like a white wave against the browner fawn-yellow of Africa. Gradually, however, one passes up onto the stony ridge, to see the sea half a mile away or so. By sunlight, it is an incredible colour, shallow over white sand; it has a pale, fierce greeny tinge of prussian blue inshore. Today, it is a very rich blue with mauve and yellow clouds hanging over it. Ahead stretch the irregular low ridges of rolling country. One cannot see inland much, but ahead, with the rains, are a series of narrow lagoons between the sea shore and the ridge. One switchbacks, crashes and bumps, in a monotony of jolts up and down. There is a broad valley which opens up inland, a long, bow-shape, with ourselves going round the circumference. In the valley, the tufts of vegetation increase to great mounds, some of them very green, some dark, some grey. Good feeding for cattle.

And then, in the distance, one sees the shape so well known to everyone out here for the last five years. The beginning of the Desert Campaign area. The two long sheds and the two spindly water towers of El Alamein station on the curving sea-ward side of the low valley. A mile to the west of it the southern ridge descends to meet the lower hog's back to the north, and together they form a very undulating moor, which rises slowly to a point about seven miles beyond, near the sea, with its famous Mosque, which was about 300 yards within our Forward HQ between the two battles, July to October.

[1] In fact, these defences were completed in time and General Auchinleck stopped Rommel there, as he had intended to do.

[2] Sandy Barclay-Russell, a professional artist, was employed by the Army as a camouflage specialist.

[3] Where George had force-landed with engine trouble on 11 July.

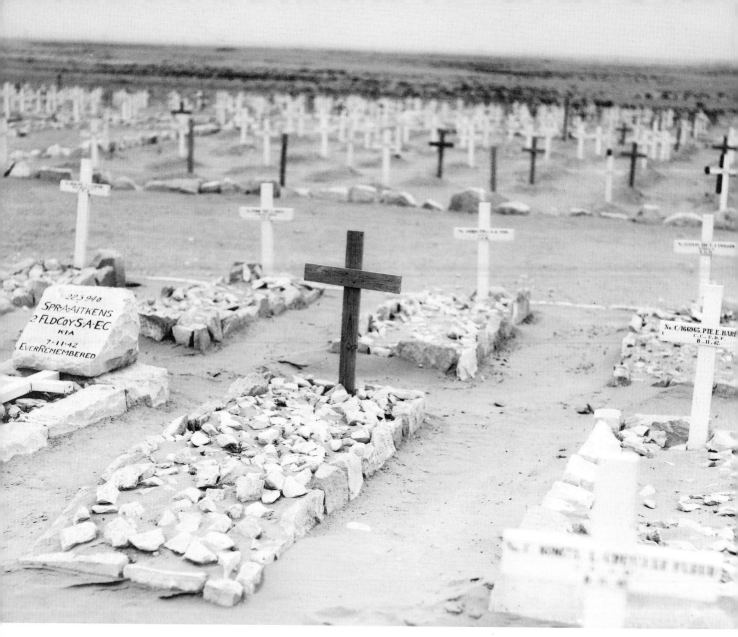

Today, the land with its scant vegetation is brown and grey, with patches of creamy yellow and a richer brown, where the clouds cross the valley and under the rocks. It would doubtless all seem very bare to anyone out from England, seeing it for the first time, but it has a rich bareness and character. About half a mile north-west of the station, as the low northern ridge curves towards the juncture, is the main cemetery. About fifty yards below the road and the top of the ridge. A low wall has already been built on the northern side, and the enclosure is about 200 yards square, falling quite steeply to the south, and the south-east corner pointing towards the station.

Here lie 7,000 of the Desert Army, together with "Monty's Boys", a wonderful galaxy of those who held

George's original grave marker at El Alamein – as described by his Godfather Sandy Barclay-Russell – with its cross marked 'Unknown Airman' (which is now in Cromer Church); and later [opposite] replaced by a new cross and with his identity finally established.

the Empire for two and a half years, "with resources" – as Hitler has said – "which other people would consider entirely inadequate". This little plot, and the others along the desert road, in their complete simplicity, stand with their proud lines – those who knew every phase of triumph and disaster, but never of defeat, not sad or even solemn, quiet and at rest in the calm peaceful sweep of the down, within sound of the sea, near to the final battlefield. There can be no richer field or finer place to lie within the Empire. No braver,

The order of service for George's Service of Remembrance at Cromer Church on 23 August 1942.

—A—

SERVICE OF REMEMBRANCE

IN

CROMER CHURCH

SUNDAY, AUGUST 23rd, 1942

*Verse of Scripture in the Times
for July 17th 1942.*

" He that overcometh, the same shall
be clothed in white raiment I
will confess his name before my
Father, and before his angels."

Rev. iii. 5.

or more battle-proved company – Indian, Australian, New Zealand, South African, Scottish, but mostly English. They stood until at last the reinforcements came, and the final battle was won, just to the west of them.

At the Cemetery one stands about 50 feet below the steepish brow of the ridge, and the brown and grey tufted land falls gently down to the station, and then a mile beyond it to the low encircling ridge. Nearby are a few tents of the Graves Commission, and that is all.

George's grave is a little to the east and to the north or upper side of the centre. There are two roads which cross at the centre, and his grave is three rows up from the centre and about tenth in that row from the road running north and south. It was numbered wrongly, so at first I could not find it, but the very charming captain in charge found that it was one of quite a number still with the original burial cross. Marked rather finely, I thought, "Unknown Airman", almost unfindable now; however, I found the original name practically disappeared in pencil just above the crosspiece. The new white inscribed cross had just come in a new consignment. The OC got it for me and I was able to plant it myself. I had brought some simple marigolds and small single chrysanthemums, which I preferred to the hot-house flowers of Alex, and which smelt beautifully fresh and sweet. These I put in the damp earth on the grave. They were the only flowers in the Cemetery that day, and as water is not yet laid on, I do not think the very few people who stop there bring them as yet.

I got two photos taken, but these will have to wait a little to be developed, etc. I brought the original cross, with which George was buried in the desert, with me and I will bring it home to you when I come. It is a simple deal battle cross, bleached by the desert.

Unfortunately, I had no option but to leave, after saying a prayer, and making a fleeting sketch of the view; but the sun came out while we were there, and I could not help feeling how proud and fitting it was that George, who had always been in the forefront of the fiercest battles, the one which saved England and the one which saved the Empire, should march on the El Alamein road among those others who held

"the last ditch", as he had done, to the end. I had to go, as the trucks were going on to the battle-field, and would probably not come back the same way. We were already late, because of the rain, etc.

The final scheme for this Cemetery is to have a low cloister built along the road for the whole length of the North side, and then a series of flights of steps down to the graves. It certainly will become a place of pilgrimage from all over the world, but I was glad to see it in its present simplicity, just part of the calm, fresh down, with the incredibly rich sky above, blue and mauve storm clouds, with ochre and white ones above, and between them all the blue of the sky, green-blue on the horizon, milk-blue and wind swept further up, and almost violet overhead, like some rich symphony of music.

With me were about a dozen men who had fought through the desert campaign and the second battle of El Alamein, come to find their friends here – they were a friendly lot. It was a very great privilege to be able to visit George's grave in this way and to fulfil a hope that I had had for so long. To find the care and skill that makes all the War Cemeteries I have seen in the ME things of such dignity and standing with such a simple eloquent pride. I felt that there was nothing else that I could do, or which needed to be done. George is not there we know, and his remains rest in good company in that field which is indeed 'for ever England', while overhead his aeroplanes pass backwards and forwards from England and Italy and salute the battlefield as they pass. The main convoys are gone, but still a lot of transport goes that way along the road just above.

In January 1943 George Barclay received a posthumous salute from England, when he was mentioned in Despatches in the New Year Honours.

CHAPTER SEVEN

My Brother George –
Stories of the Resistance

Richard Barclay

George aged about 12.

I have so much to tell about my brother, George, that I hardly know where to begin. What follows are extracts from recollections written in recent years that were initially intended for my family. There is no doubt that George was an unusually charismatic and charming person and that I hero-worshipped him. He was seven years older than me, which made any assessment of him by me inadequate. After his death this is what some of his peers had to say of him. Marshal of the Royal Air Force Sir John Grandy, who was George's CO on No 249 Squadron said:

Barclay rapidly became one of the most balanced and sensible, yet dashing, highly courageous and skilful fighter pilots … modest in the extreme, invariably courteous, brimming with humour … his infectious personality and flair for leadership would undoubtedly have moulded him to become one of our most distinguished fighting commanders. It was a great privilege to have known him. His family are rightly very proud of him.

In a letter to a former schoolmaster at Stowe School, fellow fighter pilot and Old Stoic W.B. Hay wrote: 'One of my friends in 238 Squadron said that although he didn't believe in hero worship he would follow George anywhere because he felt George was giving everything he'd got. Nearly everyone in the ground crews I have talked to has mentioned him at one time or another with real devotion. In short he made the most tremendous impression on everyone on the Squadron. ...'

The chaplain of his unit had this to say of George:

What I know best is what the ordinary airmen of 601 Squadron thought and still think of him. Only this week some of the airmen at church parade were speaking to me of him and of their real admiration and affection for him. I think that is the biggest tribute a man can have in the Service.

These are wonderful appreciations of George's outstanding qualities from fellow Servicemen, but perhaps I should add one more from a rather different source. After the First World War A.J. Evans wrote a famous bestseller about outstanding escapes, *Escapers All*, which I first heard at Sunday evening readings by my prep school headmaster. In the Second World War, Evans was used by MI9 to interview current escapers. Afterwards he wrote another book, *Escapes and Liberation 1940–1945*, in which he describes George's actions after crashing in German-occupied France. He concludes with: 'I know of no better example than this of spontaneous skill on the part of an evader. Barclay was an outstandingly good escaper; cautious, bold and intelligent.'

Of course the most interesting sources of George's story are his own diaries of the Battle of Britain and his escape through German-occupied France. My remarks will be additional to George's own account!

What can I add as George's youngest brother? Well, I do have many memories of someone I hugely admired, and vivid memories of the extraordinary aftermath of George's escape, which emerged many years after the war.

George's home leaves during the Battle of Britain

It must have been pretty astonishing to be fighting for your life over Kent one day and on the next be at home with the family, going to church if it was Sunday, or shooting pheasants on neighbours' land. That was in August and September 1940, but before that, George had to endure the frustrations of completing his training. When war broke out on 3 September 1939, he received a telegram to report at once to the RAF at Cambridge and our elder brother, Charles, offered to drive him there. Nannie and I were given a ride on the back seat, which was quite an adventure for us! In fact almost a real one, as a tyre burst when we were travelling fast along a high embankment, and it was only Charlie's skill as a driver that kept the car on the road as it careered from one side to the other and back again.

I had the second half of that year at home as my parents were worried about my health, so I was able to observe, and to some extent share, their worries and joys over an occasional telephone call or letter. But the best for me was on one weekend leave George had to share a room with me, as all the family had come home to be with him. In the morning he would follow his habit of 'standing to' at dawn, but staying in bed he would describe to me his aerial adventures with all the enthusiasm and excitement that he hid from the others. It was totally thrilling for me and added to my great admiration of George as a true hero and warrior.

Then on 29 November 1940 there was a telephone call from his Commanding Officer to say George was wounded and in hospital at Pembury in Kent. He had a bad wound in his calf but should fully recover. As he was still in hospital for his 21st birthday on 7 December, my Mother and I went down to visit him. While she was out of the room George told me of the escape from his burning aircraft and free drop of 15,000 feet before he opened his parachute. Having left his cockpit with some difficulty and nearly hitting the still spinning propeller, he found himself falling through space on his back with his feet higher than his head. There was no feeling of falling apart from the wind rushing by. His boots had been sucked off and appeared to be falling upwards from him. His plane, trailing black smoke, was spinning down, but less quickly than him.

He thought of having seen the 'birdman' at flying displays who connected his arms and legs with fabric like a flying squirrel and seemed able to change the direction of his fall and even loop-the-loop. So George put out an arm and found this turned him face down, but as he could not see anything in the wind he kept his arm out and returned to his original position. He then drew up his legs and found himself rolling head over heels – interesting but

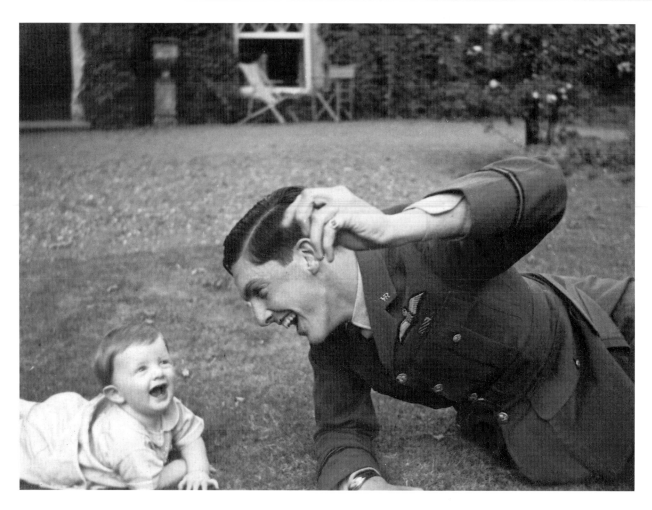

George with his Godson, Leo, in the summer of 1940.

not very comfortable. Realising he was getting close to the ground he pulled his ripcord, remembering not to drop it to avoid any accusation of being windy![1] His parachute obediently streamed up between his legs and, with a severe jerk, turned him heels over head.

So there he was, serenely floating and looking about him. Suddenly his boots went shooting past him and then his Hurricane streaming flame and smoke – fortunately not too close. Down it went to explode on the ground. Below him he saw a Kentish orchard and began to pull on his 'chute shrouds to try to avoid the trees. His leg began to pain him and he realised he was wounded – how bad was it? Suddenly – bang – he was on the ground, winded and shocked. Moments later

[1] *George states in his diary entry for 29 November on page 86: 'The pilot who drops his ripcord is said to have been 'windy' and it would probably take a long time to live down!'*

two Land Girls ran up and began to kiss him, but his response was unromantic – he only asked them to get him to hospital quickly. The farmer himself soon arrived with his car and took him off to Pembury Hospital. In due course both of his boots were found and returned to him. Curiously, our Aunt Christina Barclay, who had helped meet George's school fees, had seen a pilot descending by parachute that very day, though we cannot be sure it was George she saw!

To my embarrassment, as I had never seen a grown-up naked, George proudly showed me his bottom, spattered with scratches and little black spots left by particles from the exploding cannon shell. As my mother had not reappeared I went in search of her, and found her in a scullery washing the blood out of George's tattered uniform, weeping as she did so.

Escape from France

George had four months in a series of hospitals and nursing homes before returning to North Weald and

A profile drawing of George in 1940 made by Eric Kennington,
an Official War Artist. Kennington produced some of the finest
portraits of RAF pilots and aircrew in the Second World War.
(*Imperial War Museum*)

249 Squadron. It is worth recording that the major wound in his right calf caused by the head of a cannon shell (we still have it, on view with his medals at Tangmere Museum) could have been worse but for two things. According to his surgeons the shell head would have wrecked his ankle and foot had his Achilles tendon not acted like elastic and absorbed its force. The method of curing his large open wound was even more amazing, and had been discovered during the Spanish Civil War – the whole leg was encased in a plaster cast and the wound was allowed to rot out. It smelt horrible and itched terribly, but when the plaster came off the wound had healed beautifully clean.

The family first heard that he was flying again through a telegram asking them to send his flying helmet and gloves. His boots and Irvin flying suit (the last word in leather and fur zip-up jacket and trousers) remained at home, and after the war they were worn by me when I rode a motorbike. I passed them on to our nephew, David, and when he was killed in a car crash no one thought to reclaim them.[1] Within weeks, George was posted to be an instructor at an Operational Training Unit at Debden commanded by his old CO John Grandy. John and his charming wife, Cecile, and their dog, Boys, were to become great friends of our family, and I still use a hairbrush that they gave me for my 21st birthday seven years later.

Training green fighter pilots was not George's idea of fun and he itched to return to a squadron on active service. He was delighted in August to be posted to one of the famous Auxiliary Air Force Squadrons, No 611 at Hornchurch, East London. He was promoted to Flight Lieutenant and would command one of the Squadron's two flights. The Station was commanded by the famously aggressive, yet effective, Group Captain Victor Beamish. By 18 August George was on his first 'sweep' over France escorting bombers in an effort to draw up the enemy fighters. They refused to commit numbers to the fight and sent up only small units of four fighters, Messerschmitt 109s.

George made many new friends in the Hornchurch Wing. One that I met was another flight commander, Duncan Smith, whom he brought home to Cromer one weekend. I remember him as someone who, unusually for our visitors, seemed somewhat uneasy. Perhaps it was the lack of heavy drinking in our house, unlike the squadron

messes he was used to. Certainly George whisked him off to a session in the pub – something totally unheard of to the rest of the household. Wilfred Duncan Smith (later Group Captain, DSO, DFC) became the father of Iain, the future leader of the Conservative party.[2]

George was flying almost every day on sweeps, but on 20 September it was his turn to be 'picked off'. Four 109s were hovering over the British armada and George was keeping an eye on them. Suddenly, they began to dive into an attack directly at George. He called out a warning on his radio, but getting no acknowledgement concluded it was not working. To give an immediate lead he broke formation and turned abruptly to meet the 109s head-on, firing as he went. The enemy fired too and George heard 'ping, ping', the sound of two machine-gun bullets hitting his plane. Normally this would not be a matter of concern, but to his dismay his engine lost most of its power and as he fell behind his squadron, the 109s set about him. Every time he was attacked he used all his skill and experience in flying manoeuvres to throw off the enemy and was not hit again. But each manoeuvre cost more height and there was no chance of his gliding back to England. Now, instead of returning to lunch in his mess, he was obliged to force-land in a large field inland from Calais.

It is amazing to record that no one in the British formation saw him go. As far as they were concerned he just vanished into thin air. That evening our parents received a telephone call from George's CO, Squadron Leader E.A. Thomas, then a telegram, 'Deeply regret to inform you that your son Flight Lt R.G.A. Barclay DFC has been reported missing this evening' [see telegram on page 100]. But there was nothing they could say except that he and all the Squadron had already become very fond of George and hoped he landed unhurt. He would probably become a prisoner of war, or just possibly evade capture. Our elder brother, Charlie, a Lieutenant in the Royal Norfolks, arranged to go to Hornchurch to collect George's car and personal possessions. While there he was made very welcome, but once again there was no evidence of what had really happened.

These events occured while I was at school in Cornwall and I don't remember how I was informed

---

[1] *Miraculously, since I wrote this I have recovered the suit.*

[2] *Subsequently I learnt that Smithy was a Roman Catholic and lived in India, so no wonder he found it strange to be in a C of E vicarage.*

that George was missing. Perhaps my parents thought it better not to say anything at the time as I was so cut off from them. By the time the term was ended they had heard that he had 'evaded capture' and reached Spain. Then on 11 December there was another telegram; 'information just received states your son … has reached England today'.

George spent two days being debriefed in London, meeting everyone from the Air Minister downwards, and then returned to Hornchurch where Broadhurst told me many years later there was a celebration by the entire Wing that beat all other celebrations! The following day George came home to the assembled family and, typically, when in the train he changed out of uniform into his French clothes and proceeded to ring the front doorbell looking like a French onion seller! He was at home for Christmas but under strict orders from the medics to eat very lightly after three months of near starvation. In the course of one meal I had a second helping, which was on our Mother's over-generous scale in spite of wartime rationing, whereupon one of my waistcoat buttons burst off and went spinning across the table. This caused George to tease me then express his disappointment that he could not do the meal justice.

Four months later, George was promoted Squadron Leader in command of 601 (County of London) Squadron, the most prestigious of the Auxiliaries. He was to take it out to the Middle East as a fully equipped mobile squadron transported by sea around the Cape of Good Hope. Soon after arrival in Egypt, a series of catastrophic events occurred. First, there were no aircraft for them. They were sent to Alexandria. In fear that Rommel would be successful in his attack, their job was to investigate all the equipment stored there and select what should be given priority to be saved. The story that I heard was that they found sealed crates of Hurricane aircrafts, which they opened and rebuilt to enable them to become an effective fighter squadron again. Curiously enough, I was reading recently of someone on convoys through the Mediterranean to rearm Malta and Egypt, and his ship had delivered crated Hurricanes to Alexandria – so that seems to click.

Next, in from an intense spell of operations on Malta came the aircraft and pilots of the original 601 Squadron with a commanding officer much senior to George, who naturally expected to take over. George was called to Cairo and ordered to take command of another squadron, No 238, which had been much shot up and suffered from low morale. What a blow to leave his devoted team in 601 and to take over a unit in disarray! Needless to say George rose to the occasion and soon restored morale and made his new command effective. Their job was to fly at relatively low altitudes to protect the Army on the ground from enemy attack, and our own hurri-bombers (fighters equipped to strafe the enemy army) from enemy fighters. Between 7 and 17 July they broke up several German air attacks and George himself destroyed three enemy aircraft. On the last day, as they were about to attack more dive bombers, a German ace who had been prowling at high altitude hurled himself at the leader of the squadron – George – and killed him in one burst of fire. The German continued his steep dive and disappeared before anyone could react. George's aircraft diving vertically to the ground was observed by an army padre who wrote to our parents [see letter on page 148].

When I came home for my summer holidays, to my surprise my sister Ann, not my Mother, met me at the railway station. In the taxi Ann said, 'Mum is very upset. We have just heard that George is on his escapes again.' I realised he must be 'missing in action' and obviously hoped for a repeat of his previous escape. A few days later I joined my parents in their bedroom for early morning tea and prayers when the phone rang and Father answered it. He listened briefly and then said in a voice choking with emotion, 'Yes, send it up please.' The Post Office manager had rung to say they had received a telegram reporting George's death in action.

Madame Deram, Ian Garrow and Harold 'Paul' Cole

A number of happenings several years after the war reveal even more extraordinary events than George's great escape.

Soon after the liberation of France in the late summer of 1944, short notes began to arrive addressed to George from surviving Escape Line helpers, saying in effect, 'Are you alive, George? We would love to see you!' My Mother replied immediately and sent little presents each year in appreciation of what we knew the helpers had done for George at the risk of their own lives. It must have been late 1949 or early 1950 when a letter arrived from Mme Deram saying she wanted to get in touch with a Colonel Garrow, and could we help? We knew from George's diary that Mme Deram had hidden him for some days and the

Underground used the café she ran for passing on 'parcels'. The parcels were escapers who would be left at the café by one escort and picked up by another, thus ensuring neither escort saw the other – a matter of security.

My Mother immediately invited Mme Deram to come and stay at Langley Rectory. Rather to our astonishment, she arrived smartly dressed and bearing what we considered expensive presents: a bottle of Armagnac (we weren't quite sure what that was!) for my Father and an extraordinary stone mini-tombstone-like plaque bearing an engraved photo of George with suitable writing.

Mme Deram explained that soon after George went 'down the line' she was arrested and sent to a concentration camp. She clearly was of tough stock and had survived, but on return, instead of being treated as a returning hero she had been labelled a collaborator. As most of the French people of the Escape Line had been killed, no one could vouch for her. However, she believed that Colonel Ian Garrow would be able to restore her reputation and indeed gain for her a highly valued British 'thank you letter' and the consequent French awards and recognitions.

The question was how to find Ian Garrow. Mme Deram believed he had escaped from the 51st Highland Division that had been cut off and captured in France in 1940. I was given the task of following this up, so found out that his regiment was the Seaforth Highlanders and rang them up. I asked to speak to Colonel Garrow and was told he was on leave. I asked if I could have his telephone number and was told, 'no'. So I said, 'I am Sub-Lieutenant Richard Barclay and Colonel Garrow helped my brother escape from France in 1941. I really need to speak to the Colonel.' This did the trick and I was able to ring a number in Scotland. A military voice with a strong Scottish accent answered and in response to my appeal explained that he was Ian's father, and gave me Ian's address in London to which he had now returned. Now for it – I rang up, got Ian and said that he had helped my brother George escape so my Mother and I would like to meet him. He replied, 'I don't want to have anything to do with all that', and put the phone down.

What to do? Next morning I got up an hour earlier than usual and went to Ian's address in Mayfair. At his

Opposite: The Café au Calice, where 'parcels' were exchanged between helpers along the Line.

flat I rang the bell (it was about 8am) and someone who looked like a 'daily' answered. I said, 'Colonel Garrow is expecting me', and she let me in. A few minutes later Ian appeared with a towel round his middle looking furious. 'What the hell is all this?' I replied, 'My Mother so wants to meet you and has hung a brace of partridges, would you come to dinner tomorrow night?' He paused for a long time and then said, 'Well, I do love partridge', and agreed to come.

I passed on the good news and Mum agreed that if I would get all the ingredients she would come up in the afternoon and do the cooking. I left early for work next day leaving everything ready. Returning home about 6:30pm, I was horrified to find no Mother. I rang Father and he said she had left as planned and he was at a loss as to what had become of her. Garrow was due in half an hour! Rather hopelessly I began to prepare the vegetables until the doorbell went. There he was and I let him in. Rather embarrassed, I explained my predicament, and that I could not cook. Ian was quite unfazed and remarked that he loved cooking, so why shouldn't we go to the kitchen. (It was a very primitive one by modern standards.) He promptly took off his jacket and put on an apron. My part was to fill his glass at frequent intervals, I forget what with – I had laid on a good choice and I think he drank whisky. As he cooked, he talked. After asking about George's history he began to tell of the extraordinary events which surrounded their meeting, all unknown to George.

George and about 10 others had been smuggled through the frontier between the Occupied Territories and Unoccupied or Vichy France by Cole. Then on to Marseilles where they met the famous Pat O'Leary and Ian Garrow in a magnificent flat owned by Louis Nouveau. Pat O'Leary was a doctor of the Belgian Army who had been doing naval intelligence work for the British and joined forces with Ian to run the Escape Line. He would be awarded the George Cross for his work.

They knew of the good work Cole had done, but had been concerned at the non-delivery of funds entrusted to him for the Line's agents in the north. As soon as the escapers had been settled from the rigours of their trip – their feet sore from badly fitting shoes – Ian and Pat began to question Cole. It quickly became evident to them that Cole had spent the funds in high living and they became ever more furious. Cole suddenly collapsed

Richard Barclay and Madame Deram, who ran the Café au Calice and who sheltered George in her home between 24 and 26 September 1941. Mme Deram was the lover of Paul Cole. This photograph was taken in 1989.

on the floor weeping and promising to repay everything. As he grovelled and gripped their feet he besought them not to kill him – he knew full well that was the only penalty for untrustworthiness in the Underground.

Over his body, Ian was telling Pat that they must deal with Cole at once, and Pat was saying that they had to consider Cole's good work in the north. Rather than argue over the weeping wretch, they locked Cole in the lavatory. This had a tiny window looking into a wide ventilation shaft serving the flats around it. Quite quickly they decided he must be finished off and went to fetch

him. To their astonishment they found he had somehow squeezed himself through the window and was perched on the tiny window sill outside. As they opened the door, Cole jumped – right across the void – and caught hold of an open window opposite, a couple of floors down (they were on the fifth floor). Ian and Pat raced down the stairs to try to intercept him, but he had vanished.

At once Ian and Pat made fast tracks up the Line to warn the agents of Cole's unreliability, but they never imagined how extreme it would prove to be. Cole had returned to the north and immediately began to appear in the company of uniformed Germans. No one knows exactly what happened, but as members of the Resistance began to be arrested, it became apparent that Cole had sold out to the enemy to save his own skin. He was far too clever to give away his ex-colleagues all at once, and ensured his continued value to the Germans by leading them to Resistance workers one-by-one over a considerable period.

Worse still, the pro-Nazi Vichy French were given the names of Allied agents in Unoccupied France, and Garrow himself was arrested. He received terrible treatment, was tried and condemned to death. Amazingly, after six months with the sentence still not carried out, the few agents who had escaped arrest were able to bribe a guard to 'spring' Ian from prison. When he was fit enough, he followed the many escapers he had sent over the Pyrenees to Spain and Gibraltar and so back to England.

Just as supper was ready, and Ian's story was completed, in walked my Mother. I never understood what had happened – did she feel she could not face the meeting? Or did she realise that two chaps together would 'click' and talk more freely if left alone? Anyway, Ian and I were in a mellow mood, my Mother's Irish charm and good humour responded and we had a most enjoyable meal together. By its conclusion Ian had agreed to come to the Rectory in Kent for lunch a few days later to meet Mme Deram.

He duly arrived, and although their relations were cool (I don't think they had met before) all went well over lunch until they retired to another room for Mme Deram to make her case. After quite a short interval we heard raised voices, and then Ian came storming out saying he did not wish to see Mme Deram ever again. My Mother applied all her charm and persuaded Ian to arrange for her to at least meet someone from the War Office (MI9, I suppose) over the lack of British recognition of her work.

A couple of days later, my Mother and Mme Deram reported to the War Office and were shown into a small interview room. In came two senior Army officers looking very serious and carrying two thick files. They let Mme Deram make her case and then addressed my Mother, 'Mrs Barclay, you must understand that all our information points to this woman sharing in Cole's traitorous behaviour and we advise you that you should have nothing more to do with her.' My Mother felt terrible to think she was being treated as a friend of a traitor, but also that her attempt to help someone who undoubtedly risked her life in hiding George for several days was being denied recognition. Before she took her home she took Mme Deram to a jeweller nearby and bought her a gold RAF brooch.

That evening the phone rang and the caller asked for my Mother. It was her nephew, Roddie Barclay, who worked in the Foreign Office and was currently private secretary to the Foreign Minister, Ernest Bevin. After the usual exchange of family news, Roddie said, 'Aunt Dorothy I have a message from Mr Bevin for you. Would you kindly send Mme Deram back to France tomorrow. Her activities are at risk of causing an international incident'! Off she had to go, unsatisfied, the next day.

The famous MI9 agent 'Sunday' (Donald Darling) was astonished when he heard all this, and said he considered the Ministry of Defence officers completely out of order in their actions. He believed Mme Deram was 'all right'!

What happened to Cole? Apparently shortly after the end of the war, an English Intelligence Officer approached a senior American in the American Zone in Germany. He explained he had been behind enemy lines working for Britain identifying the key people in the German Gestapo, and if the Americans were trying to find any in their Zone, he was in a good position to help them. The Americans were delighted and hastened to give him every support – finance, a house with staff and a car with a driver.

Of course, you will have guessed that the 'English Officer' was Cole, and he now reversed the operation of betraying French Resistance agents to the Germans by betraying Germans to the Americans at intervals, one by one. All seemed to be proceeding quite satisfactorily until two senior French policemen turned up at the American HQ. They explained that they had been searching for an English collaborator called Harold Cole: a traitor responsible for the deaths of many in the Resistance. They believed he was the man the Americans were employing. Cole was sent for, arrested and taken to Paris for judgment before a magistrate.

While awaiting the compilation of the case against him, Cole was held in a police station. He spoke fluent French and was an amusing chap. He was soon on good terms with his jailers and used to be brought from his cell to join them for cards. One evening he excused himself to go and relieve himself – once in the corridor he walked into the jailers' dressing room, took a uniform greatcoat and cap and walked out through the front of the station into the street – to disappear completely.

Some months later, the authorities in France decided they must abolish the black market that had grown up in the days of the Occupation and was now distorting the economy. As a start, they decided to arrest the main black marketeers. Accordingly, two policemen were sent to arrest one of these in the early hours. They broke into the marketeer's flat and found him in bed with a woman. As they burst into the room the man produced a gun and shot one of the policemen, but the other police officer returned the fire, killing the marketeer. It was some days before they realised that they had killed Cole.

Several members of the Resistance, including Garrow, have made it clear to me that Cole got off far too easily. If he had been in their hands his death would have been long, drawn-out, and exceedingly painful.

I will add to this long story the explanation of why Cole was hiding in France at the time of the German invasion in May 1940. Cole had a history! In his early life he was a thief and served a sentence in prison. On release he joined the Army, and through his intelligence and attractive personality, was duly made the Colonel's driver. The unit was sent out to Hong Kong and some months later the Colonel's car disappeared. Through good relations on the frontier with China, the police learnt that the car had been sold to the Chinese on the mainland – by Cole, of course. He was duly charged, served another prison spell and was discharged from the Army.

Before the start of the Second World War, thanks to a vigorous recruiting campaign, Cole joined up again without, of course, mentioning his previous service. His unit was soon in France and Cole's age and expertise resulted in his promotion to Sergeant. He found himself responsible for the Sergeant's mess funds and, surprise surprise, they went missing! Cole was arrested and under guard shortly before the German attack in May 1940.

When his unit was sent into Belgium, Cole was released from arrest and took the opportunity to 'scarper'. He made his way to Lille where he had a girlfriend – none other than Mme Deram, who ran a café, and whose husband had become a prisoner of war in Germany. The café was a centre for early Resistance operations, of which there were very few in those days.

Cole soon began to demonstrate his skill at dodging the Germans and French police, and played a valuable role – except, as it proved, where the Line's funds were concerned. The official view afterwards was that Mme Deram could not possibly have failed to know that Cole was spending large sums of money on himself – and probably on her – so despite her also being betrayed by Cole and imprisoned by the Germans, she was tarred with Cole's brush.

Mauricette Ghoris

Can there possibly be another story arising from George's escape from France? Yes, indeed, and one worth telling.

We had known from George's diary that the first few nights of his escape had been spent with the Ghoris family in Cassel. Furthermore, Maurice Ghoris of Cassel and his 14-year-old daughter, Mauricette, had escorted George on a train journey to Lille. My Mother's efforts to make contact with them after the Liberation brought no response, and thanks to the carefully maintained division of the Line into cells unknown to each other, those we did contact were unable to help. We were left wondering whether they had returned to Belgium, or, more likely, been executed by the Germans.

Then 30 years later, in 1973, I had returned to my home in Woldingham from my job in the bank in Croydon, when one evening I received a phone call. The familiar voice of Anthony Gurney of Cromer spoke in characteristic military manner – 'Richard, does the name Mauricette Ghoris mean anything to you?'

I thought a moment and replied, 'Yes, I think it does. I believe she helped George on his escape.'

'Well, she is staying in Lowestoft and wants to meet you – this is her number.' Anthony rang off. I immediately rang the number and found I was talking to the proprietor of a bed and breakfast establishment. He explained that Mme Ghoris was not confident enough of her English to do more than exchange greetings on the phone but he would interpret. The outcome was an arrangement that I would pick her up for lunch the next day.

I immediately read up George's diary for the Cassel period, 20–22 September 1941, and then prepared for an early start as I had to cross through London from south to north.

I duly found the house in Lowestoft and out came a short, plump little woman with a round, smiling face and shy manner. We exchanged kisses and I whisked her off to a nearby restaurant. There she told me her remarkable story.

Her father, Maurice Ghoris, was the owner of a petrol filling station on a main road to Cassel. He had five children, the eldest being Mauricette. In May 1940, the German Blitzkrieg attack on Belgium and France brought calamity to the family. Within a week the battle had reached Cassel, and the Ghoris family found their house was in a 'no-man's land' between German and English soldiers.

Maurice rushed his family into the cellar as the Germans shot directly at their house and the petrol pumps.

Suddenly, exploding shells set the petrol pumps alight and there was every chance that the fuel tanks would blow up. As the children choked in the smoke, their coughing drew further small-arms fire on them. So with shells and bullets flying in every direction, the family had to escape from the cellar and hide in a ditch. Maurice told his family to take off their shoes and creep away from the burning house into the fields of standing crops. The British were forced to retreat and the battle passed on.

After the battle, nothing was left of their possessions, and they became refugees, swept along, over the Franco–Belgian border. Mauricette's main concern was that she had left her shoes in the cellar and had to go bare foot – for several months in fact, as it was impossible to replace them. Eventually the French authorities provided them with an empty house in Cassel. Life gradually returned to 'normal' and Mauricette went back to school, but the atmosphere was one of despondency and defeat, with most French people trying to reconstruct their lives on whatever terms the occupying Germans allowed.

Maurice was enraged by what the Germans had inflicted on him and his family, and immediately began to explore what he could do to get his own back. As George recorded in his diary, 'Maurice was absolutely flat-out against the Hun.' At that time, and until the Allied landing four years later, resistance to the Germans was highly unpopular, for fear that it would result in life being made more dangerous for everyone. Maurice was one of the very first in France to become an active 'resister'.

The opportunity to work against the Germans that presented itself was to aid British troops who had avoided capture after the fall of France return to England. It soon became clear that the coast was too heavily guarded to offer any chance of passage in a stolen boat. The only route would have to be south across the border into Vichy France, which was heavily involved in co-operation with the Germans, then over the Pyrenees to fascist Spain, where the bulk of people also co-operated for a quiet life, followed by the long journey to British-held Gibraltar. A formidable prospect and near impossible for those who spoke little or no French.

Gradually, a chain of small groups, formed through personal contacts of active individuals, became an 'Escape Line' stretching the length of France. In the Pas de Calais area this was led by Sergeant Cole, and in Marseilles, by Captain Garrow, who both remained in France to run the Organisation. A Belgian military doctor, Albert Guérisse GC, joined them in due course, using the now famous nom de guerre Pat O'Leary, and it was by this name that the Line was known.

Having got the British troops who were in hiding away southwards, the Escape Line of which Maurice had become a part, found plenty more 'customers' as airmen descended from the skies by parachute following air battles. In addition to night bombing raids, there were high-profile 'sweeps' by large numbers of British fighters, usually escorting a few daylight bombers raiding airfields and factories in western France. Their main object was to bring the German Air Force into action, destroy their aircraft and, if possible, prevent their movement away to other 'fronts' such as Greece, North Africa and later Russia.

If the parachuting airmen were to be saved from capture by the Germans it was vital that the Resistance reached them first and whisked them away before the enemy search parties arrived. So when the 'sweeps' were overhead Maurice would set off on his bike with a change of civilian clothing in his saddle bag. His young daughter, Mauricette, accompanied him to make him less conspicuous. If the airman was not badly wounded he was quickly changed into 'civvies', and he and Maurice would set off on the bicycles for Cassel, leaving Mauricette to walk home.

Mauricette told me they had several successes, but on one occasion had a real shock. They found a parachutiste, as the French called them, who was wounded and unconscious. They began to strip him of his overalls, only to find he was wearing German uniform! At this point a German search party arrived and Maurice had to quickly justify his interest in the airman as an effort to give first aid. They got away with it – and if they hadn't, this story would never have been told.

George was sent by the curé of Nordpeen to hide at the Ghoris's borrowed home in Cassels on the evening of 20 September 1941. He had crash-landed that afternoon and successfully evaded capture. Within a few days George and Maurice walked to the railway station at Bavancore with Mauricette acting as scout ahead of them for German search patrols – as opposed to individual German soldiers who paid them no attention. They changed trains at Hazebrouck after a nerve-wracking wait, and then travelled to Lille, where George was passed on, like a 'parcel' as evaders were called, to Madame Deram, followed by Fernand Salingue.

It was not until 1943 that the blow fell and the Gestapo arrested both Maurice and his wife. Mauricette told me that her father could have avoided arrest as he had received a warning that morning, but he was so concerned about the incriminating documents left in the house that he returned to destroy or hide them, telling Mauricette of the hiding places. Through this action, he and his wife were caught at home, and Mauricette was left with responsibility for the three younger children, the youngest still a toddler. The first Mauricette knew of it was on returning from school to find her younger siblings crying and saying that their parents had been taken by the Germans. Mauricette's first attention had to be given to the children, to comfort and feed them and then put them to bed. But what next?

Their house was somewhat isolated and the neighbours were opposed to the dangers Resistance workers brought to them. When the children were asleep, Mauricette went to the police station in the centre of Cassel where she knew the Germans held prisoners for interrogation. It was late evening and the doors were all shut, so Mauricette banged on the door. After a time an angry policeman appeared saying, 'Go home, little girl' and closed the door. Mauricette continued to knock and eventually the policeman returned and asked, 'Well, what is it you want?' Mauricette explained she must speak to her mother about where to find food for her younger siblings. The policeman disappeared, no doubt to consult the resident Gestapo, and returned saying, 'Your mother will probably be released tomorrow, go home and wait.' Fortunately, they returned her mother about a fortnight later. The Germans were anxious in those early days of the Occupation to behave very properly. When they could not extract enough evidence to charge Maurice before a court, he was also released.

Maurice was a brave and determined Resistance worker and was soon back to his old practices and even went further – he organised sabotage. In due course he was arrested again, tortured, and condemned to a concentration camp. There he was part of a group of Flemish Resistance workers, some of whom survived the war, but Maurice never came back. It is believed that he

survived to within two weeks of the end of the war but then 'disappeared'. It was the practice of the Gestapo to kill those they had tortured to prevent their giving evidence against them when the war ended.

Mauricette's grandparents helped her with the children until her mother's return. During this period, two women from the Gestapo visited the school on frequent occasions to question Mauricette about her knowledge of her father's activities: 'We know you went out with him, what did you do? Who did you meet?' The pressure on a teenager must have been colossal.

Maurice's arrest terrified his wife – she had been against his Underground work for fear of the family's situation if he was arrested. Both she and an aunt felt Mauricette would still be a German target and decided to send her to live with her grandparents to study to be a typist. To remove any evidence from her parents' house Mauricette sewed secret documents into the shoulder pads of her coat. These were later found by her grandparents who, thinking they might be love letters, read them – only to burn them in panic, thus destroying the evidence of Maurice Ghoris's work and the names and addresses of those they had helped. This is why Mauricette was unable to write to us.

As soon as Mauricette had qualified as a typist, she was sent to a relation – a Parisian businessman – to join his operation, and she left for Paris. After some months she fell ill and her doctor contacted the employer to say she was severely malnourished – starving, even. The employer found out that Mauricette was sending half her pay to her mother to support her and the younger children, which left an insufficient amount for her own food. When Mauricette fainted at work her employer realised the problem and increased her trainee salary to allow for both Mauricette's minimum needs and something for her mother. Her situation was worse than most as she had to pay for a room, unlike the local employees who continued to live at home.

As Mauricette no longer had George's address, she decided to take her holidays in England in an effort

Mauricette Ghoris with evader Squadron Leader John Mott at Tangmere Museum in Sussex. In 1941 Mott (d.2002) was an RAF bomber pilot who was shot down over France and evaded capture with the help of the Resistance. On his return to England he later became a Lysander pilot flying SOE agents in and out of Occupied France.

to learn English and to find the Barclays. All she remembered of George's address was 'Cromer', which she thought was part of London. She found several streets with Cromer in their names and trekked out to explore them, but of course found no Barclays.

Then years later in September 1987, when she was on holiday in Lowestoft, she took a bus tour of north Norfolk country houses. One day they stopped in a small town and the guide said, 'You have an hour here. There is a good tea room for a meal. The town is known for its fine church and its famous lifeboat. It is called Cromer.' Mauricette felt as though struck by lightning and went straight to the church. There on the War Memorial she saw the names of George and our brother Charlie (killed at Kohima), together with the rough wooden cross that originally marked George's grave in the desert, but she had to rush back to catch her bus. She did not know how to visit Cromer again, except by booking the same tour the next day. When she reached Cromer again she went straight to the church and broke down in tears.

It so happened that the organist had just finished a practice. He saw this woman weeping and felt he must speak to her and ask what the trouble was. Mauricette told him, 'I knew George Barclay in France. I thought he must be dead as he never got in touch.' She then said she would like to meet the Barclay family if possible, only to learn that they had left Cromer at the end of the war. Then the organist had a brainwave: 'The Barclays still have relations in the area. If you give me your telephone number I will try to pass it to them.' That is how my cousin Anthony Gurney was told about Mauricette and consequently rang me up that night.

Mauricette and I got on well and in July 1988 she came to stay with us at Hill Head near Lee-on-Solent and met two local retired Air Force officers connected with Tangmere Museum at the famous, but now disused, Air Force station. There she presented George's wings and buttons from his tunic to the Museum and was interviewed by the local press, who reported her experiences with appreciation and sympathy. I was able to introduce her to the Royal Air Force Escaping Society, who laid on a reception for her on her way back to Paris through London.

Visit to France, 1989

In 1988, during Mauricette's visit to England, we decided that perhaps some of my family and I would go over to France, and Mauricette would contact the Resistance helpers so that we could meet them once more (some of them had been to England for the launch of the first edition of this book, *Fighter Pilot*). I duly contacted my three sons and they all jumped at the opportunity. I forget what my daughter Juliet was doing, but she was unable to come. So my last paragraphs will describe how the visit went.

Before going I contacted the RAF Escaping Society to get their advice and was told, 'I do hope you know what you are doing. Do you realise you are going to a hotbed of old antagonisms and hates which you may stir up?' Having got so far I was not to be put off and merely said I was aware and would tread carefully. It turned out that taking the boys was the best thing I could have done to remove any fears or suspicions about my visit. Those who had helped George treated us royally everywhere we went, as they felt we were honouring them and responded accordingly. They seemed to remember him with great clarity and appreciation.

On Sunday 25 June 1989 we drove to Cassel via the Calais ferry and met Mauricette at L'Hotel de Ville, once the German Headquarters, on the main square. We were to stay there and give a dinner to those who had supported Mauricette and George, including Mme Leurs who found the workman's overalls for George on his first afternoon in France, and whose daughter led him to the curé.

But the great triumph of the evening was the presence of a nun, Sister Antoine, who was allowed to leave her convent and join us as a very exceptional matter. She had been Maria Demol, the diminutive choir girl who led George from Nordpeen to Cassel and the house of Maurice Ghoris. She was utterly thrilled to be 'out' and excitedly recalled every detail of their epic walk – the heat, their exhaustion, walking through the town centre full of German soldiers, some busy, some relaxing, losing their way twice trying to find the Ghoris house etc. At first George had trotted alongside her 'fairy' bike, but both of them ran out of energy, so George carried the bike on his shoulder and held her hand. Sister Antoine was so carried away by these recollections that she nearly passed out and a doctor had to be called, but soon decided she was all right.

A visit to Dorothy's home in Wheathampstead, Hertfordshire, July 1972. Standing, from left: Hélene Fardel, Alison Barclay, Ann Asher (sister of George), Richard Barclay. Seated, from left: Henriette Fardel, Dorothy Barclay (George's mother), Fernand Salingue and Elisa Salingue.

Stories of the Resistance came from all round the table – most of them second-hand. But Mauricette described how her father had continued his Underground work, not only helping escapers, but taking instruction and orders from a Capitaine Michel for sabotage operations. The Capitaine was cornered by the Germans and tried to shoot his way out, killing four of them before he himself was shot dead.

The next day we visited Nordpeen and the large field in which George force-landed. We were entertained by the niece of the curé (I believe he was arrested and died too), and given champagne. This drink, considered the height of luxury by us in England, seemed to be a requirement of generous hospitality everywhere we went in France.

Our friends reminded us of three events in particular. Mauricette told of escorting George on the trains from Bavancore, an out-of-the-way station near Cassel, to Lille. They had to change trains at Hazebrouck and it was there that George showed his nous when he saw that a German officer was taking too close an interest in him – George was a foot taller than the rather short mining families of the area. George rushed up to some country women carrying baskets of goods for the market and embraced one of them with loud cries of delight at seeing his *tante*, to which they responded likewise without hesitation and bustled him onto the train.

We also met the widow of the schoolmaster, Fernand Salangue. They had put George up at Burbure near Lille for 15 nights. Soon after George left for the south,

Bavancore Station, to where Mauricette and her father escorted George on 22 September 1941, and from where he took a train to Hazebrouck. This photograph was taken on 26 June 1989 when Richard Barclay and his sons visited France.

Fernand was taking his class in the village school, writing on the blackboard, when he saw his neighbour coming pell-mell down the cobbled street on his bicycle, throw it on the ground and run towards the school door. He realised what this meant, laid down his chalk and walked out of the class to tell his headmaster that the Germans were at his house and he must leave. The headmaster said, 'Take off your glasses – they will be looking for someone known to always wear glasses.' Fernand did so and left the school, his house and family and did not return until after the Liberation, over three years later.

Another of our visits was to Le Touquet to meet the Fardels, another of George's hosts for a period of a fortnight or so. Monsieur Fardel, a butcher, had died, but Mme Fardel was delighted to see us, and her son André recalled at length the anxieties and alarms of having a German officer billeted on them in a room next door to the one in which George was hiding. It appeared that André, who was then 12 years old, was given the role of playing his accordion continually, partly to drown any noise George and his companion (another airman, Squadron Leader Henry Bufton) might make, and partly to persuade the German he should find a more peaceful billet elsewhere.

Perhaps the most dramatic of our meetings was the last one with Mme Deram. I had been in two minds whether to visit her, bearing in mind the view of some of the others about her playing a double-game, or at least benefiting from Cole's thieving. However, she had undoubtedly risked her life in housing George and had been close to death in a concentration camp, so I felt she deserved our thanks too. When we arrived at her small house at the end of a long passageway, we found her accompanied by a rather severe-looking man of about 30, who she introduced as her nephew. He was rather unresponsive to our greetings and enquiries and we wondered afterwards whether he was from French security or the police.

After exchange of compliments and memories of George, Mme Deram suddenly remarked that Cole had done excellent work including escorting George to Marseilles and she felt strongly that this had never been properly recognised. Of course this was like an electric

shock to us all and when I glanced at Mauricette (whose father had been betrayed by Cole) I saw she had gone as white as a sheet. Fearing a Gallic explosion I rose and we quickly made our departure. Mauricette shot out of the door and off down the passageway without waiting for us. Her head was bent forward and she was muttering – oaths, I think. I felt I should not just follow behind but should try to show some support.

As I caught up with her, she turned to me and said: 'You know what's wrong with that woman? She's still in love with Cole!'

We kept in touch with those gallant French men and women until they died.

In October 1945, when I was passing through the Suez Canal, I was able to make my way across Egypt to visit George's grave at El Alamein. It was difficult to relate to a mound in the sand of the desert, especially believing, as I do, in the life after death. It is only now, in my eighties, that I grieve for my loss of George, Charlie and Lionel.

The butcher's in Burbure where George was taken in by Joseph and Henriette Fardel and their son André, between 13 and 19 October 1941.

Bibliography to the first edition

Bloemertz, Gunther, *Heaven Next Stop: Impressions of a German Fighter Pilot* (William Kimber, 1953)

Brome, Vincent, *The Way Back: The Story of Lieut-Commander Pat O'Leary, GC, DSO, RN* (Cassell, 1957)

Darling, Donald, *Secret Sunday* (William Kimber, 1975)

Duncan Smith, Group Captain W.G.G., *Spitfire into Battle* (London, John Murray, 1981)

Evans, A.J., *Escape and Liberation 1940–1945* (Hodder & Stoughton, 1945)

Mason, Francis K., *The Hawker Hurricane* (Macdonald, 1962)

Moulson, Tom, *The Flying Sword: The Story of 601 Squadron* (Macdonald, 1964)

Neil, Tom, *Gun Button to Fire* (Stroud, Amberley, 2010)

Nowarra, Heinz J., *The Messerschmitt 109, A Famous German Fighter* (Harleyford Publications, 1963)

Ramsey, Winston G. (ed), *The Battle of Britain Then and Now* (London, Battle of Britain Prints International, 1985)

Rawlings, John, *Fighter Squadrons of the RAF and their Aircraft* (Crécy Books, 1993)

Richards, Denis, *Royal Air Force 1939–1945, Vol I: The Fight at Odds* (HMSO, 1953)

Shores, Christopher and Ring, Hans, *Fighters over the Desert* (Neville Spearman, 1969)

Shores, Christopher, and Williams, Clive, *Aces High: A Tribute to the most notable fighter pilots of the British and Commonwealth Forces in WWII* (London, Grub Street, 1994)

Sutton, Sqn Ldr H.T., *Raiders approach! The Fighting Tradition of Royal Air Force Station Hornchurch and Sutton's Farm* (Gale & Polden, 1956)

Thetford, Owen, *Aircraft of the Royal Air Force since 1918 (4th edn)* (Putnam, 1968)

Young, Gordon, *In Trust and Treason: The Strange Story of Suzanne Warren (Warenghem)* (Studio Vista, 1959)

Details of Aircraft Mentioned

Type and powerplant	Max speed (mph)/Alt (ft)	Service ceiling (ft)	Bomb load (lb)	Armament
Avro Tutor (ET)				
Armstrong Siddeley Lynx JVC of 215–240hp	122	16,200		
Boulton Paul Defiant (F)				
Rolls-Royce Merlin III of 1,030hp or XX of 1,260hp	303 or 315/16,500	30,350		4 × 0.303in
Bristol Beaufighter II (NF)				
Rolls-Royce Merlin XX of 1,280hp	330	29,000		4 × 20mm and 6 × 0.303
Bristol Blenheim IF (NF)				
Bristol Mercury VIII of 840hp	260	27,280	1,000	1 × Browning and 1 × Vickers 'K'
Consolidated Catalina (F-B)				
Pratt & Whitney Twin Wasp R-1830 S1C3-G of 1,200hp	190/10,500	24,000	2,000	4 × 0.303
Curtiss Tomahawk (F)				
Allison V-1 710-33 of 1,040hp	345/15,000	29,500		6 × 0.303
de Havilland Tiger Moth (ET)				
de Havilland Gipsy Major of 130hp	109/1,000	13,600		
Dornier Do17 (B)				
Bramo Fafnir 323 of 1,000hp	255/15,000	21,000	Up to 2,200	7 × 7.9mm and 1 × 20mm
Dornier Do215 (B)				
Daimler-Benz DB601 A of 1,150hp	275/15,000	28,000	Up to 2,200	7 × 7.9mm and 1 × 20mm
Douglas Boston II (NF)				
Pratt & Whitney Twin Wasp S3C4-G of 1,200hp	295/13,000	26,000		8 × 0.303in
Fairey Battle (B)				
Rolls-Royce Merlin I, II, III or V of 1,030hp	241/13,000	23,500	1,000	1 × Browning and 1 × Vickers 'K'
Fiat CR.42 (F)				
Fiat A.74R.1C.38 of 840hp	270/13,100	32,000		2 × 12.7mm
Gloster Gladiator (F)				
Bristol Mercury IX of 840hp	253/14,500	33,000		4 × Browning
Hawker Audax (AC)				
Rolls-Royce Kestrel IB of 530hp or X of 520hp	170/2,380	21,000	Up to 224	1 × Vickers and 1 × Lewis
Hawker Hart (B/AT)				
Rolls-Royce Kestrel IB of 525hp or V or X of 510hp	165/3,000	21,320	500	1 × Vickers and 1 × Lewis

Type and powerplant	Max speed (mph)/Alt (ft)	Service ceiling (ft)	Bomb load (lb)	Armament
Hawker Hector (AC)				
Napier Dagger IIIMS of 805hp	187/6,500	24,000	Up to 224	1 × Vickers and 1 × Lewis
Hawker Hind (B)				
Rolls-Royce Kestrel V of 640hp	186/16,400	26,400	500	1 × Vickers and 1 × Lewis
Hawker Hurricane I (F)				
Rolls-Royce Merlin II or III of 1,030hp	324/18,000	33,200		8 × 0.303in
Hawker Hurricane II (F)				
Rolls-Royce Merlin XX of 1,260hp 161	320/21,500	36,000		12 × 0.303in
Heinkel He59 (S)				
BMW VI of 750hp	161			
Heinkel He111 (B)				
Junkers Jumo 211D of 1,200hp	240/15,000	26,000	2,200	7 × 7.9mm and 2 × 20mm
Heinkel He113 (F)				
Daimler-Benz DB601N of 1,200hp	380/17,000	37,500		2 × 7.9mm and 2 × 7.9mm
Junkers Ju86 (B)				
Junkers Jumo 205C of 700hp	224		2,200	3 × 7.9mm
Junkers Ju87 (D-B)				
Junkers Jumo 211 of 1,150hp	245/15,000	26,000	1,110	3 × 7.9mm
Junkers Ju88 A4 (B)				
Junkers Jumo 211G of 1,200hp	287/14,000	22,700	4,400	7 × 7.9mm and 1 × 20mm
Macchi C202 (F)				
Daimler-Benz DB601N of 1,200hp	330/18,000	34,500		2 × 12.7mm
Messerschmitt Bf109E (F)				
Mercedes-Benz DB601A of 1,150hp	355/19,500	36,000		2 × 7.9mm and 2 × 20mm
Messerschmitt Bf109F (F)				
Mercedes-Benz DB601E of 1,300hp	390/22,000	37,000		2 × 7.9mm and 2 × 20mm
Messerschmitt Bf109G (F)				
Daimler-Benz DB605A of 1,475hp	395/22,000	38,500		2 × 7.9/13mm or 2 × 12.7mm
Messerschmitt Me110 (F)				
Daimler-Benz DB601N of 1,200hp	360/20,000	34,000		6 x 7.9mm and 2 x 20mm
Miles Magister (ET)				
de Havilland Gipsy Major I of 130hp	132/1,000	16,500		
Miles Master (AT)				
Rolls-Royce Kestrel XXX of 715hp	226/15,000	27,300		
North American Harvard (AT)				
Pratt & Whitney Wasp R-1340-49 of 550hp	205/5,000	21,500		
Short Stirling (HB)				
Bristol Hercules XVI of 1,650hp	270/14,500	17,000	Up to 14,000	8 × 0.303
Supermarine Spitfire I (F)				
Rolls-Royce Merlin II or III of 1,030hp	355/19,000	34,000		8 × 0.303 or 2 × 20mm plus 4 × 0.303in
Supermarine Spitfire VB (F)				
Rolls-Royce Merlin 45/46/50/50A of 1,440hp	374/13,000	37,000		2 × 20mm plus 4 × 0.303in
Westland Lysander (AC)				
Bristol Mercury XII of 890hp	219/10,000	26,000	Six light bombs	4 × 303in

Abbreviations: AC, Army co-operation; AT, advanced trainer; B, bomber; B/AT, bomber/advanced trainer; DB, dive bomber; ET, elementary trainer; F, fighter; F-B, fighter-bomber; HB, heavy bomber; NF, night fighter; S, seaplane. Data given (derived from Jane's *All the World's Aircraft*, *Aircraft of the Royal Air Force since 1918* and *Royal Air Force 1939–1945* Vol I) relate to aircraft marks flown by Barclay or mentioned in his diaries or log book. Absolute accuracy is not claimed, as some authoritative figures differ in detail.

Index

Abbeville 99, 106, 119-120, 122, 126
Ack-ack (anti-aircraft artillery) 38, 42, 52-53, 55, 59-60, 72, 82, 85, 97, 105, 110
Aden 142
Adolphus, King Gustavus of Sweden 12, 14
Aero engines
  Packard Merlin 98
  Rolls-Royce Merlin 136; XX 66

Aircraft 175-176
Avro Tutor 21, 23-24, 30
Bell Airacobra 137
Boulton Paul Defiant 31, 134
Bristol
  Beaufighter 98, 134
    Mk II 136
  Blenheim 33, 71, 84, 94-99, 106
    Mk IV 122
Consolidated Catalina 130-131
Curtiss
  Kittyhawk 98
  Tomahawk 98-99
  Warhawk 98
de Havilland Tiger Moth 134, 136
Dornier 50
  Do17 42, 85
  Do215 41-43, 45, 48-49, 51, 54-55, 59, 65, 74, 97
  Do217 39
Douglas Boston II 136
Fairey Battle 31, 93
Fiat CR.42 84
Hawker
  Audax 30
  Hart 27, 30
  Hector 30
  Hind 22, 24, 27, 29-30
  Hurricane 13, 24, 30-33, 38, 45, 47-49, 51-52, 55, 58, 60, 62, 64-66, 69, 71, 74, 79, 82, 84-87, 91, 93, 96, 120, 122, 134, 137-138, 139, 142, 144, 145, 147, 158, 161
    HD 144
    Mk I 32, 37, 136
    Mk II 66, 97, 136; IIB 143, 145
  Typhoon 1 136
Heinkel
  He59 84
  He111 43, 51, 53-54, 113-115, 122
  He113 46, 55, 58, 65, 72

Junkers
  Ju52 113
  Ju86 84
  Ju87 Stuka 44, 82, 115, 145-147
  Ju88 33, 54-55, 58, 60, 62, 89, 145
Macchi C202 145
Messerschmitt 42
  Me109 (Bf109) 36, 44-46, 48-49, 52-53, 55, 60, 62-67, 71, 73-74, 79, 82, 84, 86, 101, 122, 147, 160
  Bf109E 76, 146
  Me109F (Bf109F) 13, 94-96, 99, 106, 145, 147
  Me110 (Bf110) 34, 37, 41, 52-53, 60, 62, 80, 82
Miles
  Magister 31, 48, 59
  Master 30, 93
North American Harvard 31
Short
  'C' class Empire flying boat 67
  Stirling 136
Supermarine Spitfire 13, 23-24, 30-32, 38, 41, 49, 54-55, 58, 60, 65, 67, 72, 79-80, 93, 95-99, 101, 106, 113, 119-120, 122-123, 134, 137-138, 139, 142, 144
    Mk I 24, 31
    Mk VB 93-94, 96, 136-137
Vickers Wellington 118, 122
Westland Lysander 30, 96, 136, 168

Air League 21
Air Ministry 56, 100, 125, 131
Alamein Line 132
Albi 119
Alexandria 142, 144-145, 150, 151, 152, 161
Allouagne 121-122
Amiens 96
Anzio 18
Appleton, FO 97, 100
Arles 119
Ashford, Kent 60, 62-63
Atlantic Ocean 140
Auchel 120
Auchinleck, General 151
Azai 126

Baker, PO 145
Balfour, Captain Harold 66
Bancroft, Sqn Ldr 136
Banyuls 119

Barcelona 122, 127-130

Barclay, Alison 171

Barclay, Ann (sister, later Ann Asher)) 12, 17-18, 41, 105, 131, 161, 171

Barclay, Charles (brother) 14, 16-21, 88, 100, 105, 132-133, 137, 157, 160, 170-171

Barclay, Christina O. (aunt) 44, 46, 87-88, 158

Barclay, Col. David 12, 14

Barclay de Tolly, General 12

Barclay, Dorothy (mother) 2, 16-17, 75, 85, 87-89, 91, 93, 102, 133, 137, 143, 161, 163, 165-166, 171

Barclay, Reverend Gilbert A. (father) 14, 16-18, 20, 85, 88, 91, 93, 99-100, 102, 131-133, 136, 137, 142, 143, 144, 148 161, 163

Barclay DFC, George Arthur
  aircraft shot down or damaged 45, 48-49, 51, 54, 60, 62-63, 74-75, 82, 84, 88, 139, 140, 142, 147, 149, 161

  appearance 112, 123, 133, 147

  baling out 86-87, 157

  called up 12, 14

  charm, personality and popularity 7, 95, 99, 101-103, 142-143, 148, 156-157

  childhood 14

  Christian faith 44, 142

  Combat Report 27 September 1940 63

  commemorative plaque, Cromer 18

  courage, determination and flying skills 7, 16, 24, 30-31, 99-100, 142, 144, 148

  crash (forced) landings 27, 29, 45, 48, 62, 144-145, 147, 151
    in Occupied France 8, 99-100, 106, 108, 136, 157, 160, 171

  diaries 7-9, 13, 24, 36, 72, 116-117, 128, 157, 166

  Distinguished Flying Cross (DFC) 9, 81, 84-85, 88, 90

  education 16, 19, 44, 46, 90

  escape through France and Spain 7, 13, 16, 99, 103-133, 136, 138, 140, 157, 161, 163-168, 170-173

  first operational flying 33

  flying instructor duties 91, 93-94, 142, 160

  glandular illness and operation 19, 21

  grave in El Alamein War Cemetery 13, 149-152, 155, 170

  hobbies and interests 14, 19, 21, 46

  holidays in Germany 64

  interrogated on return from France 131, 161

  killed in action 83, 140, 144-146, 148, 161

  leadership qualities 7, 99, 103, 147, 149, 156

  log book 27, 31, 36, 38, 93, 96, 98-99, 130, 137

  mentioned in Despatches (New Years Honours 1943) 155

  passing out at RAF Cranwell 14

  promotions:
    to commanding officer 13, 137, 138, 143-144, 160-161
    to Flight Lieutenant 93, 134, 160
    to Flying Officer 84
    to Pilot Officer 26
    to Squadron Leader 26, 128, 137, 140, 142, 144, 145, 161

  reported missing 99-102, 160
    presumed dead 125

  road accident 76

  Service of Remembrance 154-155

  shooting game 19-20, 68, 82, 157

  shot down 62, 84, 86, 88
    El Alamein 12-13, 18, 21, 142, 147-148
    France 12-13, 94, 97-99, 102,106, 120, 134, 138, 148
  wounded 84, 86-89, 148, 157-158, 160
  21st birthday party 88, 157

Barclay, Juliet 170

Barclay, Leo (nephew and godson) 88, 133, 158

Barclay, Mary (sister) 14, 16-19, 75, 80, 85, 87-90, 93, 98, 105, 127, 131-134

Barclay, Richard F. (brother) 8-9, 14, 16-17, 25, 27, 44, 52, 87-89, 93, 105, 107, 128, 132-133, 156-157, 163-164, 171-172

Barclay, Robin (uncle) 19, 85

Barclay, Roddie 165

Barclay, Rome (sister-in-law, née Davidson) 105, 133

Barclay T.D. (cousin) 85

Barclay-Russell, Sandy (Alexander) 19, 21, 150-155

Barclays Bank 85

Barker, Sgt Douglas 122

Barnes, 69

Barrage balloons 38, 44, 46, 58-59, 72, 96

Bartleman, 2nd Lt 138

Barton Hall, Preston 134

Barton FO/FL R.A. 'Butch' 31, 40, 42, 44, 51, 53, 55-56, 67, 71, 73-74, 79, 82, 84-85, 91

Barrow Deep 98

Batten, Jean 24

Battle 60

Battle of Britain 7-9, 12, 18, 24, 90, 102, 120, 122, 134, 137-138, 148, 157

Battle of France 137

Bavancore station 171-172

Bayley, Sgt 72

Bay of Biscay 140

BBC 120, 122

Beachy Head 39, 98

Beamish DSO, DFC, AFC, Group Captain/ Wing Commander Victor 44, 64-65, 79, 81, 102, 131, 160-161

Beard DFM, Sgt 45, 53, 55, 62, 67, 71, 73, 78

Beattie, Sgt Tudor 122

Beazley, PO John 41, 54-56, 58, 60, 64, 66

Beedham, FL D.W. 145

Belgian Army 163

Bell, Sgt Patrick V. 110, 118, 123, 126, 128, 130

Béthune 115, 120, 122

Betts, Rev. S.W. 102

Bevin, Ernest 165

Bisdee DFC, Sqn Ldr J.D. 137, 138, 142

Bishop's Stortford 98

Bitter Lake 142

Blakeney Point 20

Bloemertz, Gunther 56

Bondues aerodrome 112

Boozy and Paizen, kittens 67

Bosanquet, Mary (née Buxton) 94

Bosch, PO Roeper 98-99

Bouquillard Sgt 74-75

Brent Pelham 93

Brentwood 67
British Army 21, 42, 123, 151, 161, 165
  8th Army 132, 142, 145
  Coldstream Guards 134
  Royal Norfolk Regiment 18, 100, 133, 137, 160
  Seaforth Highlanders 118, 163
  13th/18th Hussars 73
Broadhurst, Group Captain Harry 102, 105, 144
Brome, Vincent 126
Buckingham Palace 84, 90-91
Bufton, Sqn Ldr/Wing Commander Henry E. 118, 121-127, 129-
  130, 172
Burbure 115-117, 119-123, 128, 172-173
Burgh El Arab 145, 151
Burnham-on-Crouch 44, 46
Burnett, FL 84
Burton, PO/FO Percy 36, 41, 48, 56, 60, 62, 64, 71
Buxton, Alfred (uncle) 74-75
Buxton, Arthur (cousin) 93, 105
Buxton, Blanch and Theresa 73
Buxton, Edith (aunt) 74-75
Buxton, Harry 82
Buxton, Jean 90
Buxton, 2nd Lt Lionel (cousin) 16, 18-19, 75, 90, 134
Buxton, Murray (uncle) 75, 90
Buxton, Susan (cousin) 75, 90, 134
Buyschoeure 99, 108

Café au Calice, Lille 161, 163-164
Cairo 140, 142, 149, 161
Calais 98, 122, 125, 160
Cambridge, University of, Trinity College 19, 21, 68, 73, 90
Cameron, FL Neil 140-142, 144, 148
Campbell, Sgt Ken 94, 129
Canterbury Cathedral 74
Carew-Gibbs, FO K.A. 142
Carpentier, Abbé 119-120, 126
Cassel 108-111, 113, 123, 166, 168, 170-171
Cassidy, FO 83, 85, 91
Caterpillar Club 87
Chateauroux 126
Chelmsford 67
Cherry, Sqn Ldr John 40
China 166
Chocques 94-95, 122
Church House, Westminster 75
Churchill, PM Winston 138
Clacton 42, 45-46, 55, 98
Clapham, Joseph 123
Clairmarais aerodrome 108
Cobham, Sir Alan 21
Coen, PO Oscar 118, 123, 129
Cole, Harold 'Paul' 115, 123, 126, 128, 161, 163-166, 173
Cologne 122
Commonwealth War Graves Commission 150-151
Cordwell, Sgt 145
Corner AFC, Wing Commander 99

Coventry 84-85
Crampton, Sgt William 118, 122, 126, 128-129
Crawley, PO L.G. 26
Croft, John 120
Cromer, Norfolk 9, 14, 17-18, 21, 93-95, 105, 131, 137, 160,
  166, 170
  Vicarage and Church 14, 16, 18, 26-27, 59, 100, 102, 131,
    140, 150, 152, 154, 170
Crossey, PO Terry 'Ossie' 43-44, 53, 56, 74, 78, 91

Dallington, East Sussex 62
Darling, Donald 128-129, 165
Darwen, Wing Commander 139
Davidson, 86, 91
Dawn Patrol film 52
Dawson, Wing Commander 131
Deal 54
de Gaulle, General 111
de Jonge, Rev. F. 143
Delpierre, Dr 119
Deram, Mme 114-115, 120, 161, 163-166, 168, 173
Deram, Marcel 114-116
Desert Campaign 151
Didery 119
Dimes, Edward 123, 129
Dixon, Wing Commander Jimmy 129-130
Dogfights 49, 60, 82, 98, 134
Donovan, Sgt Joseph 122
Doorly, PO Pat 30
Douai 122
Douglas, Air Vice-Marshal Sholto 64
Dover 55, 71, 73, 85-86, 96, 98
Dowding, Air Chief Marshal Sir Hugh 66, 81
Dundas, Sqn Ldr H.S.L. 136
Dungeness 96
Dunkirk 96-99, 110, 117-118
Durban 140, 148
Dutch islands 105

Eagle, PO L.C. 142
Easneye estate, Ware 82
Eastchurch 44
Eddy, Norman 44, 46
Edwards, FO 130
Egypt 138, 142-144, 161
El Alamein 12-13, 97, 132, 142, 144-145, 147, 149-151, 155
El Alamein War Cemetery 13, 149-152, 155
El Daba 142
Empire Air Days 21, 23
English Channel 52, 59, 65, 74, 80, 85-86, 96, 98, 123
Epping 59, 67, 80
Epping Hospital 66
Epping Place 73
Escape Line 9, 161, 163, 166
Eton 14
Evans, Captain A.J. 157, 171
Evans, Sgts 51, 97-98

Fardel, André 123-125, 172-173
Fardel, Hélene 171
Fardel, Henriette 123, 125, 171-173
Fardel, Joseph 123-124, 126, 172-173
Far East 149
Fauquembergues 119
Fen Causeway 25
Fifth Columnists 52, 116
Figueras 126-127, 129
Fillerin, Norbert 119
Finch, FL Mike ingle 136
Finlandia by Sibelius 148
Flak 94-97, 99, 105-106
Flamborough Head 33
Fleming, PO Robert D.S. 30-32, 45, 64
Flushing 99
Flying clothing 12, 29, 66, 135
   helmets 29, 135
   Irvin suit 48, 62, 67, 69, 160
   Mae West 34, 66, 68-69, 71
   Sidcot suit 29-30
Folkestone 55, 74
Forbidden Sector, France 8, 120
Foreign Office 130, 165
Fouquereuil 115, 120
France, Occupied 8, 16, 100, 102, 109, 118, 126, 133, 157, 163, 168
France, Unoccupied 8, 163, 165
France, Vichy 118, 126, 163, 165
Franco, General 129
Franks, Norman L.R. 147
Fraser, Arthur 122
Freetown 140
French Army 73, 124
French coast 65, 76, 96, 98, 106

Gardner, PO 98
Garrick Club 9
Garrow, Captain/Colonel Ian 118, 128, 161, 163-166
Gazala 132
Geneifa 142
George VI, King 84, 90
German Army 38
Germany, American Zone 165
Gestapo 113-114, 119, 123, 165, 168
Ghoris, Maurice 109-111, 113-114, 125, 166, 168, 170-172
Ghoris, Mauricette 9, 111, 166, 168, 170-173
Gibraltar 13, 99, 122, 126, 128-131, 165
Gilbert, PO 147
Gillan DSO, DFC, Wing Commander 96
Gneisenau 65
Goodwin Sands 98
Gosnay 94
Gossage, Walter C. 131
Grandy, Cecile 160
Grandy GCB, KBE, DSO, Sqn Ldr Sir John 7, 9, 31-32, 34, 36, 43, 51, 56, 92-93, 102, 138, 149, 156, 160
Gravelines 95-96, 98

Gravesend 43, 64
Graves Registration Unit 149
Gray, Sgt 95-96
Great Glen, Leics 21
Great Holland Rectory, Frinton-on-Sea 14, 16-17, 19, 21, 46, 55, 59, 75-76, 84
Gresham's School, Holt 89
Grey, FL 131
Gris Nez 99
Guilbert, Fleury 120
Gulbenkien, Nabor 128-129
Gurney, Anthony 166, 170

Hailsham 62
Hammond, PO W.R. 26
Hanks DFC, Sqn Ldr Prosser 105
Happisburgh 105
Hardelot 97
Harris, 'Streak' 98
Harvey, Sgt Len 26
Harwich 55, 76, 85
Hawtreys prep school, Westgate-on-Sea 16, 46
Hay, PO W.B. 145, 149, 157
Hayter, FL Spud 94, 96, 99, 106
Hazebrouck 96, 99, 106, 110, 112, 168, 172
Higginson DFM, FL Taffy 105, 114
Higham 19, 59, 68, 80, 85
Hilgarth, Captain 130
Hillary, Richard 30
Hill Head nr Lee-on-Solent 170
Hinkler, Bert 21
Hitler, Adolf 122, 152
HMS *Ark Royal* 131
HMT *Mauretania* (Cunarder) 140
Hoare, Lady 129
Hoare, Sir Samuel (cousin) 128-129
Holland 62, 99
Hong Kong 166
Horsey 76
Horsley MC, Group Cpt C.F. 34
Hotel du Commerce, Lillers 115-116, 120
Howard, Leslie 131
Hughes, Desmond 95 95
Hyde, H. Montgomery 9

Ingram, Sgt 94, 99
Ipswich 55
Iraqi Desert 151
Irish Sea 134
Isle of Sheppey 44, 46
Isle of Wight 36, 76
Ives, Sgt 129

Jackson, Sgt Maurice 122
Jenner, Sgt 99

Kellett DFC, DSO, FL R.G. 'Boozy' 31-33, 54, 74
Kennington, Eric, official war artist 159
Kent, HRH The Duke of 36
Killingback, Sgt 45
King Sqn Ldr Bruce 37
King's Cup Air Race 21
Kohima, Burma 18, 21, 137, 170
Kola Peninsula 138

La Bassée aerodrome 115, 120
Lake District 134
La Madeleine station 112-114, 120-121
Land Army 18, 133
Langley Rectory, nr Maidstone 9, 163, 165
Langley MC, OBE, Captain 131
Le Brimier, Captain 131
Leigh Sgt 98
Leigh-Mallory, Air Vice-Marshal Trafford 34, 102, 131
Leighton Buzzard 76
Lemille, M. 120
Lens 96
Le Touquet 172
Leurs, Madame 107-108, 170
Lewis DFC, PO/FL Albert 'Lew' 51, 53, 56, 59-60, 64, 67, 69, 78, 91
Lewis, Rev. R.D. 148-149
Liberation of France 9, 161, 166, 172
Libyan Desert 149
Lille 96, 107, 110, 112-114, 116, 119-120, 122-123, 126, 166, 168
Lillers 114-115, 120-121, 123
Limpsfield 90
Link trainer 71, 74
Liverpool 97, 138, 148
Loches 126
Lofts DFC, PO/FL Keith 51-52, 56, 66-67, 73-74, 76, 86
Lohmeyer, PO/FL/FO 40, 68, 91
London 46, 55, 58, 60, 62, 71, 73-76, 82, 84, 105, 161, 170
  East End 46, 48
  South 65, 73, 75
  South East 71
London Docks 46
Louden, Sqn Ldr 96
Love, Wing Commander R.C. 144
Lowestoft 166, 170
Loweth, PO 55
Luftwaffe 12, 32, 36, 38, 56, 98, 122, 132, 139
  JG27 146
  8./JG27 146
  111/JG27 145
  7/JG54 76
  9./KG76 39
  4./StG2 146
Lund, PO Tom 30
Lydd 76

Madrid 126, 128-130
  British Embassy 128

Maidstone, Kent 44, 46, 52, 72, 76, 82, 85-86
Malta 132, 138, 142, 161
Maplin Sands 98
Mardyck 97-99
Margaretting, Essex 64
Margate, Kent 82
Maries 126
Marine Court Flats, St Leonards, Hastings 26
Marquise 94
Marseille, Hans Joachim 147
Marseilles 118-119, 122, 126, 128, 163, 173
Mathers, Sqn Ldr 139
Matthews, PO 145
Mazingarbe 97-98
McConnel PO 74
Meaker DFC, PO Brian 59-60, 62
Mediterranean 138, 161
Mediterranean Fleet 132
Medway 72
Mellersh, FO Clive 97, 102-103, 105, 144
Mensecq 120
Mersa Matruh 142
MI5 18, 80
MI9 128, 157, 165
Michel, Capitaine 171
Midlands 134
Middle East 7, 18, 21, 98, 126, 128, 132, 134, 137-138, 140, 142-143, 148, 151
Middleton DFC, PO 67
Mid-Wales 134
Millington DFC, PO/FO William Henry 'Bill' 43-44, 59, 68, 71-74, 80, 82
Military Training Act 24
Mills, Sgt 78-79, 85, 91
Ministry of Defence 165
Mollison, Jim 21
Montpellier 119
Moody and Sankey, missioners 16
Morris, Sqn Ldr 95
Moscow 12
Mott, Sqn Ldr John 168
Mottram, FL 96
Mount, Vice Sqn Ldr C.J. 144
Mowatt, James 122
MTBs 96
Munich Agreement 24
Munro, Ian (cousin) 16, 18
Murmansk 139
Murray DFC, DFM, FL 136
Mussolini 12

Napoleon 12
Naze, the 76
Neave, Airey 128
Neil DFC, PO Tom F. 'Ginger' 32, 43, 52-53, 56, 59, 65, 68-69, 74, 78, 82, 84, 91
Newall, Sir Cyril 54, 64

Nicholas, Air Com. C.H. 33
Nicolson VC, FL E.J.B. 34, 37
Nitelet, PO Alexandre 118-119, 123, 126, 128, 130
Nocker, Roddie 95
Nordon, PO 145
Nordpeen 108, 110, 170-171
North Foreland 98
North Sea 55, 98
Nouveau, Louis 119, 126, 128, 163

Oft 96
O'Leary, LT Commander Pat (Albert-Marie Guérisse) 105, 118, 126, 128, 163-164
Olver, FL F. 145
Operation 'Newman' 138
Oram, PO 147
Organisation, the 118, 123, 126
Ormiston, Sgt 96-99, 106
Orton DFC, Sqn Ldr 'Fanny' 105
Osborn, Dick 89
Ostend 96
Ourse, Madame *see* Leurs, Madame
Oxford 76, 80, 93

Palace Pier, St Leonards, Hastings 26
Palliser, Sgt G.C.C. 'Titch' 51, 60, 62, 83, 91
Paris 120, 122, 126, 165, 168, 170
Parish, Sgt 69, 83
Park, Air Chief Marshal Sir Keith 74, 81
Parkinson, Richard 129
Parnall, FO/PO Denis 36, 40, 51, 53, 64
Parsons, Phyll 76, 85
Pawson, PO 137
Payton, Sgt 128-129
Pellys, Jack 73
Pembury Hospital, Tunbridge Wells 87-90, 157-158
Percy, Hugh 95
Perpignan 119, 122, 126, 128
Perrin, Sgt G.C.M. 73
Phelan, PO 145
Phillips, Corp. Eddie 26
Phillips, Sgt 107
Pipsqueak the puppy 67-68, 73, 83
Playford, Humphrey 149
Portsmouth 34
Port Suez 140
Port Tewfik, Suez 140
Potterstreet village 45
Powell, FL Kenneth Coryston 101
Preston 134
Prevot, FL 98
Prinz Eugen 65
Pugeot, M. 112
Pyrenees 126, 128, 165

Qattara Depression 148

Radar 38
RAE Farnborough 136
RAF Pageant, Hendon 21
Read, Sgt/WO Kenneth B. 118, 122, 126, 128-130
Red Cross 103, 121
Redhill 62
Red Sea 142
Reeves, PO 98
Renty 119
Resistance 118-119, 164-166, 168, 170-171
Reveillon, André 119
Reveillon, Giséle 121-122
Reveillon, 'Poupette' 121-123
Robecq 121
Roberts, Sqn Ldr 86
Robertson, Sgt Pilot 147
Robillard, Sgt Larry 122
Robinson RFC, FO 'Robbie' 79-80
Rochester 44, 46
Rochford 41, 44
Rodoccanachi, Dr 119
Rommel, Field Marshal 145, 151, 161
Roosevelt, President 138
Rouen 99
Rowe, Frank 122
Rowell, Sgt (Flash Alec) 55
Royal Air Force (RAF) airfields and bases 39
    Aboukir 142
    Aston Down 30-32, 82, 95, 102
    Barkston Heath 27
    Biggin Hill 73, 75
    Boscombe Down 34, 36-37, 40-42, 51, 59, 67
    Brize Norton 32
    Catterick 33
    Church Fenton 31, 33-34, 48, 53
    Colerne 41
    Coltishall 93
    Debden 73, 86, 91-95, 102-103, 137, 160
    Digby 137-138
    Duxford 21-25, 105, 114, 136, 149
    Halton 93
    High Ercall 136
    Hornchurch 59, 75, 79, 93-99, 102, 105, 108, 131, 134, 143-144, 160-161
    Kenley 39, 65, 136
    Leconfield 7, 31-33
    LG No 12 Sidi Haneish North 142
    LG No 13 Sidi Haneish South 142
    LG 92 El Amiriya 143-145
    LG 154 144
    Manston 84, 96, 98, 105-106
    Martlesham Heath 80, 85, 95, 138
    Maryut 140, 142
    Middle Wallop 34, 36
    Northolt 32, 136-137
    North Weald 14, 36, 38, 40-41, 43-47, 49, 53-54, 56, 64-65, 68-70, 78, 82-86, 89-91, 93, 96-97, 99, 102, 105, 136-138, 158

Oakington 136
Old Sarum 30
Samlesbury 134
Sealand 30
South Cerney 27
Stapleford Tawney 65, 80, 138
Tangmere 170
Valley 136
Wattisham 122
West Malling 60, 95
Royal Air Force Air Historical Branch 9
Royal Air Force College Cranwell 7, 14, 27, 30, 32-34, 45, 64-65, 75, 93-94, 100
Royal Air Force Escaping Society 119, 170
Royal Air Force Hospitals
Ely 88-89
Torquay 88-89
Royal Air Force (RAF) squadrons and units
Advanced Training Squadron (ATS) 27
Air Fighting Development Unit (AFDU) 136
No 8 (Army Co-operation) War Course 30
Auxiliary Air Force (AAF) 21, 93, 137, 160-161
Bomber Command 130
Desert Air Force 98, 132, 142
Elementary Flying Training School 27
Fighter Command 12, 31-32, 34, 36-38, 66, 81, 90, 134, 137
HQ Stanmore 134, 136-137
No 9 Group 32, 134
No 10 Group 32, 34
No 11 Group 32, 36, 74, 81, 93, 102
HQ Uxbridge 144
No 12 Group 32
No 13 Group 32-34
No 14 Group 32
Gunnery Research Unit 136
No 3 Initial Training Wing (ITW), Hastings 26-27
No 10 Maintenance Unit (MU) 32
Middle East 142, 144
No 5 Operational Training Unit (OTU) 30-32, 82
No 52 Operational Training Unit (OTU) 91 -93, 137
Pathfinder Force 123
No 1 School of Army Co-operation 30, 136
No 5 Service Flying Training School (SFTS) 30
No 1 Squadron 58, 65
No 1 (SAAF) Squadron 145
No 6 Squadron 144
No 9 Squadron 118, 122
No 17 Squadron 138
No 19 Squadron 24
No 25 Squadron 71, 85
No 46 Squadron 51, 53, 55, 60, 65-67, 72, 74-75, 80, 82, 84
No 54 Squadron 94-98, 105-107
No 56 Squadron 36, 40, 51, 59, 96, 105, 136
No 66 Squadron 24
No 71 'Eagle' Squadron 118, 123
No 73 Squadron 53
No 74 Squadron 138

No 80 Squadron 145
No 81 Squadron 139
No 110 Squadron 122
No 111 Squadron 97, 99
No 134 Squadron 139, 144
No 213 Squadron 145, 148
No 219 Squadron 31, 33
No 222 Squadron 97, 99
No 238 Squadron 140, 142-145, 148, 149, 157, 161
No 242 Squadron 97
No 249 Squadron 7, 31-34, 36, 38, 42, 47, 49, 51, 56, 62, 64, 66, 71-73, 78, 84, 90-91, 93, 102, 136, 138, 149, 156, 158
appointed Gold Coast squadron 82
formation 64
personnel 38
No 257 Squadron 71-74, 80
appointed Burma squadron 82
No 274 Squadron 145, 147
No 303 (Polish) Squadron 31-32, 54, 74
No 403 (Canadian) Squadron 94-96
No 600 (City of London, AAF) Squadron 137
No 601 (County of London, AAF) Squadron 128, 137-140, 143, 144, 157, 161
No 602 (City of Glasgow, AAF) Squadron 110, 123, 137
No 603 (City of Edinburgh, AAF) Squadron 95-97, 101, 105-106, 137-138
No 609 (Belgian, AAF) Squadron 118-119, 123
No 611 (West Lancashire, AAF Squadron) 93-103, 105-106, 134, 136, 143-144, 160
No 616 Squadron 31
No 243 Wing 144
No 244 Wing 144
Royal Air Force Volunteer Reservists (RAFVR) 14, 21, 24, 26-27, 30
Royal Canadian Air Force (RCAF) 122
Royal Navy 18
Runnymede Memorial 80
Russia 139
Russian Army 12

St Gennys, Cornwall 64
St Hippolyte internment camp 114
St Omer 94-95, 97, 119, 122-123
St Paul's Cathedral, London 73
St Peter's Church, Wheathampstead 152
Salingue, Elisa 116-117, 119-121, 123, 171
Salingue, Fernand 114-116, 118-121, 123, 168, 171-172
Salingue, Jean 116-117, 119-123
Saul, Air Vice-Marshal R.E. 34
Scharnhorst 65
Schneider Trophy 21
Schroer, Lt Werner 145-147
Scott-Maiden, PO/FL David 30, 95-96, 105, 137
Sheerness 59, 82
Shellhaven 44, 51
Sherfield 85
Shoeburyness 53-54
Simmons, H.C. 122

Sinai Desert 151
Sinclair, Sir Archibald 54, 64, 131
Sister Antoine (Maria Demol) 170
Smith, Babington 130
Smith, Iain Duncan 160
Smith DFC, PO/FL Wilfred 'Smithy' Duncan 94-95, 105, 160
Smithson, Sgt 45, 74
Smyth, Sgt 84
Snider, PO 145
Solak, George 'Jersey' 64, 71
Somme Estuary 76
Sorley, Group Cpt Ralph 36
South Africa 140, 142
Southampton 34
Southend 54, 98
Spain 8, 13, 99, 118-119, 121, 123, 126, 128-130, 136, 160, 165
Spanish Civil War 12, 129, 160
Special Operations Executive (SOE) 30, 168
Spitfire Fund 89
Squadron code letters 51, 53
SS *Rangitata* 139
Stalag XII 111
Stapleton DFC, Wing Commander Eric D.C. 94, 96, 99, 105-106
Stowe School 16, 19, 44, 90, 148, 149, 157
Straits of Dover 96
Stranraer 130-131
Studd, Buffy 90
Studd, C.T. 14
Studd, Sir Eric 89
Studd, Lady Stephanie (cousin) 90
Sulpnagel, General von 122

Tangmere Military Aviation Museum 9, 160, 168, 170
Templewood, Viscount 128
Thames Estuary 41-42, 46, 48, 53-55, 58, 62, 65, 71-73, 82, 84-86, 98
Thames, River 49, 82
Thatch, The, Epping 59, 67
Thirty Years War 14
Thomas, Sqn Ldr E.H. 93, 97, 99-100, 106, 160
Thompson, PO A.R.F. 'Tommy' 74, 79, 82, 91-92
Thorburn, FL W.B. 143
Times, The 9, 149
Tobruk 132, 142
'Torch' expedition 132
Toulouse 119, 122, 126
Tours 122
Townsend, Sgt 'Tubby' 97
Transjordan Desert 151

Trenchard, Lord 9
Trimingham 93, 105
Tuppence the cat 44, 46
Turlington, Sgt 97

U-boats 131
Union Defence Force (UDF) 151
University Air Squadrons 7, 24, 27
    Cambridge (CUAS) 19, 21-23, 25, 82, 95, 136, 150, 157
    Oxford 30
USS *Wasp* 138

Vange 51
Vesely, FL 136
VHF radio 40, 53
Victoria Cross 18, 34, 37
Vincer, Sqn Ldr 129-130
Volunteer Reserve Town Centre, Cambridge 14, 25

WAAFs 42, 98, 105
Waddell, PO 147
Walcheren 99
Walker Cup 26
Warenghem, Suzanne 126, 129
War Office 165
Watford 85
Way, Leslie 131
Wells, PO/FO Pat H.V. 30-33, 36, 45-46, 49, 53, 64, 66, 68, 84, 86, 91
Went, Douglas 46
West Africa 140
Western Desert 13, 97, 137, 139, 142-144, 148, 151
Wheathampstead 152, 171
Whiskey the dog 19
Wilfred the duck 82-83
Winskill, PO A.L. 122
Woldingham 166
Woodger, PO 134
Woolmer, 91
Worrall, PO 71
Wright, Sgt 97
Wright, Marjorie (governess) 16
Wynn, FO Dickie 83
Wynn, Humphrey 7, 9
Wynn, Nelg 41, 91

Zeebrugge 99, 105
Zimmermann, Unteroffizier Arno 76
Zuytpeen 108